STO

ACP ☙ **S0-BXL-966**
3 1833 00303 3377
DISCARDED

4-2-75

KARL MARX

KARL MARX

Michael Evans

Indiana University Press
Bloomington and London

First published in the United States by
Indiana University Press

Copyright © Michael Evans 1975
All rights reserved
No part of this book may be reproduced or utilized in
any form or by any means, electronic or mechanical,
including photocopying and recording, or by any
information storage and retrieval system, without per-
mission in writing from the publisher. The Association
of American University Presses' Resolution on Permis-
sions constitutes the only exception to this prohibition.

Printed in Great Britain

Library of Congress Cataloging in Publication Data

Evans, Michael, 1936–
Karl Marx

Bibliography: p.
1. Marx, Karl, 1818–1883.
HX39.5.E9   1975   335.4'092'4 [B]   74-15712
ISBN 0-253-33172-2

1865947

To My Mother

IRD2947

PREFACE

This book is an introduction to the social and political thought of Karl Marx. As an introduction, it is necessarily selective, and in some places compressed in treatment. I regret the omission of any extended analysis of the problems surrounding the Hegelian elements in Marx's thought, but as Hegel once said, these are not ideas that lend themselves to brevity. The discussion of Marx's economic theory is limited to that sufficient to relate his economics to his politics. My interpretation of Marx steers a course between the Scylla of neo-Hegelian intuitionist Marxism and the Charybdis of positivist Althusserian Marxism without, happily, mentioning either. To establish Marx's intellectual position requires study of the relevant texts, but it is a fruitful approach to get away from purely textual exegesis, and consider his thought in the context of his activities within the labour movement in England, France and Germany. In this area political theorists should utilise the work of labour historians far more than they have done hitherto. Marx's ideas changed and developed in response to influences both theoretical and practical.

I should like to acknowledge my own intellectual debts to George Lichtheim, whose *Marxism* remains the outstanding work of interpretation and synthesis written in the post-war period; and to David McLellan, from whose work on the early Marx I have derived much profit.

My thanks must go to Miss Marilyn Dunn, of the Department of Government; to Miss Gillett and the staff of the Secretarial Reserve in the Faculty of Economic and Social Studies for their patient translation of a difficult manuscript into an elegant typescript.

I should like to express my gratitude to those who read and commented on some part of the work: to Geraint Parry, the editor of this series, for his patient assistance; to David McLellan, Ursula Vogel and Robert Wokler; and, most especially, to Norman Geras, for his penetrating and painstaking comments on earlier drafts. For the defects that remain I am responsible.

Finally, one's family is usually the main casualty in the writing of a book. I hope they will find the result worthwhile.

Manchester, January 1974

LIST OF ABBREVIATIONS

Full titles will be found in the Bibliography, Part I

A–D	*Anti-Dühring*
Cap. I–III	*Capital* I–III
CGP	*Critique of the Gotha Programme*
CM	*Communist League* (ed. D. J. Struik)
CPE	*Critique of Political Economy*
Critique	*Critique of Hegel's Philosophy of Right*
CSF	*Class Struggles in France*
CWF	*Civil War in France*
CWUS	*Civil War in the United States*
Documents I–IV	*Documents of the First International*
EB	*Eighteenth Brumaire*
EG	Easton and Guddatt
EPM	*Economic and Philosophical Manuscripts*
Freymond I–III	Freymond (ed.), *La Première Internationale*
G	*Grundrisse*
GI	*German Ideology*
HF	*Holy Family*
JQ	*Jewish Question*
LA	*Letters to Americans*
MEGA	*Marx-Engels Gesamtausgabe*
MEW.EB	*Marx-Engels Werke. Ergänzungsbände*
N	Nicolaus (ed.), *Grundrisse*
PP	*Poverty of Philosophy*
SC	*Select Correspondence* (Moscow, 1965)
SC (1956)	*Select Correspondence* (Moscow, 1956)
SW	*Select Works*, 2 vols
TSV I–III	*Theories of Surplus Value* I–III
WLC	*Wage-Labour and Capital*
WPP	*Wages, Price and Profit*
NRZ	*Neue Rheinische Zeitung*
NYDT	*New York Daily Tribune*
IISH	International Institute of Social History (Amsterdam)
IWA	International Workingmen's Association

CONTENTS

Marx's Life and Work

1 EARLY YEARS

Karl Heinrich Marx (1818–83) was born in Trier, the centre of the Moselle region in the Prussian Rhineland, an area which had been occupied by France from 1795 to 1815. Marx's parents were Jewish. His father, Heinrich Marx (1782–1838) was forced to change his religion in order to retain his legal post in the Prussian civil service.[1] Karl was deeply attached to his father, and always carried an old photograph of him.[2] Heinrich was a liberal much influenced by the French Enlightenment. Indeed, the intellectual influence of French thought remained strong in the Rhineland and Trier became a centre for the spread of the ideas of Saint-Simon. The Fourierist, Ludwig Gall, lived in Trier during Marx's period at high school (1830–5). Baron von Westphalen (1770–1842) was certainly abreast of the latest social and political ideas and communicated his enthusiasm to Karl. The Westphalens lived next door. Ferdinand, a son by Westphalen's first marriage, later became Prussian Minister of the Interior (1850–5) in Manteuffel's cabinet and as such, one of the prime movers in the Cologne Communist Trial of 1852. Jenny, a daughter by Westphalen's second marriage, became secretly engaged to Karl before he left for the University of Bonn in the autumn of 1836.

At school Marx proved himself to be of sound intelligence, versed in Greek and Latin, but, surprisingly, deficient in history. He was much influenced by the headmaster, Hugo Wyttenbach, a Kantian liberal. Marx's essays for the *Abitur* have been preserved. One sentence has especially interested commentators: 'Our social relations . . . have already begun to form before we are in a position to determine them.' [3] Of this Riazanov claimed: 'Here one may discern the germ of the Materialist Conception of History.' [4] This is stretching the evidence. Suffice it to say that at the close of his school career Marx had been exposed, both at home and at school, to the ideals of 1789, a rational liberalism, and the social ideas of Fourier and Saint-Simon. Not that he immediately put into practice his unctuous advice about choosing 'the vocation in which we can contribute most to humanity'. His year of carousal at the University of Bonn caused his father some anxiety, Karl's main preoccupation being the writing of poetry rather than the study of law.

After a year Marx moved to Berlin. He gave an account of his first year in Berlin in the only letter to his father which now survives.[5] We must be wary of assuming the literal truth of all his claims in this letter. Marx seeks to persuade his father that he is genuinely forwarding his legal studies despite apparent detours through poetry (now a 'side line') and philosophy (a 300-page philosophy of law; 'a new basic system of metaphysics'; 'I had got to know Hegel from beginning to end, together with most of his disciples'); as well as translations of Aristotle, Tacitus and Ovid, and a study of the English and Italian languages. Much is written for effect, and his father's reply, renewing his complaints about his son's indiscipline and extravagance, shows that he was not taken in.

Nevertheless, the letter shows that by the end of 1837 Marx had become a Hegelian, possibly encouraged by the lectures of Edward Gans, a Hegelian much influenced by Saint-Simon. Hegel had died in 1831, but his thought remained dominant. It was his perspectives that ruled philosophical discussion. Briefly, Hegel believed that we see the world as we do because of the necessary categories of our thought. Our concepts form the net in which 'all the concrete matter which occupies mankind in action and impulse, is grasped'.[6] A central place is given to the inherent creativity of the human mind in all cultural experience. The Kantian distinction between *phenomena* and *noumena* has no meaning: for Hegel there is no world apart from our conceptualisations of it. Yet 'this web and its knots in ordinary consciousness . . . are not drawn up and made explicitly the objects of our reflection'.[7] This is the task of the philosopher. But his task is the labour of Sisyphus and must be undertaken anew in every age. For Hegel emphasised the historical nature of all concepts. The world is essentially subject to change through processes of contradiction and opposition. What Kant took to be changeless and necessary categories are concepts subject to alteration and change, whose necessity can only be fully explicated in the light of the totality of historical experience. The meaning of history lies within history. It is a process of development of human self-consciousness to some final state of absolute truth. 'The truth is the whole. . . . Of the absolute, it must be said that it is essentially result, that it is only in the end what it is in truth. . . .'[8] But even the philosopher can explicate only the past, and never the future: 'The Owl of Minerva spreads its wings only with the falling of the dusk.'[9]

In Berlin Marx met Bruno Bauer, who encouraged him to think in terms of an academic career. He joined the *Doktorklub*, a forerunner of the Young Hegelians, who were especially impressed by Hegel's teleological view of history, interpreting his dictum '*What is rational is actual and what is actual is rational*' in a radical fashion.[10] Among German intellectuals there was at this period a general sense of crisis and impending catastrophe, with a good deal of talk about the inevitability of a social revolution and the necessity for a fundamental reconstruction of society.[11] The Young Hegelians saw this situation reflected in philosophy. Parallels were drawn between the position of Greek philosophy after Aristotle and that of the Young Hegelians after the total philosophy of Hegel. Marx shared these general preoccupations. His doctoral dissertation was intended to throw light on the post-Hegelian situation in philosophy by an examination of a parallel period in post-Aristotelian Greek thought, comparing the philosophies of Democritus and Epicurus. The preface to the dissertation reflects his radical humanism:

> Philosophy makes no secret of it. The confession of Prometheus: 'In one word, I hate all the Gods' is her own confession, her own sentence against all heavenly and earthly gods who do not recognise human self-consciousness as the supreme divinity. There shall be none other beside it.[12]

Marx began his studies for the dissertation towards the end of 1838, spurred on by his father's death, financial worry and the hope that the gaining of a doctorate would open the way to a career and a secure basis on which to marry Jenny. The writing was completed in March 1841. In April, Marx was made a Doctor of Philosophy by the University of Jena. His prospects seemed good: but Bauer's dismissal from his Bonn post for irreligious views ended Marx's own hopes for a university career.

Marx turned to journalism. He began to write for the *Rheinische Zeitung*, a newspaper founded and backed by liberal industrialists like Camphausen, Mevissen and Oppenheim in order to take advantage of the recent lightening of censorship and campaign for measures which would forward commerce and industry.[13] In fact, the newspaper soon became the leading exponent of the ideas of the Young Hegelians, and Marx himself became editor in October 1842. He increased the circulation, but was very cautious with his material and especially with the articles he was getting from the Berlin *Freien*, 'pregnant with world revolutions and empty of thought . . . flavoured with a little atheism and communism'.[14] Marx had warned Oppenheim that the striking of attitudes gained nothing but closer attention from the censor. Ill-digested communist and socialist ideas would do the paper no good. Indeed, 'we are annoying a large number . . . of liberals engaged in political activity'.[15] Mevissen, however, thought the *Rheinische Zeitung* too negative in its approach, while Camphausen complained to his brother of the lack of any 'clear and definite principles' because the editor refused to allow a positive expression of the political views which had inspired the founding of the newspaper.[16] But despite Marx's caution, his own contributions were finally sufficient to get the paper banned. In looking back at this period Marx singled out as of most importance to his

17

development the experience of finding himself 'in the embarrassing position of having to discuss what is known as material interests', in dealing with the wood-theft laws in Prussia and the economic plight of the Moselle wine-growers.[17] But it was an attack on Russian absolutism that proved the last straw for the Prussian government, and in March 1843 the *Rheinische Zeitung* ceased publication, interestingly one of the last liberal newspapers to do so. In June, Marx married Jenny and retired to a summer interlude at Kreuznach.

The months at Kreuznach are of great importance in Marx's early intellectual development. Perhaps spurred on by Gans's lectures on the history and influence of the French Revolution, Marx began to delve deeply into the literature on this subject. At the same time he not only read extensively in political theory, but also began an extended critique of Hegel's political thought. The manuscript seems to be an attempt by Marx to clarify his own thinking on political matters before he took up work on the *Deutsch-Französische Jahrbuch*, which he and Arnold Ruge, a radical publicist, hoped to edit in Paris. Marx arrived in Paris on 11 October 1843.

In his first months in Paris, Marx furthered his knowledge of the French Revolution. We know from Ruge's letters that Marx decided to abandon his critique of Hegel's political thought in order to write a history of the Convention of 1793. He studied the speeches of Saint-Just and Robespierre as well as the minutes of the Convention debates and the memoirs of Levasseur de la Sarthe, a Convention member who witnessed the struggles of Girondins and Montagnards.[18] The events of the revolutionary period were strongly to colour Marx's image of revolution for some years to come. In addition, Marx learnt from the French bourgeois historians the conception of class struggle in history. J. H. Hexter has criticised those who write 'the social history of Western civilisation for every century up to the nineteenth in terms of the rise of the middle class and the decline of the aristocracy, in those strictly Marxist terms and in no other'.[19] But in fact the terms are those of the liberal historians of the French Restoration period after 1815. Marx saw in the histories of Thierry and Guizot, as well as those of English popular historians like John Wade, a history of class struggle written from the point of view of the 'rising middle classes'.[20]

Thus Marx was being no more than strictly accurate when he later wrote that

> no credit is due to me for discovering the existence of classes in modern society or the struggle between them. Long before me the bourgeois historians had described the historical development of this class struggle and bourgeois economists the economic anatomy of the classes.[21]

Indeed this is also true of the idea of successive historical economic formations, which had already received a clear statement by, among others,

Richard Jones in his criticism of the culture and time-bound character of classical political economy.[22] Hyndman relates that Marx had described how 'the whole idea came upon him, as he was studying in Paris, like a flash. . . .' [23] What appears to have happened is that Marx began to see a set of systematic links between several ideas which had been born more or less independently of each other: the notions of class conflict, of successive economic formations in history, and the economic role of classes in production. It was an essay in the *Jahrbuch* by Friedrich Engels that first directed Marx's attention to economics. He dropped his plan to write a history of the Convention and began to study political economy. The *EPM*, written in the spring and summer of 1844, is a set of manuscripts reflecting the early intellectual struggles of a Hegelian confronted with political economy having assimilated the ideas of the French socialists. But it was not only intellectual influences which finally persuaded Marx of the truth of the communist standpoint. The emotional impact upon Marx of his experiences with the artisan societies in Paris is vividly recorded in the *EPM*: 'The brotherhood of man is no mere phrase with them, but a fact of life, and the nobility of man shines upon us from their work-hardened bodies.' [24] The Marxian synthesis of the ideas we have mentioned was directly related to the perspective of a new social class, the industrial proletariat.

Marx and Ruge had hoped that the *Jahrbuch* would be a collaborative effort between French and German intellectuals. But it appeared in February 1844 without a single French contribution. The failure of the journal was compounded by the confiscation of many copies by the Prussian government. Personal relations between Marx and Ruge became increasingly strained. The final political break came when Marx attacked Ruge's petty bourgeois radicalism in an important article in August 1844.[25]

On the twenty-eighth day of the same month came Marx's momentous meeting with Friedrich Engels (1820–95). The two had met in Cologne in September 1842, but Engels was then connected with the Berlin *Freien*, and the meeting was short and cool. But now the two hit it off immediately, and there began the collaboration that was to last nearly forty years. The extensive financial and psychological support given by Engels needs no emphasis. The only known rift in their personal relationship occurred in 1863, when Engels had informed Marx of the death of his mistress, Mary Burns, to receive in reply perfunctory condolences and a lengthy account of Marx's own troubles.[26] There are indications that Marx was not completely open with Engels: 'I shall take the utmost care to prevent our good General from seeing anything that is likely to give him pain,' wrote Eleanor of Marx's papers.[27] There is no evidence, however, that Marx's reserve ever concerned matters of an intellectual or political kind.

The working relationship between the two men was extremely close. It was Engels, first through his *Jahrbuch* article and then through his personal knowledge, who turned Marx's attention to economics. Engels had spent most of 1843-4 in his father's cotton-spinning factory in Manchester, writing for Robert Owen's *New Moral World* and gathering material for his *Condition of the Working Class in England in 1844*. At this time he was probably a communitarian communist and wrote enthusiastically about the American communist communities. Marx was not so impressed.[28] The essential point is that Engels knew at first hand the condition of the working class about whom Marx had been theorising as a philosophical instrument of liberation. Engels' practical business knowledge of the money market, of trade trends and industrial conditions was always available to Marx. There was only a minimal collaboration on *The Holy Family*, but the major detailed statement of their view of history, in *The German Ideology*, is mainly in Engels' hand.[29] Between November 1850 and September 1870 Engels worked in Manchester and direct daily collaboration ceased. But the two visited each other regularly, and the exchange of nearly 1,350 letters is not only a major source for Marx's views in these years but is also revelatory of an extensive and continuing working and intellectual relationship, which was by no means a one-sided affair.

Engels also gave Marx considerable assistance in his journalistic activities. Because of Marx's inability to write English it was Engels who wrote Marx's first articles for the *New York Daily Tribune*.[30] The correspondence reveals considerable assistance by Engels in the provision of material and the proposing of points of view. As examples we can cite Marx on the nature of Oriental government; and their exchanges concerning the course of the American Civil War.[31] When Marx was hard pressed, Engels was usually willing to oblige with an article. When Marx lost his only son Edgar in April 1855, Engels took over and wrote the next four sets of articles for the *Neue Oder Zeitung*.[32] Engels always considered Marx his superior intellectually, but discussion was manifestly between equals, in which Engels gave as good as he got.[33] The two did, of course, tend to specialise, and Marx normally deferred to Engels' opinions on military matters and on scientific questions. Engels had a circle of scientific friends in Manchester, among whom Carl Schorlemmer, a founder of organic chemistry and later a professor at Owens College, was the most important. Marx and Engels exchanged many letters concerning the material, structure and arguments of both Marx's *Critique of Political Economy* (1859) and *Capital* I, in which Engels' advice was sometimes accepted and always evaluated with care. 'Your satisfaction . . . is more important to me than anything the rest of the world may say of it,' wrote Marx.[34] The latter also scrutinised Engels' writings, the most notable example being *Anti-Dühring* (1877), which, for all its flaws, remained the only systematic exposition of the 'Marxist' position.

In addition, it was Engels who, after Marx's death, assembled *Capital* II and III from a mass of manuscripts. It is through Engels' work that we know these volumes. True, Marx once wrote to Engels that 'although finished, the manuscript, gigantic in its form, could not be prepared for publication by anyone but myself, not even by you'.[35] But it is not necessarily the case that what might have been true in 1866 remained so in 1883. One volume from the manuscript had been published; Marx did engage in some reshaping of his material; and he did leave some directions on how to handle and select from the manuscripts for publication purposes.[36]

These facts should remind us of another feature of their relationship. For a long period Marx's sole intellectual audience was Engels. His views remained unknown outside a small group of personal friends. Marx's pamphlet on the Paris Commune had established him only as the notorious Red Doctor; in the SPD he was known, but not read, as the man who had proved, in a big book, the inevitability of the collapse of capitalism. Despite the publication of *Capital* I in 1867, it was not until the publication of *Anti-Dühring* a decade later that Marx's views became at all well known, and then only through the medium of Engels.

In sum, much of Marx's work has come to us through the medium of Engels, and much written by Engels passed through Marx's hands before publication. We can trace many disagreements on matters of politics, history and natural science in the correspondence, but these concern detail rather than substantive theory. Neither Marx nor Engels ever appears aware that they might entertain different views on matters of theory. This is important, as differences of major theoretical significance have been detected by commentators in the areas of ontology, epistemology, history and politics. Marx was especially adept at detecting major differences of principle in what might appear to the unwary as minor differences of detail. Yet there is no evidence that Marx ever scented those differences which are said radically to differentiate his views from those of Engels. Marx may, of course, have simply been mistaken. The theoretical issues will be taken up as and when they arise in the course of our later exposition.

2 THE COMMUNIST LEAGUE AND THE REVOLUTIONS OF 1848

In February 1845, having received an expulsion order because of his connection with *Vorwärts!*, the radical German-language newspaper published in Paris, Marx went to Brussels. The three years he spent there saw his first concentrated efforts at working-class organisation. Marx and Engels visited London and Manchester for six weeks in the summer of 1845, and the latter introduced Marx to his contacts in the Chartist movement and the London branch of the League of the Just,

21

the secret German artisan organisation. On his return to Brussels, Marx decided to institute a network of communist corresponding committees, an idea he probably borrowed from similar methods used by the artisans of the German Workers' Educational Society in London.[37] The Brussels committee was set up in February 1846. Marx set about persuading prominent socialists to take part.

Among those approached was Pierre-Joseph Proudhon (1809–65), whom Marx had met briefly in Paris in late 1844.[38] Proudhon had sprung into prominence in 1840 with his famous book *What is Property?* and the notorious answer, 'Property is theft'. In fact, his socialism assumed an economy of peasants and artisans: he attacked large-scale ownership and defended the small owner. For Proudhon, economic equality did not mean either communism, in whatever form, or equal ownership, but simply that there should be no extremes of wealth or poverty. Political liberty involved a state of anarchy: there would be no government and no hierarchical organisation. Society would consist of small owners bound together by freely entered contracts. The social revolution that ushered in this state of affairs would come through force of principle: 'No hatred, no hatred: eliminate by principle.'[39]

In a letter to Proudhon Marx explained that the object of the committee project was to organise a regular correspondence on matters of theory, propaganda and organisation, and thus to establish regular contacts between French, German and English socialists. He emphasised the need for the socialist movement to rid itself of national limitations of knowledge and outlook. Because of German political conditions, however, the correspondence would have to be secret.[40] Marx might have secured Proudhon's help if he had left matters there. But in a postscript he added a warning. Proudhon must beware of 'a literary swindler, a charlatan . . . the man is dangerous . . . beware of this parasite', namely Karl Grün, friend of Proudhon. In his reply, Proudhon agreed 'willingly . . . to become one of the stages of your correspondence'. But he hoped that it would not be used to spread a new dogma in emulation of Luther. 'Let us set the world an example of wide and far-seeing tolerance.' Proudhon warned against 'an appeal to force and arbitrariness . . . I would rather burn property little by little than give it renewed strength by making a St Bartholomew's Day of property owners'. He concluded with a lengthy defence of Grün, and urged Marx to assist the sale of the latter's translation of Proudhon's forthcoming book on economics.[41] No reply by Marx is known. When Proudhon's book appeared, Marx savaged it in *The Poverty of Philosophy*. The episode is a good example of a youthful lack of tact which Marx was later to curb. It is also representative: Proudhon's ideas were to reappear as a lifelong form of opposition to Marx's views.

Indeed, the general response to Marx's scheme was disappointing. There were some desultory contacts with Silesia, the Wüppertal (G. A. Köttgen), Kiel and Cologne. No new contacts of importance were made, and the hope of giving wide circulation to new developments in socialist theory (and especially the theory of *The German Ideology*) was not fulfilled. The Just in London and Paris, internationally organised but confined largely to German artisans, together with G. J. Harney of the Chartist Left, remained the only real hope of contact with what Marx was to call later the 'real movement'.

The Just had originated in the milieu of the Paris secret societies of the 1830s as a secret, conspiratorial society linked to similar French ones, notably the *Société des Saisons* of Blanqui and Barbès. Early doctrinal influences had included the artisanal communism of Babeuf and the Christian populism of Lamennais. According to the 1838 statutes of the Just, however, the main objective was the achievement of the Rights of Man and of the Citizen in Germany.[42] The organisation consisted of the basic unit, the *Gemeinde* (commune of 5 to 10 members), the *Gau* (region of 5 to 10 communes), with an elected *Volkshalle* as a central committee, from which a commission of three was elected.[43] All officers were elected annually and were subject to recall.[44] There was no lateral communication: members were to know each other only within their commune. As a secret society, the Just usually existed within a larger, public organisation. Tailors, cabinet-makers and shoemakers made up the bulk of the membership, which was confined to those of German speech and customs.[45]

Many Just members were implicated in the abortive Blanquist *coup d'état* of 12 May 1839 in Paris. Some, Schapper and Moll among them, fled to London. Bauer joined them in 1842. These three became the leaders of the Just in London. The German Workers' Educational Society, founded by Schapper, soon became not only the milieu within which the London *Gau* of the Just existed, but also the centre of the social and political activities of the three major émigré groups in London: German, French and Polish. The central committee of the Just was not transferred from Paris to London until 1846, but London throughout the 1840s was the most alive and active centre.

Wilhelm Weitling (1808–71) was the early formulator of Just doctrine with his 1838 pamphlet *Mankind As It Is and As It Should Be*. His formulations were squarely in the Lamennais tradition, equating communism with primitive Christianity and attacking religious and social hierarchy. In the new order there would be community in all things, equal work and rewards for all, equal education and so on. There is a pervasive chiliastic fervour: a call for Messianic leadership in the holy war for the liberation of mankind. All this goes well beyond the objectives of the 1838 statute. In May 1841 Weitling left to spread the message in Switzerland, leaving Ewerbeck, a doctor with literary pretensions, in control of the Paris Just. Weitling's views became more and more violent, talking of the need to release the 'thieving proletariat' upon mankind and bring about the millennium with 'one violent push'. But despite the publication of his *Guarantees of Harmony and Freedom* in December 1842, a book much praised by Marx, Weitling was fast losing ground as the ideological leader of the Just. A general revulsion from the methods of conspiracy and *coup d'état* had occurred after the disaster of 1839. Ewerbeck had become a follower of Cabet, translated *Voyage en Icarie* into German, and converted the Paris Just to his views. The London Just also found more in common with Cabet than with Weitling. Thus when the latter arrived in London in September 1844 after a term of imprisonment in Switzerland, he found that the leaders of the Just were opposed to his views.

Cabet, like Weitling, also appealed to Christian sentiment: 'Communism is Christianity in its original purity.' But the goal was to be attained through peaceful, mass propaganda and the changing of hearts. Cabet appealed to all classes, though in fact the French Icarians consisted overwhelmingly of traditional skilled artisans.[46] Icarianism had spread rapidly after a political trial of Icarians at Toulouse had ended with their acquittal. The London Just had sent a letter of support to Cabet, declaring 'our entire adhesion to the Icarian doctrine'.[47] More specifically, they pledged themselves to use peaceful propaganda rather than force in pursuit of their goal. It is significant that no commitment is made to *communauté*: the London Just rejected every attempt by Cabet to get an experiment in Icarian communism off the ground. His emigration proposals ignored the difficulties ahead and the fate of the Europe left behind.[48] However, the selective acceptance of Cabet did not aid Weitling. The surviving records of the GWES show that he was defeated on every issue that received discussion between June 1845 and January 1846.[49] His advocacy of one great cataclysmic upheaval, superintended by a dictatorship of a well-organised revolutionary elite, found favour among neither leaders nor rank and file. Some time in February 1846 Weitling went to Brussels.

In Brussels, Marx and Weitling soon clashed.[50] Marx, having argued the need for a common doctrine among socialists, had then challenged Weitling to make clear the theoretical principles upon which he had based his actions. The latter replied that he merely wished to open people's eyes. Marx: 'The stimulation of fantastic hopes . . . led only to the ultimate ruin, and not the salvation, of the oppressed.' Weitling's anti-intellectualism came to the fore. He retorted that his preparatory work was more important 'than criticism and closet analysis of doctrines in seclusion from the suffering world and the misery of the people'. This caught Marx on the raw. He jumped up, slamming his fist on the table, and exclaimed, 'Ignorance has never yet helped anybody.' The meeting closed soon afterwards. Weitling alleged that Marx had demanded a purge (*Siftung*) of the '*Kommunistische Partei*', and had threatened the withdrawal of finance from those who failed to pursue 'a suitable form of criticism' in their writings. For Marx the main theoretical enemies were 'artisan communism' and 'philosophical communism'. Finally, there could be no question of the immediate realisation of communism:

the bourgeoisie must first take the rudder.[51] This was a repudiation of a belief common to Weitling and the True Socialists like Karl Grün, namely, that industrialisation could be avoided.

Marx attached considerable importance to ridding the German artisan circles in London and Paris of the widespread influence of artisanal communism. Such a doctrine reflected the beliefs of the old-style guild craftsman who sees his way of life threatened by the massive socio-economic changes taking place, which are gradually forcing him into the ranks of the urban proletariat. There is a radical impulse here, but from the Marxian viewpoint it is essentially reactionary.[52] Further, the social gap between Marx and Weitling – the one an educated intellectual from a professional family, the other an illegitimate, self-taught journeyman tailor – symbolised a perennial difficulty confronting Marx: the distruct many workers felt for the bourgeois intellectual of socialist views. In the end, each side was to complement the other. Marx had a doctrine and was in search of a genuine workers' organisation to convert; the Just had an organisation and were in search of a doctrine. Despite these mutual interests, however, it is clear that Marx could expect no uncon-ditional adherence. The letters from the London corresponding com-mittee to Brussels are evidence of this. For them the main difficulty in the relationship of worker to intellectual lay 'in the arrogance of the intellectual . . . and you *Brüsseler Proletarier* possess this damned intel-lectual arrogance in a high degree'.[53] Marx does not appear to have replied to this. In November 1846 relations reached breaking-point when the *Volkshalle* of the Just called for a League congress in May 1847 in order to thrash out a unified doctrine and construct a 'simple communist creed' to guide the membership.[54] The leaders of the Just wished to arrive at some agreed position before proceeding further with Marx. The latter's annoyance is made clear in a letter written to him by Engels, who advised caution, for a direct break with the Just would destroy Marx's chance of exercising influence in working-class circles. His reasons are interesting. There were no theoretical reasons worth breaking over. Further, 'Against the literati we could proceed as the party, but not against the straubingers. After all, these people are a couple of hundred strong and are accredited to the English through Harney. . . .' [55] The two needed the Just more than the Just needed them. Joseph Moll's visit to Brussels in January 1847 seems to have effected some kind of reconciliation.[56] The leaders of the Just were evidently disappointed with the poor response to their call for a congress, and probably hoped that Marx would provide them with a stable intel-lectual platform. The call to a June congress warned against conspira-torial tactics, condemned 'sentimental communism', and pointed to the Chartists as a model of a mass working-class organisation and to their Charter as having the kind of format suitable for a communist credo.[57]

At the congress in June 1847, the Just became the Communist League. Drafts of the organisational statutes and of a confession of faith (the latter written by Engels, but bearing strong marks of artisanal communism) were circulated to members of the League.[58] For Engels, the congress was the occasion on which conversion of the Just leadership to Marxian views was consummated by the conversion of the membership as a whole. But the drafts show that this was not the case. The June statutes are significantly different from those finally accepted in December, in terms of both organisational structure and theoretical commitment.

The proposed organisation was to be ultra-democratic. Below the central committee there were two levels, the basic unit of the commune (3 to 12 members) and the circle (2 to 10 communes). A congress was to meet once a year as the final authority, consisting of one delegate from each circle. All officials were to be elected for one year, could be re-elected, but were always subject to recall (Article 29). Each commune member had to be unanimously elected to membership (Article 3), but there was to be no restriction on language or nationality. Communication remained primitive. No commune was allowed to contact another (Article 10), but everyone had a duty to keep in regular touch with the central committee or their circle committee (Article 32). Finally, each commune had the power to accept or reject congress resolutions (Article 21).[59] However, the statutes accepted at the December congress were changed in several important respects. Article 21 of the June statutes disappeared; a new level, the leading circle, was inserted between the circle and the commune. These two changes strengthened the higher levels of the League as opposed to the grass-roots. All messages to the central committee were now to be channelled through the leading circles, which thus controlled the information flow from the lower levels of commune and circle between congresses. The ban on contact between individual communes remained. The principle of election and recall of officials was also retained.[60]

The December statutes were therefore far more hierarchical than those passed in June, though even the latter allowed room for an unscrupulous circle committee to ignore the views of its communes. Thus, in September 1847 the London central committee had sent its draft Communist Confession of Faith to the circles and communes. This remained impregnated with artisanal communism. Moses Hess had also presented his version to the Paris circle, the communes of which accepted it. For a time it looked as though Engels' June draft was to drop out of sight. But in October Engels informed Marx: '*Just between ourselves*, I have played a hellish trick on Mosi.' He had persuaded the circle committee that the Hess version was not good enough, and that he should sketch a new one – 'which will be discussed next Friday in the circle and will then be sent to London *behind the backs of the communes*'.[61] Engels could attempt this because the communes were forbidden to contact each other and were therefore unlikely to be in a position to compare notes on what they had decided. In a later letter Engels supposes that at the forthcoming congress, '*this time we shall have it all our own way*'.[62] But there were ten days of strenuous debate before the statutes were finally approved and Marx and Engels commissioned to write a manifesto.[63] This in itself indicates that opposition remained strong. Marx was at this point a dominant figure in the League, but at no point in its history could it be said to have been his organisation. Nevertheless, Article 1 of the December statutes, after the June version had replaced the objective of 1838 by that of community of property (*Gütergemeinschaft*), a typical artisanal phrase, was now squarely written in Marxian terms:

> The aim of the League is the downfall of the bourgeoisie and the ascendancy of the proletariat, the transcendence of the old bourgeois society based on class conflict, and the foundation of a new society without classes and without private property.[64]

Yet this was an objective posed for an organisation composed in the main, not of factory proletarians, but of backward-looking artisans seeking escape from the factory situation. Marx was now to write a manifesto which informed the majority of the members of the organisation on whose behalf it was written that their way of life was doomed to extinction.

The *Communist Manifesto* was written in the nick of time, though it was to have no effect on the course of events. In late February 1848 came the revolution awaited by radicals throughout the 1840s. The mandate of the London central committee was transformed to the Brussels circle committee, and thence to Marx personally, authorising him to organise a central committee in Paris. This he did. In April the members returned to Germany. At first a central committee appears to have functioned in Cologne. But there is no known document later than 11 May to prove that the committee was still in existence.[65] 'The League is dissolved: it is everywhere and nowhere,' wrote Stephen Born to Marx.[66] There is no evidence of the organisational existence of the League until late in 1848 when Joseph Moll travelled to several German cities on behalf of a reconstituted London central committee.

An explanation for this gap in the record was given by P. G. Röser, a leading League figure in Cologne (1849–50), whilst under police interrogation.[67] He claimed that Marx had been given discretionary power at the Brussels meeting 'to govern the affairs of the League according to his own convenience'.[68] At a meeting of the Cologne central committee Marx had proposed dissolution. For him the League, as a secret organisation, was no longer necessary, as the freedoms of speech, press and assembly were now available. Marx was supported by a local leader, Andreas Gottschalk, and opposed by the old Just leaders, Schapper and Moll. There has been a controversy over the reliance to be placed on Röser's claims; and about whether the League was in fact dissolved.[69] The absence of evidence that the League did exist in the second half of 1848; the fact of its reconstitution in London under a new set of statutes (December 1848); and the testimony of Röser and (indirectly) Born, all suggest that the League was dissolved. But why?

The reason attributed to Marx, that the League was superfluous in a time of civil freedoms, lacks plausibility. Both he and Engels emphasise that the League was a propaganda society whose need for secrecy was contingent. That there appeared to be no reason for secrecy was an argument for an *open* League organisation, not for dissolving it altogether. Indeed, by hindsight, it could be argued that the possible temporary nature of these freedoms implied a need to keep a secret organisation in being. But there was a more pressing motive than the one attributed to Marx. He was concerned solely at this time with the publication of the *Neue Rheinische Zeitung* (*NRZ*), a democratic newspaper with a policy in keeping with the *Manifesto*, namely, one of alliance with the radical bourgeoisie in Germany's 1848 equivalent of the 1789 revolution. It notable that Engels was at this time very worried about the distribution of a seventeen-point flysheet bearing demands far less radical than those of the *Manifesto*: 'If a single copy of our 17 points appears here . . . it will be all up with us.' [70] That is, there would be no backers for the *NRZ*, or worse, the backers would refuse to allow Marx to run it. If the League remained in being, those to whom control of the organisation would devolve might well pursue policies at variance with those of Marx. Indeed, the whole Cologne period up to April 1849 was to see a continuous struggle between Marx and those, like Gottschalk, who felt that a more radical and independent course should be pursued.

For a few months it did seem as though Marx was right in his estimate of the situation. From Paris the unrest had spread in March to Berlin. Camphausen formed a liberal government. These events, for Marx, constituted Germany's 1789, the chance arrived at long last for the German people to catch up with the French in terms of political development. The role of the *NRZ* seemed to be one of encouragement and exhortation to the liberal bourgeoisie in the fulfilment of their historic role as the leaders of the long awaited bourgeois revolution. But by December 1848 Marx was denouncing the policies of the government.[71] The liberals had preferred to ally themselves with the forces of order rather than give countenance to the demands of a rising urban proletariat. For Marx, as indeed for many radical liberals, the only way out appeared to be a revolutionary war against Russia, to save the revolution in emulation of the events of 1792. But the June Days in Paris were followed by the October reaction in Vienna and the recovery of nerve by the Prussian government in Berlin by December. Russian bayonets shored up the counter-revolution. Despite Marx's changing appreciation of the situation, however, he clung to the policy of alliance. Only in April 1849 did he admit his mistake and break off political relations with the radical democrats.

The *Neue Rheinische Zeitung* closed in May 1849. Marx returned to

Paris, where he witnessed the June Days of 1849. In July he received an order expelling him from Paris. He was, however, to be allowed to go to Morbihan, in 'the Pontine marshes of Brittany', a phrase Marx clearly relished, since he repeats it in three successive letters to Engels. 'You realise, I shall not endure this cloaked attempt at murder.' [72] Marx went to London instead, where he had hopes of establishing a new journal. He was followed by his family in September 1849.

It seems that it was only after his arrival in London that Marx rejoined the Communist League, and helped in the task of reorganisation at the same time as he edited his journal and awaited a fresh outbreak of revolution. For a brief period optimism reigned, with much talk of new contact and groups being formed. Marx considered that 'a tremendous industrial, agricultural and commercial crisis' was brewing in England. But he considered that the revolutionaries should wait until this crisis broke out:

> A premature outbreak of the revolution – provided it is not provoked directly by Russian intervention – would be, in my opinion, a misfortune, for at the present time, when trade is expanding more and more in France, Germany, etc., the labouring masses, as well as all the small shopkeepers, may be revolutionary in phrase, but not so *en réalité*.[73]

In short, the possibility of a successful revolution is predicated only on the event of some kind of economic crisis. Throughout 1850 Marx closely watched commerce and industry for signs of such an event. In March the revolution is said to be imminent; in June, that it 'can no longer be very far away'; but by the time Marx came to write the survey of developments which forms the last part of *The Class Struggles in France*, he is clear that, for the moment, any talk of immediate revolution is futile.[74]

Although Marx was not clear about the details, his basic position concerning the economic prerequisites of a successful revolution in Western Europe is consistently held at this period, though the theoretical basis of the position was beginning to shift. This should be emphasised, as it has often been claimed that Marx at this time was under the influence of Blanqui.[75] In April 1850 a shadowy organisation, the *Société Universelle des Communistes Révolutionnaires*, was set up, composed of the London leaders of the Blanquists, the League and the Chartist Left (Harney). The goal of the society was 'the overthrow of all privileged classes, to subject these classes to the dictatorship of the proletariat by sustaining the revolution in permanence until the realization of communism . . . the final form of organisation of society'. [76] In the first part of *CSF*, published in March 1850, Marx talks of 'communism, for which the bourgeoisie has itself invented the name of Blanqui'. The March *Address to the Communist League* is said to bear the hallmark of conspiratorial Blanquism.[77]

The *Address* is both an appreciation of what occurred in 1848–9, and a statement of policy in view of an impending new revolution, which it was thought would be made by the 'democratic petty bourgeoisie'. The latter would need the help of the proletariat, as the liberal bourgeoisie had gone over to absolutism. The League must aid the democrats against the bourgeoisie, but attack them whenever they seek to consolidate their position in their own interest. The revolution must be made permanent 'until the proletariat have conquered state power'.[78] What tactics should be pursued in such a situation? The mistake made in 1848 must not be repeated. 'An independent, secret and public organisation of the workers' party' must be established alongside the democrats. There must be no organisational fusion of the kind which occurred in 1848–9; a secret organisation must be maintained alongside the public one; and there must be none of the slackening of organisation which occurred in the revolutionary enthusiasm of 1848. When the revolution arrives, the League must do all it can to keep 'the direct revolutionary excitement . . . alive as long as possible', and encourage a disciplined use of force and even 'excesses' in pursuit of their aim. The workers must arm themselves, put forward their own demands, and alongside the official government establish 'simultaneously their own revolutionary workers' governments'. After the revolution a representative national assembly will be elected. Here the League must aim at full electoral rights for workers, the adoption of workers' candidates, a 'single and indivisible German republic', centralisation of state power, and also prevent ex-feudal lands from falling into the hands of the peasantry, a measure which Marx felt had immeasurably strengthened conservatism in France after 1789. The *Address* envisages 'a lengthy revolutionary process' before the German workers could attain power, a process which would hopefully be accelerated by the 'direct victory of their own class in France'. Until then, the battle-cry must be: 'The Revolution in Permanence.'

All this may appear to have a Blanquist ring. But we must be careful. The strategy laid down in the *Address* is predicated on familiar Marxian grounds. There is no suggestion that a self-appointed revolutionary elite can seize power independently of favourable socio-economic conditions.[79] The impending revolution will be begun by other agents – the petty bourgeois democrats. The League is told that it must avoid identification with those who are soon to become its enemies. The aim is to develop a working-*class* party, with independence in both organisation and policies; to arm the whole 'proletariat'. There is no elite action here. To see a need for a secret as well as public organisation seems only sensible in the prevailing political situation in Germany. The readiness to capitalise upon 'excesses' if harnessed to disciplined party activity cannot be considered peculiarly Blanquist. To eschew the use of force in a revolutionary situation would be pointless.[80]

The historical conditions in which the *Address* was written should also be kept in mind. The revolution had been defeated. The surviving revolutionaries were back in London licking their wounds. The *Address* is written to rally the faithful and provide a framework within which the situation could be understood to the advantage of the revolutionaries. Marx himself may have been under pressure at this time. Why, otherwise, enter into such an amorphous alliance as SUCR with the Blanquist refugees? The *Address* itself is a *mea culpa* by Marx. He had dissolved the League, claiming that there was no need for a secret organisation. It had been others who had reorganised it. He had pursued in Cologne what was to prove the will-of-the-wisp policy of alliance with the democrats. Finally, Marx's involvement in working-class politics in Cologne or the rest of Germany had been slight. In the *Address* Marx shows great skill in satisfying the revolutionary romanticism of the rank and file within the framework of his theoretical views, and yet managing to skim over some of the defects apparent in his own political activities. Not that the *Address* was a realistic appraisal of the situation. The idea that there was a revolutionary 'proletariat' to arm was simply not true; even more chimerical was the belief that the petty bourgeois democrats would, or could, begin a new revolution. As the 1850s wore on, Marx was to become aware of the capacity of West European societies to sustain without essential damage commercial and industrial crises which his earlier economic theorising had told him must lead to the collapse of those societies.

By September 1850 Marx had become tired of the empty pseudo-revolutionary declarations of the German and French exiles. The effective end of the League came at the famous central committee meeting of 15 September. Marx proposed to move the CC to Cologne, to form two leading circles in London independent of each other, and to declare the December 1848 statutes void. The Cologne CC should draw up new statutes. In his view, the revised statutes were too conspiratorial. Further, the minority in the CC (who were clearly in a majority in the League as a whole) held views contrary both to the *Manifesto* and to the March *Address*.

> The revolution is seen not as the product of the realities of the situation but as the result of *will*. What we say to the workers is: you have 15, 20, 50 years of civil war to go through, in order to change social relationships and to train yourselves for the exercise of power, whereas they say, we must take over *at once*, or else we may as well go to sleep.

Schapper, Marx's main opponent, agreed that the CC should be transferred to Cologne and that new statutes should be drawn up. But to have two separate leading circles in London meant an end to unity and indeed 'the end of the League'. As to the current situation, he argued that revolution was imminent; that once the French workers had come to power, the same would happen in Germany and there would be a

31

proletarian government. 'I do not share the view that the bourgeoisie will come to power. . . .' The split in the League meant two Leagues, one for the intellectuals and theoreticians, the other for 'those who organise the proletariat'. Marx replied that he had 'always defied the momentary opinions of the proletariat'. 'Our party can only gain power when the situation allows it to put *its own* measures into practice.' [81]

The next few months are a story of bickering and recriminations. Marx and his followers resigned from the *GWES* – 'the Great Windmill street gang'.[82] A certain amount of effort was made to secure the appearance of a legitimate succession for the Marx fraction, but Marx himself appears to have given up League work in January 1851.[83] He turned increasingly to his economic studies. These were interrupted by the trial in Germany of members of the Communist League. Marx spent much of his time in preparing evidence, refuting police forgeries and finally writing *Revelations of the Communist Trial in Cologne*. In November 1852 the League was dissolved on Marx's motion.[84] By the end of the year exile had become a reality. Except for visits to the Continent in his later years Marx was to remain in England for the rest of his life.

3 *CAPITAL*

The 1850s were to prove a time of poverty, anxiety and disappointment. Three of the six children born to Jenny died, Guido in 1850, Franziska in 1852 and Edgar in 1855. There was also a still-born child in 1856. Periods of near-starvation diet must have been partly responsible for this. Marx summed up the situation in the summer of 1851: 'My wife is ill, little Jenny is ill, Lenchen has a kind of nervous fever. I cannot call the doctor, as I have no money for medicine. For eight to ten days I have been feeding the family on bread and potatoes.' [85] More succinctly, '*Beatus ille*, he who has no family'.[86] To cap an uneasy domestic situation, Helene Demuth (Lenchen), the maidservant and general factotum of the household, gave birth to an illegitimate son by Marx.[87] The family was evicted for non-payment of rent in 1850, and for the next six years lived in two squalid rooms in Dean Street, Soho. A small legacy following the death of Jenny's mother enabled them to move in 1856, but was soon spent. Marx's only regular income came from the ill-paid work he did for the *New York Daily Tribune*.[88] He never had a regular job. With an immense, single-minded determination Marx held to his belief that his theoretical work took priority: 'I must pursue my goal through thick and thin and I must not allow bourgeois society to turn me into a money-making machine.' [89] In this he certainly succeeded. But he delighted in hard work. Indeed, there seems little doubt that the deprivations of the 1850s and the overwork to which he subjected himself were both major factors in the ill health which dogged Marx's later years. After one bout of illness, he wrote, 'They assure me that after I return I shall be able to work again, and being *unable* to work is indeed a death sentence for any man who is not a beast.' [90]

The Marx family were very largely dependent on the irregular help provided by Engels, who in 1869 was finally able to settle an income of £350 a year on Marx. Until then, the life of the household was punctuated by financial crises. A wry comment to Engels sums up Marx's situation: 'How right my mother was! "If only Karl had made Capital, instead of. . . ."' [91] Yet an attempt was always made to keep up appearances. A housemaid was added to the household in 1858; and the daughters Jenny, Laura and Eleanor were given lessons in all the usual accomplishments deemed suitable for young ladies. In 1864 bequests were received on the deaths of Marx's mother and Wilhelm Wolff. This simply encouraged Marx and his wife to move to a much larger house and the £1,600 received was spent within the year. Marx probably felt that he owed it to his family. He was very aware of the sacrifices which he had made his family endure while writing *Capital*. One of Marx's major worries about Lafargue's wish to marry Laura was his lack of any apparent economic prospects:

> You know that I have sacrificed my whole fortune to the revolutionary struggle. I do not regret it. On the contrary. Had I my career to start again, I should do the same. But I would not marry. As far as lies in my power I intend to save my daughter from the reefs on which her mother's life has been wrecked. [92]

Marx shows more than a touch of the Victorian paterfamilias in this letter. Protesting about Lafargue's familiarity with Laura, Marx adds that 'should you plead in defence your Creole temperament it becomes my duty to interpose my sound sense between your temperament and my daughter'. [93]

Marx's major occupations after 1850 lay in journalism, the writing of *Capital*, and the organisation of the International Workingmen's Association (IWA). As soon as he was established in London, he took up once more his study of Ricardo and other political economists. 'I am most often at the British Museum, from 9 in the morning until 7 in the evening.' [94] This reading, which can be traced in his extant notebooks, led to major changes of direction in his economic theorising. Marx was optimistic that the work would be finished quickly: '. . . the job is rapidly approaching completion. One must break off somewhere or other by main force. . . .' But he never did. Engels remarked that as long as Marx had not read a book he considered important, he did not get down to writing. [95] As we have noted, his work was interrupted by political events. Further, the insistent need to earn a living meant that much time was spent in journalistic activities. The result can be traced in Marx's extant notebooks for this period. His economic reading ceases at the end of 1852. Between 1853 and 1856 his reading was mainly on diplomacy (in respect to Russia, Greece and Turkey) and history (especially Spain and India). Marx does not appear to have taken up economics again until 1857, impelled by a belief in the imminence of revolution: '[I am] working madly through the night on a synthesis of my economic studies, so that I have at least the main principles clear before the deluge.' [96]

Marx most succinctly stated his scheme of work in a letter he wrote to Lassalle.[97] He listed three projects. The first was his *Economics*, 'a critique of the economic categories', which he divided into six books: namely Capital, Landed Property, Wage Labour, the State, International Trade, and the World Market. The second project was 'a critique and history of political economy and of socialism as a whole'; and the third, a 'brief historical sketch of the development of the economic categories or relationships'. The distinction drawn between these three projects gives a misleading impression, for Marx did not in fact keep them separate in those manuscripts written up to 1863.

The *Grundrisse* manuscripts constitute the first draft of the *Economics*, and afford us an unrivalled opportunity to observe the working of Marx's mind as he began to reformulate the major concepts of his economic theory (August 1857 to June 1858). The importance of the *Grundrisse* in any account of Marx's intellectual development is manifest. It is here that the notions of labour power and surplus value, involving the distinction between the exchange value and the use value of labour power; the theory of the equalisation of the rate of profit as an answer to the contradiction in Ricardo's theory between his determination of value and his theory of profit; and the theory of the tendency of the profit rate to fall, are all given clear expression for the first time.[98] In addition, the manuscripts add considerably to our knowledge of Marx's views on the nature of work and free time in a communist society, and show that the concept of alienation, given a first expression in 1844, remains central to Marx's concerns in the late 1850s. However, the importance of the *Grundrisse* should not be overestimated. Before we see it as the central theoretical work from which all else in Marx's theorising stems, we should note that much of the economics of the *Grundrisse* was re-worked in the 1860s; that certain important parts of the economic theory were first worked out in the 1860s; and, perhaps of most importance, that there is very little material concerning politics, the state and revolution in the notebooks. Indeed, the agency of the proletariat in bringing about a revolution is not mentioned.

The second surviving set of manuscripts [99] reveal Marx still mixing historical material on the development of economic theories with his theoretical discussions of the nature of the contemporary capitalist system. One reason for this is that Marx is still developing some of his own theoretical positions in the course of writing up the historical material. A more fundamental reason lies in Marx's own methodological viewpoint, in which the history of economic theories has a logical status

1865947

equivalent to Hegel's conception of the history of philosophy. In a letter to Engels, Marx stresses that he wishes in his work to develop the economic categories both *dialectically* and *historically*. Thus David Ricardo's views concerning the concept of value could only be conceived in a society in which all pre-bourgeois modes of production have been dissolved. 'Although an abstraction, this is an historical abstraction which could only be adopted on the basis of a particular economic development of society.' [100] Thus the full enterprise involved a dialectical elaboration, involving a method of immanent critique, of the economic categories of the classical political economists, together with a historical investigation of the socio-economic conditions of society in which such categories originated and developed. The enterprise was viewed by Marx as a strictly 'scientific' one; but the results of the task would be to place a theoretical tool in the hands of the proletarian class, both to situate it within bourgeois society and to help define in general terms the kinds of strategy and tactics likely to win political success.

Marx had set himself an enormous task, and in the event, the 'nightmare' as he once called it, grew at an alarming rate. In 1863 he decided to simplify the structure of his work by separating out the material concerning the history of economic theory, envisaging a fourth book in which such material could be published.[101] Marx also dropped the plan to issue his work in separate parts. In 1865 he summed up the position in the following manner:

> There are still three chapters to write in order to complete the theoretical part (the first 3 books). Then there is still the 4th Book, the historico-literary one, to write, which is relatively the easiest part to me, as all the questions have been solved in the first three Books and this last one is, therefore, something of a repetition in historical form. I cannot decide to send any part of the book to the printer until the whole work lies ready before me. Whatever shortcomings they may have, the merit of my writings is that they form an artistic whole, and this is only attainable thanks to my decision never to print them until they are quite finished. This is impossible with the Jacob Grimm method, which is of use only for writings which have no dialectical articulation.[102]

Perhaps because of this over-scrupulousness, only a part of the first book of the *Economics*, namely *Capital* I (1867), was to achieve publication in Marx's lifetime. Part One of *Capital* I incorporated the argument of *A Contribution to the Critique of Political Economy* (1859). Before the publication of *Capital* I Marx had completed the first drafts of what were to be published by Engels as *Capital* II (1885) and III (1893). It is evident from the latter's valuable prefaces to these two volumes that little material essential to them can be dated later than 1867.

What place do Marx's political writings have in all this? In his contract with the publisher C. W. Leske (February 1845) for a two-volume

Critique of Politics and Economics, politics were to have occupied a whole volume. What appears to be a draft plan of the contents survives in one of Marx's notebooks.[103] In essence, the volume would have contained the results of Marx's work at Kreuznach, namely, his reading about the French Revolution and the substance of the *Critique of Hegel's Philosophy of Right* concerning the separation of the state and civil society, bureaucracy, political parties and universal suffrage, all presumably updated in terms of Marx's Paris experiences. As time goes by, however, Marx's attention becomes more and more directed towards the technical problems of political economy, which he feels he must resolve. The whole grandiose project involved a synthesis of economics, sociology and politics. In effect, the result is a half-finished economics, with problems of sociology and politics dealt with as they arise: or, as Marx put it in his very first plan, 'the relations of political economy with the state, law, morals, civil life, etc. are . . . touched on only to the extent that political economy itself expressly deals with these subjects'.[104] In the plan of 1858, the state is the subject of the fourth book of the *Economics.* This does not mean that there is nothing of interest to political theorists in the surviving volumes of *Capital.* But it remains true that Marx's views on the state, politics, ideology, social classes and revolution are nowhere systematically set out, and need to be recovered largely from writings which are often polemical, one-sided *pièces d'occasion* requiring close examination of both text and context. A major part of the evidence for his mature political views lies in the work Marx undertook for the International Workingmen's Association (IWA) from 1864 to 1872.

4 THE INTERNATIONAL WORKINGMEN'S ASSOCIATION

Between December 1852 and September 1864 Marx had stayed aloof from organisational activity.[105] The revival of the German labour movement in the early 1860s owed nothing to Marx and much to Ferdinand Lassalle, of whom Marx had always been somewhat contemptuous.[106] But at the famous St Martin's Hall meeting Marx felt that this time 'real "powers"' were involved, and that an independent and nonsectarian initiative had been taken by working-class leaders.[107] For eight years, at a time of intense intellectual effort on his part, Marx's energies were poured into his work on behalf of the IWA. The IWA was finally to founder amid precisely the kind of sectarian strife which Marx had hoped to avoid. Nevertheless, Marx's political activities in this period are of crucial importance to the understanding of his views about political action.

Marx had played no part in the events leading up to the founding of the IWA. A letter to Engels sets out the sequence of events. Finally, Marx was to write the *Inaugural Address* of the IWA, 'a sort of review of the adventures of the Working Classes since 1845', the preamble to the Rules, and the Rules themselves. 'I was obliged to insert two phrases about "duty" and "right" into the Preamble to the Rules, ditto about "truth, morality and justice", but these are placed in such a way that they can do no harm.' [108] In the *Address* Marx paints a picture of events between 1848 and 1864.[109] The collapse of militant class organisation had been compensated by the rise of a 'political economy of labour', the principle of which had won a signal victory in the Ten Hours Act. There had also been the demonstration by the co-operative movement that production on a large scale did not require 'a class of masters employing a class of hands'. But co-operative labour by itself is not enough. The capitalist and the landowner in all countries will always use their political privileges to defend their economic monopolies. The working class must realise the international character of their struggle and the need 'to conquer political power': 'One element of success they possess – numbers; but numbers weigh only in the balance, if united by combination and led by knowledge.' Marx's general claim is that, with local variations, 'the English facts reproduce themselves in all the industrious and progressive countries of the Continent'. The subsequent history of the IWA was to show, on the contrary, that capitalism was developing in very different social contexts. Thus the anarchist views which had so much appeal in Spain, Italy, Russia and Switzerland as a reaction to industrial development had no counterpart in English experience.[110]

The *Address* could be accepted by those with quite different views about socialism or about the connection between socialism and the labour movement. To some, the 'abolition of class rule' meant the removal of institutions in which a particular class had a privileged status; to others, the abolition of classes *per se*.[111] The same is true of the call to political action, as we shall see. On some subjects of importance – the growth of trade unions, the national movement in Italy – Marx remained silent; on others, such as the co-operative movement, he decided to gloss over his own views. The *Address* also reflects genuine changes of opinion by *Marx*. The *Manifesto* argued that the working class had nothing to hope for within capitalist society. The *Address* pointed to the immense benefits obtained from the Ten Hours Act. The moral drawn is that the state can be made to legislate in favour of the working class even in a predominantly capitalist society. Marx also recognised the lack of homogeneity which now characterised the working class: while 'the great mass . . . were sinking down into a lower depth', a minority had had real wages raised.[112] This lack of homogeneity in the 'working class' was to underpin a central feature of the IWA. It claimed to represent the standpoint of the working class as a whole. Yet its membership in all countries, not merely underdeveloped ones like Italy, Spain and Switzerland, was drawn largely from the skilled artisan trades. None of the big English trade unions based on the new technologies (such as the engineers) took part.[113] The IWA mobilised elements of the past: though from Marx's perspective it was oriented to the future.

How did Marx view his own role? He began with caution. As he remarked to Engels concerning the *Address*,

> It was very difficult to frame the thing so that our view should appear in a form acceptable from the present standpoint of the workers' movement. In a few weeks the same people will be holding meetings for the franchise with Bright and Cobden. It will take time before the reawakened movement allows the old boldness of speech. It will be necessary to be *fortiter in re, suaviter in modo*. . . .[114]

The main aim was to build up an international working-class organisation, and not to engage in theoretical polemics which could only lead to disunity. In the early years, at any rate, Marx was happy to accept incremental moves towards a general theoretical programme. Of the programme for the Geneva Congress in 1866, he wrote: 'I deliberately restricted it to those points which allow of immediate agreement and concerted action by the workers, and give direct nourishment and impetus to the requirements of the class struggle and the organisation of the workers into a class.' Marx worked, as he put it, 'behind the scenes' on the General Council.[115] Mentions of him at congresses are few; [116] in the sections of the IWA he was unknown. Both his intellectual authority and his common sense enabled Marx to dominate the General Council. He was often to use his position as the man who drafted most of the Council's official documents to give them a slant of his own.[117] But they required Council approval before publication. Yet, of course, Marx's final objectives were not shared by many of those adhering to the IWA. This was obscured for some time by Marx's very success in drafting documents which would get maximum support from the IWA membership while at the same time inching forward the acceptance of his own views. We can agree with Rubel that the IWA was never, for Marx, an instrument of indoctrination, but towards the end, as we shall see, he comes close to such a view.[118] We shall consider in turn the three major issues which were finally to divide the IWA: collectivisation, political action, and the organisation of the IWA itself.

At Lausanne (1867) it was resolved that the state, variously considered as 'the collectivity of the citizens' and as 'the strict executor of the laws voted upon and recognised by the citizens', should become the 'proprietor of the means of transport and exchange'.[119] In the discussion Longuet spoke for many when he accepted the resolutions on the understanding that by state was meant 'the collectivity of the citizens'.[120] The issue of landed property was left to the Brussels congress (1868), which decided that mines, quarries, railways, arable lands, forests, canals, roads, telegraphs and other means of communication should be collective property (*propriété collective*).[121] But the discussion revealed that most of the collectivists envisaged decentralised control in the form of workers' co-operatives rather than state control. The decision that the land should become collective property was reaffirmed at Basle in 1869.[122]

The discussion at Basle revealed a major divergency. The small minority against collective property had voiced fears that no collectivist system had been put forward which had not proved authoritarian, hierarchical and centralised. Bakunin had brushed this aside, seeing collective ownership of land as a means to the abolition of 'the political and juridical state'. Eccarius countered this by arguing that 'the state could be reformed by the accession of the working class to political power'.[123] It was clear that a number of distinct views existed, concerning the means by which collective property would be attained and the method of collective organisation itself. The presence of Bakunin had aided the collectivist and revolutionary tendencies at Basle. But his views about the state led to the first defeat of the General Council on the question of the right of inheritance. Marx argued that this was an affair of the juridical superstructure, a mere effect of the economic base. Resolutions about inheritance have meaning only at a time of social transition, when the working class would be powerful enough to enforce inheritance duties and limitations on testamentary rights of inheritance.[124] Bakunin agreed that the fact of private property precedes the law which expresses it, but the law 'can cause other effects in its turn'. Inheritance is a principal basis and condition of private property in that it allows continuity of ownership. Further, merely to dispossess the peasant would be to make him counter-revolutionary. Remove the right of inheritance, and the land would become collective property within a few generations.[125] Bakunin's arguments won the day.

In this way the debate over collective property inevitably raised the problem of political action and the role of the state. The *Address* had emphasised that the conquest of political power had become 'the great duty of the working classes'.[126] The Geneva congress had accepted the Preamble to the Rules, which stated that 'the economical emancipation of the working class is . . . the great end to which every political movement ought to be subordinate as a means'. But the French omitted the '*comme moyen*' at the end of the sentence, and these words were also omitted in the French minutes of the congress.[127] The French mutualists were deeply suspicious of most forms of political activity. Nevertheless, both the Geneva and the Lausanne congresses unanimously accepted resolutions which required political action. At Geneva it was accepted that 'general laws, enforced through the power of the state' were necessary to regulate juvenile and children's labour; while in a resolution on co-operation it was stated that general social changes could be achieved only 'by the transfer of the organised forces of society, viz., the state power, from capitalists and landlords to the producers themselves'.[128]

At Lausanne, it was accepted without debate that social emancipation and political emancipation were inseparable and that the political liberties of press and assembly were an essential first step.[129] However, it remained true that the IWA had not, at any of its congresses, committed itself to any specific method of political activity. The connection between political action and 'the social movement of the working class' was a subject placed on the agenda of the projected Mainz congress in 1870.[130] But the outbreak of the Franco-Prussian War prevented the congress from taking place.

Two months later Napoleon III had been captured at Sedan, the Empire had collapsed, and the French Republic had been declared in Paris. Marx counselled caution. He urged the French workers to 'calmly and resolutely improve the opportunities of Republican liberty, for the work of their own class organisation'.[131] But the events of the next six months – the siege of Paris, the capitulation of the Government of National Defence, the national elections which returned a monarchist 'rural majority' to the Assembly, the efforts of the new government of Thiers to secure the rights of property – all this led to an atmosphere of outrage and frustration among the Parisians which was finally to explode in the short-lived Commune, crushed in the 'bloody week' at the end of May 1871. Like many radical republicans, Marx saw the Commune as a defensive measure against attempts to restore the monarchy. But he also saw something more significant than this. Many historians place the Commune as a final episode in the revolutionary tradition stretching back to 1789. For Marx, however, the Commune was a portent for the future, as the first occasion in world history when a working-class government held the reins of power. *The Civil War in France* glossed over the many criticisms privately made by Marx, and associated the Commune with the IWA, which was already being accredited with the major responsibility. In doing so the pamphlet not only increased the external pressures on the IWA, but also introduced and sanctified a myth, one which contradicted much that Marx had sought to achieve through the IWA. And indeed, an empty myth, for 'the failure of the Commune discredited the Blanquist theory of the *coup de main* and led instead to an emphasis on the need for organisation and propaganda'.[132]

Yet Marx was well aware of the deficiencies which had been revealed in the organisation of the IWA. A conference was held in London (September 1871), which, as it was not a full congress, could concern itself only with organisational questions. As Serraillier put it, the conference could not revise the statutes, but only reintegrate and tidy them up according to past congress decisions.[133] At the same time Marx argued that existing translations of the Rules were 'garbled at many points'; that the French version had falsified certain formulations; and that internal dispute had been caused because some versions of the Rules did not contain 'exactly what had been agreed at the congresses'.[134] It was decided to publish official versions in other languages. But the conference took one step which was clearly beyond its brief. Resolution IX not only reiterated that the conquest of political power was vital to the working class, but also went on to assert that 'the working class cannot act, as a class, except by constituting itself into a political party, distinct from, and opposed to, all old parties formed by the propertied classes'.[135] From Marx's point of view this was a sensible expansion of what political action entailed. But at no congress had there been any commitment to the organisation of independent, class-based political parties. This suggestion was quite new. It is significant that when Marx had been asked about the vagueness of the wording of the political question on the agenda of the Mainz congress he had replied: 'There are different ways of considering the political labour movement and we must have a comprehensive form to include them.' [136] This is to admit that no particular method of political action had yet been adopted by a congress. At London a lively discussion ensued over whether the resolution was stating a new principle. Vaillant and the Blanquists affirmed that this was not the case, and their presence ensured that there was a large majority in favour.[137]

The questions of political action and of organisation became inextricably tied together in the minds of many who opposed the London conference decisions. In the Provisional Rules the General Council had been envisaged as 'an international agency' between participating associations to facilitate the exchange of information; to carry out a general statistical inquiry; and to co-ordinate policy in the event of, for example, international quarrels. Eventually it was hoped that the Council would deal with a small number of national associations rather than with a large number of small sections, but this did not prevent any local society from directly corresponding with the Council.[138] At Geneva the Rules were put separately: only two aroused discussion.[139] The Geneva Rules made no provision to allow the Council to co-opt new members, a power given it by the Provisional Rules, but at Lausanne the Council was allowed to add to its number as it saw fit.[140] At Basle (1869) the powers of the Council were extended. It was given the rights to admit or refuse the affiliation of a new section; to suspend a section from membership; and to adjudicate in the event of disputes between different sections. These powers were exercised subject to a right of appeal to the next congress of the IWA.[141] It is noteworthy that Bakunin was strongly in favour of these provisions, which were retained without change by the London conference in 1871.[142] Yet the division between those who favoured political action and those who wanted to abstain from bourgeois politics became linked, especially in the minds of the abstentionists, with a division between authoritarian centralisers and anti-authoritarian decentralisers.

It is in the context of these disputes concerning political action and organisation that we should place the conflict between Marx and Bakunin. It is true that their uneasy personal relationship had already led to a number of misunderstandings, and was exacerbated by Marx's Russophobia and Bakunin's equally virulent hatred of all things German. The latter, while acknowledging Marx's intellectual stature, described him as 'morose, vain and treacherous'.[143] But apart from personal animosities the two men held irreconcilable political positions. Bakunin believed in the necessity of a universal revolution embracing the urban working class, the peasantry, the lumpenproletariat, the unemployed and unemployable. He gave a leading role to *déclassé* and disaffected students and intellectuals. The revolution would begin, not in advanced countries like France or Germany, but in the backward countries of southern Europe. Political participation short of revolution was anathema to him. In an important speech at Berne (September 1868), Bakunin summarised the differences between his *collectivism* and *communism*.

> I detest communism, because it is the negation of liberty. . . . Communism concentrates and seeks to absorb all social powers in the state . . . it tends necessarily to the centralisation of property in the hands of the state, while I want the abolition of the state, the radical extirpation of this principle of authority and of tutelage by the state. . . . I want the organisation of society and of . . . collective property to proceed from the bottom upwards by way of free association. . . .[144]

For Bakunin, the idea of a transitional dictatorship of the proletariat controlling the state for socialist ends was latently authoritarian. Its implementation would lead to the domination of labour by a new privileged elite of scientific experts.[145] His alternative was couched in vague terms: 'a world federation of free productive associations of all countries.'[146]

Yet Bakunin had supported the extended powers of the General Council.[147] Further, his public denunciations of the authoritarianism of Marx and the General Council sort ill with his less public commitment to the construction of secret, conspiratorial, hierarchical societies bound by strict discipline. That most of Bakunin's secret organisations remained chimeras 'formed in the clouds of his tobacco smoke'[148] is irrelevant: he did his best to make them a reality. In 1868 Bakunin's views had been rejected by the bourgeois League of Peace and Freedom. He and a few followers seceded, and founded the International Alliance of Social Democracy. In December the Alliance applied for membership of the IWA, but was rejected on the ground that the IWA did not admit other international organisations.[149] In February 1869 the Alliance tried again, agreeing to dissolve itself if its sections were enrolled as IWA sections. This time the General Council agreed, stipulating that the phrase 'equalisation of classes' be removed from the Alliance programme and that the Council be informed of the numerical strength of each section.[150] In fact, only the Geneva section was enrolled. At this point Carr interprets Bakunin as envisaging a set of concentric rings:

the IWA; the Alliance inside the IWA; the International Brotherhood inside the Alliance; and Bakunin's own directorate inside the International Brotherhood. It is evident from Bakunin's letter to Herzen in October 1869, following his victory on the inheritance issue, that he foresaw a 'life and death struggle' with Marx.[151]

The defeat on the inheritance issue convinced Marx that the IWA was confronted by a campaign of internal disruption. In late March 1870 he sent a confidential circular to the German sections relating Bakunin's activities and concluding that 'the game of this most dangerous intriguer will soon be brought to an end. . . .' [152] But events were to prove otherwise. The Genevan Alliance section applied for admission to its local federation, the Fédération Romande, which held its annual congress at the beginning of April 1870. The application was opposed by the Russian émigré Utin, a personal enemy of Bakunin who had already made overtures to Marx. A lengthy debate ended with a vote of 21–18 in favour of admission, in accordance with IWA rules. Led by Utin, the minority seceded. Each side held a congress and each claimed to be the rightful Fédération Romande. The General Council adjudicated: on Marx's advice, it decided that the majority at the original congress had been 'nominal'; [153] that the original committee, having acted correctly in the past, should not be deprived of its title; and that the organisation of the majority should adopt some other name.[154] Marx made a bad tactical error in persuading the General Council to take a decision which was not clearly in accordance with the Rules. From this point forward, the Jura sections supported Bakunin; the Geneva sections, Marx and the General Council. Bakunin had tapped a potent source of discontent within the IWA which was to come to a head with the decisions at London. Following the conference, a congress of the dissident Fédération Romande was convoked. It issued the famous Sonvilliers Circular to all the federations of the IWA.

The Sonvilliers Circular described how, by means of administrative resolutions, the General Council, originally conceived as a central office of correspondence between the various sections of the IWA, had been given dangerous powers to suspend sections and to adjudicate disputes. The Council had been unable to evade the 'fatal law' that power corrupts the holder.

> The General Council, composed for five years of the same men' always re-elected, and given at Basle a great power over the sections, has come to regard itself as the legitimate head of the IWA. . . . Little by little, these men . . . have been induced . . . to wish that their special programme, their personal doctrine should predominate. . . .[155]

Their views became the official theory, and divergent ideas were taken to be 'a veritable heresy'. The statutes did not allow for the kind of secret conference called at London. This conference sought to turn 'a free federation of autonomous sections' into 'a hierarchical and authoritarian organisation of disciplined sections' under the control of the General Council. This is, of course, a natural process so far as those are concerned whose ideal is '*the conquest of political power by the working class*'. The IWA must return to the principle of the autonomy of the sections, and the General Council to its role as 'that of a simple correspondence and statistical bureau'. Finally, the Circular closed with what was to be a familiar theme: that of prefiguration:

Future society should be none other than the universalisation of the organisation which the International has given itself. . . . How can a free and egalitarian society arise from an authoritarian organisation? It is impossible. The International embodies future human society. . . .[156]

The Circular, together with Marx's counterblast, *Fictitious Splits in the International*,[157] set the terms of the debate in 1872, and indeed for many years afterwards. The picture the Circular gave, of the Collectivists with their goal of a free federation of Communes, in desperate struggle with the Marxists, authoritarian communists who believed in state centralisation, was in many ways a caricature. Marx was never as authoritarian as he was painted; and there was no Marxist party, if by that we mean a disciplined group of followers with a clear understanding of his political and economic thought. Nor do Bakunin's libertarian claims stand close examination. Each can equally be credited with seeking to mould the IWA in his own image. Thus it was that the IWA, which before the Commune was experiencing a decline in membership and a marked apathy in the advanced countries,[158] partially concealed by radical resolutions at the congresses, and which was now being attacked from without for its supposed role in the Paris Commune, now proceeded to tear itself apart internally. Both sides desperately sought a majority at the inevitable and crucial congress. At The Hague in September 1872 it became clear that Marx had won the battle for delegates. All the resolutions of the London conference were confirmed.

Marx had also decided to discredit Bakunin. A committee was appointed to hear Engels' charge that the Alliance, supposedly dissolved in 1869, had continued to exist as a secret organisation within the IWA with the aim of imposing a sectarian programme upon the international. The IWA, said Engels, 'is composed of socialists of the most varied shades of opinion. Its programme is sufficiently broad to accommodate them all'. But a secret Alliance working against the basic principles of the IWA is another matter. All members are equal under the Rules. But the Alliance thinks in terms of 'two castes: the initiated and the uninitiated, the aristocracy and the plebs, the latter destined to be led by the first by means of an organisation whose very existence is unknown to them'. [159] The committee found that the Alliance had existed subsequent to 1869 but that there was 'insufficient evidence for its continued existence'. It went beyond its brief in convicting Bakunin of using fraudulent means to gain money and threats when asked for repayment. Guillaume attacked the proceeding as 'a political trial with the desire of silencing the minority, that is, the majority'.[160] And indeed for Marx any means were justified to crush the influence of a man he regarded as a dangerous buffoon. Bakunin and Guillaume were finally expelled from the IWA.

But Marx was able to save the IWA from Bakunin only at the cost of destroying the organisation. Engels created a sensation when he proposed that the seat of the General Council be moved to New York. A number of motives seem to have been present. The next congress, in Switzerland, was sure to have a Bakuninist majority. As Engels put it, if there had been conciliation at The Hague, 'the sectarians, especially the Bakuninists, would have got another year in which to perpetuate, in the name of the International, even greater stupidities'.[161] In his struggle with Bakunin, Marx had been supported by the Blanquists, support he preferred to do without, as they had abated none of their 'barricadology' following the Commune. If Blanquist support was conditional, that of the English members of the General Council had grown lukewarm if not antipathetic. Thus Marx could not assume Council support for his views. Engels cited party dissensions in London as a major reason for moving the seat elsewhere.[162] Further, Marx's health was worsening, and he wished to devote the time he had to the completion of *Capital*. Indeed, he saw The Hague congress as 'the end of my slavery. Then I shall become once more a free man; I will accept no further administrative function. . . .'[163] If the Council were to be moved, Brussels and Paris were ruled out on grounds of security, while a seat in Switzerland would make it easier prey for the Bakuninists.[164] New York was safe, equally from European governments and from destructive elements. In addition, it was argued that a move would be in keeping with the rapid industrial growth being experienced in the United States. Whatever the motives, however, the move effectively killed the IWA. By the end of 1873 even Engels was forced to admit that 'the anarchist International was stronger than the vestiges of the old International'.[165]

How should we account for the failure of the IWA? The move to New York spelt the effective end, but was not itself the cause of failure. The IWA comprised a temporary convergence of differing and ultimately discordant elements. The English, through trade unionism, had clear but limited goals: the franchise (1867), legal security (1871), and an end to strike-breaking through the importation of foreign workers. The aims of the first French participants were even more limited, their more radical-seeming successors just as backward-looking, and the Commune meant the end of the IWA in France. As for Germany Marx was bitterly disappointed: 'The purely platonic relationship of the German Workers' Party to the International . . . compromises the German working class.'[166] The accession of members in Spain and Italy merely reinforced the traditional artisan craft-skill basis of the IWA.

Thus Marx worked within a difficult situation. His aims were not those of the working-class leaders within the IWA. The most revolutionary-sounding elements were also the most backward-looking in their general social outlook. As we have seen, discussions about such crucial issues as collective property and political action remained at a level of generality which concealed deep divisions of opinion. These divisions were brought into the open by the advent of Bakunin and the disaster of the Paris Commune. In the context of post-Commune repression Marx concluded that the mediatory role of the General Council was inadequate and that a clear political attitude was required. Yet the new powers of the Council, granted at Basle and confirmed at The Hague, were not of a dictatorial character: indeed, they were hardly adequate to the tasks faced, in Marx's view, by the IWA.[167] But Marx made a major error in refusing to allow that the new commitment to independent working-class political parties was a matter of principle which had not been decided at a congress. This gave a lever to Bakunin and his allies in their search for support. Indeed, only the location of the congress, the decision of the Rimini congress that the Italian delegates should boycott the congress, and a number of dubious mandates for delegates favourable to Marx prevented this support from being decisive at The Hague.

However, these issues probably accelerated a decline in the IWA already apparent before the Commune. Liebknecht was right in his view that an international organisation was premature: the problems of the nascent labour movement in the various countries of Europe varied too much for any unified international direction or common programme to be possible. Rubel prefers to see in the *Address* and the Rules of 1864 a magisterial synthesis which expounds 'the tendency and the meaning of the movement in the century to come'.[168]

5 LAST YEARS

In Marx's later years, persistent illness dogged his attempts to complete *Capital*. Perhaps illness was itself a reason by which Marx could excuse his waning powers. He was always someone who felt his age. As early as 1863 we find him telling Engels how a re-reading of the latter's book on the English working class in 1844 had

> made me regretfully aware of our increasing age. How freshly and passionately, with what bold anticipations and no learned and scientific doubts, the thing is still dealt with here! And the very illusion that the result will leap into the daylight of history tomorrow or the day after gives the whole thing a warmth and vivacious humour – compared with which the later 'grey in grey' makes a damned unpleasant contrast.[169]

He was forty-five. It is ironic that the very period in which Marx was relieved of any pressing financial worry and could devote himself wholly to the writing of *Capital* was the period of least progress. Illness is certainly one reason. The sheer size and complexity of the project must be accounted another. Marx himself often explained it as the result of new theoretical difficulties and changes in the subject of study: '. . . the job is making very slow progress because things . . . constantly exhibit new aspects and call forth new doubts whenever they are to be put in final shape.' [170] This was in 1858. Marx makes a similar statement in 1879. He could not, he said, publish *Capital* II, 'before the present English industrial crisis had reached its climax. . . . It is . . . necessary to watch the present course of things to their maturity before one can "consume" them "productively", I mean "*theoretically*"'.[171] This was indeed a constant preoccupation with Marx, and constituted a rule of method.

But Marx always seemed able to find reasons for pursuing yet another line of study. For example, up to 1870 his work had been based largely on the evidence of three countries, England, France and Germany. In 1869 he developed a keen interest in Russian economic conditions, and set about learning Russian in order to read the relevant sources. The material would be useful in composing his treatment of ground rent.[172] Engels saw this as yet another excuse for not getting on with *Capital*: 'It would be a pleasure . . . to burn the Russian publications on agriculture that have been preventing you for years from finishing *Capital*.'[173] After the completion of *Capital* I Engels had been hopeful: 'This damned book . . . was at the root of all your troubles. . . . This everlastingly unfinished thing exhausted you physically, mentally and financially . . . now that you have rid yourself of this incubus you will feel a different man altogether. . . .' [174] But he was too sanguine. Engels was himself clearly taken by surprise at the unfinished state of the manuscripts when he went though Marx's papers after the latter's death.

> In addition, there is the handwriting – absolutely only legible to me and that with difficulty. You may ask, how it came about that it was kept hidden from me, how far from being finished the thing was? Very simple; if I had known about it, I should have given him no rest by day or night until it was quite finished and printed.[175]

Engels considered that Marx's delays were based not so much on intellectual scrupulousness as on 'theoretical excuses', the root cause being the state of Marx's health.[176] Probably the truth lies in both factors: Marx recognised that there were weaknesses in *Capital* but no longer had the intellectual energy to cope with them by reason of debilitating illness.

Whatever the truth of the matter, Marx wrote nothing of consequence on economics in the last decade of his life.[177] But he remained keenly interested in working-class politics, and was always prepared to see revolutionary possibilities in a situation, interestingly more and more in countries which had yet to become capitalist. In this period we should note especially the critique of the Gotha Programme of the SPD (1875), the Circular Letter on certain tendencies in German social democracy (1879), Marx's part in the drafting of the first Marxian political programme in France (1880), and his drafts concerning Russian developments (1881), which show the use to which Marx put his work on Russia. We should also note the interesting questionnaire for workers written by Marx for Malon's *La Revue socialiste* (April 1880).[178] Marx made considerable efforts to ensure that his views were not misunderstood, though his efforts met with limited success so far as the dogmatic French Marxists were concerned: 'Ce qu'il y a de certain, c'est que moi je ne suis pas Marxiste.' [179]

Marx published very little in the last years of his life, apart from a chapter in Engels' *Anti-Dühring* and a few articles in Conservative newspapers attacking Gladstone's Russian policy in 1877.[180] Technically Marx remained a political alien. He had thought of applying for British citizenship in 1869, so that he could travel on the Continent with more safety, but did not make a formal application until August 1874.[181] Unfortunately the report on Marx did not reassure the civil servants at the Home Office, citing him as 'the notorious German agitator, the head of the International Society, and an advocate of communistic principles. The man has not been loyal to his own King and Country'.[182] Marx's application was refused. The Home Office declined to give reasons. It is doubtful whether Marx had any more respect for bureaucracy at the end of his life than he had forty years earlier. After the Paris Commune and The Hague congress of the IWA in 1872, Marx seems to have retreated into family life, adored by his daughters and revered by a small circle of close friends. On one brief occasion he even seems to have been drawn into the financial system of the society whose social and economic features he so deplored, becoming a partner in the exploitation of the patent for a new copying machine.[183] Engels put up the money.

The life of the Marx family was no longer one of poverty and hardship. Laura married Paul Lafargue in 1868, and Jenny, the eldest, Charles Longuet in 1872. Marx's remark to Engels in 1882 should not be taken too seriously: 'Longuet as the last Proudhonist and Lafargue as the last Bakuninist! To the devil with them!' [184] But the lives of his daughters ended tragically. Jenny, after bearing six children in nine years, died of cancer at the age of thirty-eight, and her sisters committed suicide: Eleanor in 1898 after her protracted troubles with Edward Aveling, Laura (with Paul) in 1911.

This was how Marx appeared to a total stranger in 1879:

His talk was that of a well-informed, nay, learned man, much interested in comparative grammar. . . . It was all very *positif*, slightly cynical, without any appearance of enthusiasm, interesting, and often, as I thought, showing very correct ideas, when he was conversing of the past or the present, but vague and unsatisfactory when he turned to the future.[185]

Marx continued to study, but nothing came of it. In 1881 his wife died. Much of the next two years was spent travelling in the hope of regaining his health. But in March 1883 Marx died, appropriately, at his desk. His eldest daughter, Jenny, had preceded him by two months.

A Note on Marx's Writings

The total bulk of Marx's work is very large, though most of it is now available in printed form. We can divide up his writings in the following way:

1. Writings published in Marx's lifetime:
   - (a) Books, pamphlets, essays. Important pieces here include Introduction to CHPR, *JQ*, *PP*, *WLC*, *CSF*, *EB*, *CPE* (including *Preface*), *Capital* I.
   - (b) Organisational. For the CL (*CM*, *ACL*). For the IWA (*Inaugural Address*; *CWF*).
   - (c) Journalism.[186] The major newspapers are *RZ*, *Vorwärts!*, *DBZ*, *NRZ*, *NRZ-Revue*, *NYDT*, *NOZ*, *Das Volk*, *Die Presse*, *Free Press*, *Der Volksstaat*.
   - (d) Newspaper reports and interviews.

2. Writings known posthumously:
   - (a) Manuscripts written as drafts for work published, or with a view to eventual publication:
       - (i) Edited by Engels (*Capital* II and III; *CGP*);
       - (ii) Edited by others after 1895 (*TSV*, *Introduction*, *GI*, *EPM*, *Critique*, *Grundrisse*, etc.).
   - (b) Private correspondence:
       - (i) Marx–Engels;
       - (ii) Marx–third parties;
   - (c) Notebooks.[187]

There are good reasons for dividing up Marx's writings in this way. First, the main division (before and after 1883) separates those works prepared for publication by Marx himself, and those prepared by others. We have already noted the care Marx took over his published work. This must be borne in mind when assessing the value of manuscripts which he had not himself put into a final form.[188] The main division is also of importance when we consider the way in which Marx's influence and reputation (including what he is thought to have 'really said') have altered since his death. One reason for this lies in the publication and reception of certain of his previously unpublished writings, for example the *EPM*, or more recently, the *Grundrisse*, writings which have been successively said to be the key to Marxian thought.[189]

The threefold subdivision of the works published by Marx is also important. We should distinguish between views Marx published independently and on his own account (though even here with an eye to the censor), the views put forward in pot-boiling journalism written for a living, and the views found in items written on behalf of an organisation.

Obviously independent work must come first in terms of evidential value. But even here we need to distinguish between the theoretical writings of *CPE* (including the *Preface*) and *Capital* I, and the more overtly polemical writings which, though no doubt guided and informed by theoretical conclusions, are nevertheless one-sided *pièces d'occasion* written in reaction to specific events, or to appeal to a particular kind of audience. Thus both *CSF* and *EB*, though often referred to as historical accounts, are in fact contemporary political polemics. This distinction should not be pressed too far, of course: even *Capital* contains much that is polemical, while much of theoretical importance can only be found in overtly polemical writings.

Care is also required with Marx's writings on behalf of the CL and the IWA. Such writings may well represent a consensus of opinion within the organisation, or contain views which are not those of Marx or which have been put in such a way as to appeal to particular audiences, or indeed contain deliberate omissions. We must always expect this with any party document. We know this to be true of the *Inaugural Address* and the *CWF*, and it may well be true of the *ACL* and even of parts of the *CM* itself. Much depends here on the room for manœuvre Marx thought he had at the time. How far this general point is true, however, must be determined in the individual case.

Marx's post-1852 journalism needs to be treated with even more circumspection. Much of it was written in considerable haste, and Marx had neither the time, nor indeed the inclination, to devote the care in conceptualisation and composition he lavished upon *Capital* I. He resented the time taken up by newspaper scribbling, bound as he was to editorial predilections and publishing deadlines, dispersing his energies and in the end accomplishing little. 'Pure scientific works are something else entirely,' he wrote.[190] It should be evident, too, that newspaper reports of what Marx said in public speeches and interviews should also be treated with reserve, especially in those cases where Marx is known to have objected to the misreporting of what he said.

If we turn to the second main group of writings, further problems arise. Some of the unpublished writings, such as the *CGP* (1875) and the Circular Letter (1879) were circulated privately and were clearly of great importance to Marx. But much of the manuscript material could not be published without a considerable amount of editorial work being expended upon it. Engels' prefaces indicate the trouble he had with *Capital* II and III. Once a neat copy of a manuscript has been produced, there remains the important problem of deciding whether Marx would have written a final published version in the same form, containing the same conclusion and the same method of approach. It is pertinent to note, especially with reference to the early writings (*Critique*, *EPM*), that much of what Marx wrote was for self-clarification rather than publication. There was nothing to prevent Marx from fulfilling his contract for a two-volume *Critique of Politics and Political Economy* with

C. W. Leske by writing up the contents of the *Critique* and the *EPM* for publication, but he did not do so. What we have in these two manuscripts is the spectacle of a mind working its way through certain problems in a detailed and often obscure way. Marx is speaking to himself, not to a reader with whom he must make an effort to communicate. Instead, he plunges into the composition of the bulky manuscript of *GI*, and despite the obvious turgidity of much of its contents this manuscript was hawked around for two years before Marx and Engels gave up the attempt to publish.[191]

Enough has been said to indicate the danger of quoting indiscriminately from any part of the corpus of Marx's writings with no reference to considerations of time or place. The problems of assessing the value of particular kinds of evidence bulks very large even when we consider only what Marx himself published. The problems are multiplied with manuscript material, private correspondence and notebooks. But all such material must be considered, for Marx never published a general systematic treatise detailing his view as an ordered whole. The nearest he came to this is in the first volume of *Capital*, and in the *Preface* to the *CPE*. We must conclude, somewhat traditionally, that the analysis of Marx's views must at least start from these two sources, whatever material may be brought into evidence subsequently.

It should perhaps be said that the dangers of undifferentiated 'scriptural quotation' were long ago pointed out by Engels in connection with the Russian Marxists of the early 1890s:

> The different Russian émigré groups interpret passages from the writings and correspondence of Marx in the most contradictory ways, exactly as though they were texts from the classics or from the New Testament.[192]

II

History

The central role played by his view of history in all Marx's social, political and economic thought can hardly be over-emphasised. Socio-economic systems, the theories that seek to explain or justify them, and the social classes that exist within them, are historical and transient phenomena. Marx's approach can be viewed in two ways: as a method of historical interpretation, and as a doctrine which claims to give guidance in political practice. There are a number of short characterisations: 'historical materialism' and 'scientific socialism', both used chiefly by Engels;[1] a much more all-embracing terms, 'dialectical materialism', first used by Plekhanov;[2] and 'the economic interpretation of history', first used by Bernstein. None of these are very satisfactory.

1 HISTORY AND HUMAN NATURE

In the sixth thesis on Feuerbach, Marx wrote that 'the human essence [*menschliche Wesen*] is no abstraction inhering in each single individual. In its actuality it is the ensemble of social relationships'.[3] This can be paralleled in an earlier passage written in late 1843: 'But *man* is not an abstract being, squatting outside the world. Man is *the world of men*, the state, society. . . .'[4] It has often been concluded from passages like these that Marx thought it illegitimate to make any generalisations about 'man in general'. It is true that Marx rejected Feuerbach's notion of generic man, bereft of social relations or historical development: the man, in short, implied in the conception of civil society as a set of isolated individuals.[5] For Marx, man is a natural being living in constant interchange with the natural world; but the interchange is always mediated through society; and history itself is the record of the continuous transformation of human nature. But this historical conception does not prevent Marx from making trans-historical generalisations, about the permanent characteristics of men that distinguish them from animals, or about what is true 'under all modes of production'.

For Marx man is rooted in nature. He is an animal with a relatively stable physiological make-up and a set of physical wants which require satisfaction. Such 'natural wants . . . food, clothing, shelter, fuel, etc., differ from country to country in accordance with variations in climatic and other natural conditions'.[6] Man can be distinguished from other animals by the fact that he produces himself through his labour. As Engels succinctly remarked, 'Animals at most *collect* while men *produce*' at first for means of subsistence, later for means of development.[7] Unlike other animals, man produces when free of physical need; he produces instruments of production, that is, he is a toolmaker; he produces a whole new nature, the 'anthropological nature' of the social environment; he is a purposive and self-aware animal with a unique capacity for reason and language.[8] He can plan:

> We presuppose labour in a form which stamps it as exclusively human. A spider conducts operations that resemble those of a weaver, and a bee puts to shame many an architect in the construction of her cells. But what distinguishes the worst architect from the best of bees is this, that the architect erects his structure in imagination before he erects it in reality.[9]

These generalisations apart, however, Marx rejected neat definitions of man, which must be inevitably selective and usually rooted in a particular socio-economic formation. Thus he remarks of Aristotle's celebrated definition of man as a political animal,

> Strictly, Aristotle's definition is that man is by nature a town-citizen. This is quite as characteristic of ancient classical society as Franklin's definition of man, as a toolmaking animal, is characteristic of Yankeedom.[10]

Human history is 'the true natural history of man'.[11] But Marx reminds us of Vico's view that 'the essence of the distinction between human history and natural history is that the former is the work of man and the latter is not'.[12] The theme of history as the creation of man through labour, the idea of one (historical) science, and the views concerning the relation of natural science and industry are all present in the *EPM, GI* and *Capital* itself. The historical emphasis is clear enough in the *EPM*:

> The nature which comes to be in human history – the genesis of human society – is man's *real* nature; hence nature as it becomes . . . through industry, even though in an estranged form, is true *anthropological* nature . . . the entire so-called history of the world is nothing but the creation of man by human labour . . . his self-creation, of his own process of coming-to-be.[13]

Man is a historical product: the productivity of labour 'a gift not of nature, but of a history embracing thousands of centuries'.[14] Thus history can be seen as the 'pre-history' of mankind: the 'humanisation of the ape'. Man is increasingly conditioned, not by nature, but by what he has made of himself. At the same time history can be seen as a trend towards a single, world society through the creation by capitalism of a world market: 'World history did not always exist: history as world history is a result.' [15]

Marx's model of the labour process is central to his conception of human nature. Labour power is 'the aggregate of those physical and material capabilities existing in a human being whenever he produces a use-value of any description'.[16] The process involves three elements: the use of labour power, the instruments of labour, and the subjects of labour. It is 'form-positing purposive activity'; [17] it is

> purposive action with a view to the production of use-values, appro-priation of natural substance to human requirements; it is the neces-sary condition for effecting exchange of matter between man and Nature; it is the everlasting nature-imposed conditions of human existence, and therefore is independent of every social phase of that existence, or, rather, is common to every such phase.[18]

Labour is a process of productive consumption in which substances are given new life, a purposive transformation of the material which preserves it in a definite form: 'Labour is the living, form-giving fire . . .' which 'makes instrument and material in the production process into the body of its soul and thereby resurrects them from the dead.' [19] The physical structure of the material does, of course, impose limits to the forms it can take; within these limits, form is external to the material. Thus the form of a table is 'an accidental property of the wood' created by human labour.[20] External physical conditions can, of course, limit the productivity of labour: for example, a shortage of raw materials, or particular kinds of geographic conditions.[21] The more primitive man is, the more he is subject to these natural limitations; the more advanced he is, the more human creativity dominates nature.

But men are eternally forced by their needs to engage in the labour process. Such needs are intrinsic to human nature: 'If I am determined, forced, by my needs, it is only my own nature, this totality of needs and drives, which exerts a force upon me; it is nothing alien. . . .' [22] At first this involved merely the 'necessary needs . . . of the individual himself reduced to a natural subject': the primary needs of food, drink, clothing, housing.[23] As productivity increases, new needs are created: 'This production of new needs is the first historical act.' [24] Marx thus distin-guishes between basic and acquired needs, the latter developing and changing through time. Even primary needs can be satisfied in many ways: 'Hunger is hunger: but the hunger that is satisfied by cooked meat eaten by knife and fork differs from hunger that devours raw meat with the help of hands, nails and teeth.' [25] But it is acquired needs which are the mark of a civilised society.[26]

The multiplication of needs is, for Marx as for the classical economists, one of the major tendencies in history. But it has taken place in restricted areas of the world against a general background of scarcity. Throughout history, men have been bedevilled by scarcity: *natural* scarcity, not scarcity socially induced. Most men, at most times, have lived at the margin of subsistence. It is also true that in most societies a minority have monopolised the means of production and the labourer has therefore had to add 'to the time necessary for his own maintenance an extra working time in order to produce the means of subsistence for the owners of the means of production'.[27] In all such societies, surplus labour had produced a surplus product. But *individual consumption* had predominated: the surplus had been consumed as means of subsistence. *Productive consumption*, where labour power, in consuming raw materials, creates surplus value, is dominant only under capitalism.[28] If we view the history of production graphically, therefore, it must be seen not so much as a line moving steadily upwards, but as a more or less horizontal line which has in the space of a century climbed almost vertically. Thus 'the bourgeoisie during its rule of scarce one hundred years has created more massive and more colossal productive forces than have all preceding generations put together'.[29] The civilising influence of capital is therefore immense: 'Capital . . . drives labour out beyond the limits of its natural needs, and thus creates the material elements for the development of a rich individuality.'[30] It does this by expanding the proportion of surplus to necessary labour time expended in the production process. But this distinction is itself a historically relative one:

> This necessity is itself subject to changes, because needs are produced just as are products and the different kinds of work skills. . . . The greater the extent to which historic needs – needs created by production itself, social needs – . . . are posited as necessary, the higher the level to which real wealth has developed. Regarded materially, wealth consists only in the manifold variety of needs.[31]

Man's domination of nature remains a relative domination. 'The priority of external nature' is always emphasised.[32] Man cannot defy the laws of external nature, though he can learn them and use them to his advantage. Schmidt has pointed out Marx's significant use of the metaphor of metabolism (*Stoffwechsel*) to express 'the mutual interpenetration of nature and society within the natural whole'.[33] Indeed, one of Marx's charges against capitalism is that it has upset the delicate balance between man and nature. The creation of great urban centres has disturbed 'the metabolism between men and the soil, i.e. prevents the return to the soil of its elements consumed in the form of food and clothing; it therefore violates the conditions necessary to the lasting fertility of the soil'. It is his ecological hope that a future society will restore the natural metabolism in the form of a regulating law of social production.[34]

Marx's concept of the labour process involves a model of instrumental action abstracted from the labour process in any particular society. Yet by production is always meant 'production at a definite stage of social development'.[35] But it is possible, and indeed methodologically necessary, to talk of production in general, and of features common to *all* production. The result is 'a rational abstraction' of common features discovered by comparison. 'It is necessary to distinguish those definitions which apply to production in general, in order not to overlook the essential differences existing. . . .'[36] Thus no production is possible without instruments and past, accumulated labour. Capital can be seen as both of these things within a particular kind of society, but it is not necessary to the labour process as such. Capital is a historically transient form. At the same time, production is always social: 'appropriation by an individual within and with the help of a definite social organisation'. There are techniques and instruments of production, and these are employed in specific ways in specific societies. As the concept of production itself involves reference to appropriation of the product of labour, 'it is tautological to say that property (appropriation) is a condition of production'.[37] Thus Marx's concept of capital refers both to an instrument of production and to a specific property form at a historically specific point in time.

Marx, in rejecting any historical teleology which appears to view history as more than the outcome of individual purposes, is also making an important methodological point about the nature of social activity: '"History" is not a person apart, using man as a means for its own particular aims; history is nothing but the activity of man pursuing his aims.'[38] But in settled societies men stand in more or less stable relations with each other. Thus

> Society does not consist of individuals, but expresses the sum of interrelations, the relations within which these individuals stand. . . . To be a slave, to be a citizen, are social characteristics, relations between human beings A and B. Human being A, as such, is not a slave. He is a slave in and through society. . . .[39]

A social formation is the resultant of the reciprocal actions of men, but this formation can be seen as a social process with structural relationships independent of the will of the individuals who compose the process. Thus the circulation process of capital 'arises from the conscious will and particular purposes of the individuals', yet is 'neither located in their consciousness nor subsumed under them as a whole'. Indeed the total process appears to them as an 'objective relation, which arises spontaneously from nature. . . . Their own collisions with one another produce an *alien* social power standing above them. . . .'[40]

All social life is mediated through language. Men become conscious of themselves as individuals only through their relations with each other. Consciousness and language imply each other and arise from 'the need,

57

the necessity of intercourse with other men'. Further, 'where there exists a relationship, it exists for me: the animal does not enter into "relations" with anything. . . . Consciousness is . . . a social product and remains so as long as men exist'.[41] Men stand in social relations, and they have a conception of those relations: indeed, the conception may be partly or wholly constitutive of those relations. In general, 'relations can be established as existing only by being *thought*, as distinct from the subjects which are in these relations with each other. . . .'[42] Thus in the exchange relation, what are '*objective* dependency relations' between the individuals involved, appear in such a manner 'that individuals are now ruled by *abstractions*', or at least believe themselves to be so ruled. Such an abstraction is 'nothing more than the theoretical expression of material relations'; and as such relations are normally to their advantage, 'the belief in the permanency of these ideas, i.e. of these objective relations of dependency, is of course consolidated, nourished and inculcated by the ruling classes by all means available'.[43] Indeed, Marx sometimes speaks as though a social relationship endures solely because of the *belief* of those concerned in the relationship:

> The recognition of the products as its own, and the judgement that its separation from the conditions of its realisation is improper – forcibly imposed – is an enormous step in awareness, itself the product of the mode of production resting on capital, and as much the knell to its doom as, with the slave's awareness that he cannot be the property of another, with his consciousness of himself as a person, the existence of slavery . . . ceases to be able to prevail as the basis of production.[44]

The conceptions men have about themselves and the social and natural world within which they live are historical: they change over time. This is true of even the most abstract concept. Schmidt notes that the concept of matter has changed radically in the course of the development of natural science, 'a history very closely interwoven with that of social practice'.[45] Change is especially true of the social, political and economic concepts with which Marx was most concerned. Thus economic categories are '*the theoretical expression of historical relations of production, corresponding to a particular stage of development in material production*'.[46] Marx developed two sets of concepts of particular relevance: the general structural concepts outlined in the *Preface* of 1859, and the economic categories designed for the analysis of the capitalist mode of production. Korsch states that Marx considered 'all, even the most general categories of social science, as categories changeable and *to be changed*'.[47] This is to go too far: Marx certainly believed that the general concepts of the *Preface* (forces of production, relations of production, mode of production) would be permanently applicable to the investigation of past epochs, whatever might occur in the future to limit their applicability so far as post-capitalist societies were concerned.[48] But it follows from Marx's position that the categories deemed suitable for the analysis of capitalism in Marx's own day will be unsuitable for the analysis of past economic systems; and that as those societies deemed capitalist change, then the concepts he used for the analysis of capitalism may also require revision. Marx was also aware that all social theory must begin (though not end) with the concepts the agents themselves have about their activity; and that the categories of any such social theory may themselves help to form the spectacles through which the actors view their society and their own role in it.

To conclude these remarks we should consider the role played by the concept of nature in Marx's view of history. There are two related characteristics of all pre-capitalist societies: men's social life is dominated by external nature (*Aussenwelt*), and men in society are subjected to traditional social relations, which they regard as natural (*naturwüchsig*). Both these features have been broken down by the rise of capitalism, with the dissolvent effects of trade, the division of labour and exchange. The first feature – men dominated by nature – has received sufficient explanation, but the second requires further elucidation.

When discussing pre-capitalist economic formations, Marx talks, for instance, of the *naturwüchsige Stammgemeinschaft* (the naturally arisen, spontaneous tribal community).[49] Several related ideas seem to be involved in the use of *naturwüchsig*. The community is one which has arisen in a spontaneous, unplanned manner, in reaction to natural circumstances. Its features are not intended or controlled by the individuals composing it. It is also a natural community, in the sense that it is joined by ties of blood and custom (second nature). For a society to be tied only by language is for Marx the product of a much later stage of development. Relations between men are (at least apparently) directly *personal* relations, not relations mediated by the abstractions of exchange.[50] In a community close to the earth and dominated by natural scarcity, the aim of production goes only a little beyond subsistence, with a small surplus for barter or as revenue to ruling groups, not value-creation. Typically, the individuals produce in common, or as small, independent peasants, or as slaves or serfs: in the latter two cases, they are regarded as part of 'the *inorganic and natural* conditions' of production.[51] Marx gives only a sketchy account of the various forms of such natural communities, but his basic point is clear: 'In all forms in which landed property is the decisive factor, natural relations still predominate; in the forms in which the decisive factor is capital, social, historically evolved elements predominate.'[52]

In both the *Grundrisse* and *Capital*, Marx's basic concern is with the nature of modern bourgeois society. In the former, the history is largely illustrative, and resorted to in order to clarify the differences between the capitalist order and all pre-capitalist ones, and where a general view is attempted, it remains a sketch.[53] In *Capital* the account of the formation process of capitalism is greatly expanded, but it remains secondary to the main theme: the structural features of the capitalist mode of production. Thus Marx concentrated on the differences between the various pre-capitalist modes taken as a whole and the capitalist mode, and much less on the differences between each of the other modes.

It is not the *unity* of living and active humanity with the natural, inorganic conditions of their metabolic interchange with nature, and hence their appropriation, which requires explanation . . . but rather the *separation* between these inorganic conditions of human existence and this active existence, a separation which is only completely posited in the relation of wage-labour and capital.[54]

In all agricultural societies, whether based on slave, serf or peasant labour, there is said to be no separation of labour from its inorganic conditions (the land). In industrial societies labour has been separated from its inorganic conditions, and is only reconnected through the exchange process, which itself presupposes separation; and relations are social, no longer dominated by nature.[55] The formation process of capitalism is also a separation process. Marx must explain how this came about.

But an account of capitalist society itself, the solidified social formation as it were, requires a structural analysis of the mode as an organic whole. The order of succession in which the economic categories appear must therefore be determined 'by their mutual relation in bourgeois society and this is quite the reverse of what appears to be natural to them or in accordance with the sequence of historical development'.[56] Such an analysis will have a dialectical rather than historical character. It should be noted that Marx nowhere offers us a general law of historical development. In his view it is possible to formulate the laws of operation of a mature mode of production, but not of the formation process itself, where relations are still fluid. This does not mean that Marx had no interest in previous history. Indeed, he considered that his examination of capitalism would itself provide pointers to the past.

In order to develop the laws of bourgeois economy . . . it is not necessary to write the real *history of the relations of production*. But the correct observation and deduction of these laws, having themselves become in history, always leads to primary equations . . . which point towards a past lying beyond this system. These indications, together with a correct grasp of the present, then offer the key to the understanding of the past – a work in its own right which, it is to be hoped, we shall be able to undertake as well.[57]

In the event, what Marx had to offer us was, first, a set of structural concepts, applicable to all past societies, which he called 'the guiding thread' in his studies; and second, 'the economic law of motion of modern society'.

2 STRUCTURAL CONCEPTS

a. *The* PREFACE *of 1859*

In his classic account of his general conclusions,[58] Marx distinguished in history at least four modes of production, 'epochs marking progress in the economic development of society', namely the Asiatic, ancient, feudal and modern bourgeois modes.

> In the social production of their existence, men inevitably enter into definite relations, which are independent of their will, namely relations of production which correspond (*entsprechen*) to a given stage in the development of their material forces of production. The totality of these relations of production constitutes the economic structure of society, the real foundation, on which arises a legal and political superstructure and to which correspond (*entsprechen*) definite forms of social consciousness. The mode of production of material life conditions (*bedingt*) the general process of social, political and intellectual life. It is not the consciousness of men that determines (*bestimmt*) their existence, but their social existence that determines their consciousness.

There follows Marx's theoretical definition of a social revolution:

> At a certain stage of development, the material productive forces of society come into conflict with the existing relations of production or, what is only a legal expression for the same thing, with the property relations within the framework of which they have operated hitherto. From forms of development of the productive forces these relations turn into their fetters. Then begins an era of social revolution. The changes in the economic foundation lead sooner or later to the transformation of the whole immense superstructure.

We must distinguish between a change in the economic conditions of production, which can apparently be ascertained with the precision of natural science, and the ideological forms (legal, political, religious, artistic or philosophical) in which men become conscious of the conflict. However, the bourgeois mode will be the last 'antagonistic form', and will conclude the 'pre-history' of human society. Finally, Marx makes two general points which he takes to be applicable to all societies. No social order ends before all the productive forces which can be, have been developed within it; and new, 'higher' production relations never arrive until material conditions for them have appeared in 'the old society'.

This passage has attracted considerable attention, for as the 'guiding thread' in his studies Marx invites us to take what he says as a considered account of his views. We should note that he does not put forward a theory but only a general summary of his position.[59] As a summary, it has a number of disadvantages as a highly schematic account which lends itself to unilinear and economic deterministic interpretations. It includes an unfortunate metaphor from the language of constructional engineering, namely, the distinction between base (*Basis*) and superstructure (*Überbau*). Concepts essential to Marxian views are omitted, for instance alienation and class. There is no hint that a social revolution may be violent; nor that a communist society is a necessary outcome of the development of capitalism. Prinz has suggested that caution in the face of political censorship caused Marx to exclude some of his views.[60] This is possible: but at the level of abstraction at which Marx is writing he need not mention all these things. Not to take Marx's account seriously would be to ignore the fact of previous similar versions. Prinz makes much of the omission of violence as a means of revolution, but this is not for Marx theoretically necessary to his concept of revolution, but merely a contingent feature of some revolutions. Nevertheless, two points need to be made about the account in the *Preface*: first, there are ambiguities and obscurities of formulation which require clarification; and second, there are omissions which have to be made good from other sources.

We need to distinguish between a *mode of production* and a *socio-economic formation*. The first concept involves an abstract economic model: for instance, the model of pure capitalism Marx constructs in *Capital*. The second concept involves reference to a concrete society, such as Great Britain in the mid-nineteenth century, within which a particular mode of production holds a dominant position. A specific socio-economic formation may well have within it, not only a dominant mode, but also survivals of previous modes; or, in periods of transition, no dominant mode, but only competing ones.[61] Marx does not always formulate the distinction clearly. For instance, when he claims that higher productive relations never appear until the material conditions for them have appeared in 'the old society', does he mean within the mode of production, or within the socio-economic formation? As we shall see, an unambiguous answer to this question is important to an understanding of Marx's conception of social change. Here we need note only that the limits of a productive epoch are defined, in some sense, by the dominance of the mode of production within it, and the transitional period between epochs by the theoretical concept of social revolution. Within any socio-economic formation the major structural elements of importance are the economic structure, which involves a 'specific mode of production and the social relations corresponding to it',[62] the legal and political institutions, and the forms of ideological consciousness. Marx makes a general methodological point which should be noted:

Viewed apart from real history, these abstractions have in themselves no value whatsoever. They can only serve to facilitate the arrangement of historical material and to indicate the sequence of its separate strata. But they by no means afford a recipe, or schema . . . for neatly trimming the epochs of history.[63]

A number of key concepts in Marx's account require closer definition: productive forces, production relations, and mode of production.

The explanation of *productive forces* is relatively straightforward. It involves all that is included in the factors of the abstract labour process: labour power, its subject, and its instruments. The term means of production (*Produktionsmittel*) is used to cover both 'the instruments and the subject of labour'. An instrument of labour (*Arbeitsmittel*), is

a thing, or complex of things, which the labourer interposes between himself and the subject of his labour, and which serves as the conductor of his activity. He makes use of the mechanical, physical, and chemical properties of some substances in order to make other substances subservient to his aims.[64]

The word instrument is used very widely, to embrace the earth itself as a 'universal instrument', tools of all kinds and degrees of complexity, and also 'all such objects as are necessary for carrying on the labour process' and without which the labour process could either not take place, or do so only in a deficient manner. Marx lists such items as workshops, canals, roads and so on.[65] By 'subject of labour' Marx means the soil (and water) as 'the universal subject of human labour'; natural materials 'provided immediately by nature' (in mining, hunting, fishing); and raw materials, objects already products of labour, such as processed iron ore, seed for agriculture, and so on.[66] Whether an item is to be regarded as raw material, or as an instrument of labour, or as product, depends entirely on its 'function in the labour process'.[67]

In addition to means of production, the concept of productive force comprises also labour power and its results: natural science, technology, human skills and invention, organisation (the division and combination of labour) and so on. 'Of all the instruments of production, the greatest productive power is the revolutionary class itself.' [68] Thus the concept involves more or less blanket reference to complex phenomena. It is the totality of these phenomena which are said, at certain points in historical development, to come into conflict with existing relations of production. Thus when Marx talks of capitalism having developed the forces of production, he may be referring to the level of economic development, or to the creation of a new class, the proletariat, or to both.

By the term production relations (*Produktionsverhältnisse*), Marx means both relations between men engaged in the production process, and property relations. Thus the conflict between productive forces and production relations which is said to occur in history is not simply one concerning discrepancies between new techniques of production and

63

old job relationships. The conflict concerns property ownership. A particular property form is said to have become a fetter on the further development of the productive forces. This can entail, in line with the protean notion of productive force, that the existing property system prevents either the full development of the economic system (for instance, the capitalist mode is said to exclude 'all rational improvement beyond a certain point' [69]), or the human development of the working class; or both.

The relations between men engaged in the production process, work relations, involve, for instance, the technical division of labour in a factory. A particular method of production will require a certain technical organisation, involving a distribution of functions as well as authority relations among the workers. From the technical point of view, to adopt the method means to adopt the relations which are therefore inevitable and independent of the will of men. Changes in technology may also have larger social consequences than those of the immediately factory environment. Marx exhaustively documented the ways in which men were being replaced by machines. He also notes how the development of new kinds of machine (the automatic factory) would finally remove 'the technical reason for the life-long annexation of the workman to a detail function'.[70] That is, for technical reasons, 'variation of work' would be recognised 'as a fundamental law of production'.[71] History as the development of technology is a major theme in Marx's account.

As we have seen, production relations involve not only work relations but also ownership relations.[72] Thus the productive forces conflict with the production relations; or 'what is but a legal expression for the same thing', with the property relations of the until then dominant mode of production. By definition as production relations, property relations are also inevitable and independent of the will of men. We have seen that Marx, though he was prepared to discuss an abstract model of the labour process, always began with 'the socially determined production of individuals'.[73] In this sense, that a man is the slave of another man is just as much a production relation as the fact that he works for that man. We can agree that any enduring productive system requires *some* rules governing the relationships of men, and that these will involve rules about persons and property. But Marx in many passages appears to want to go further than this, and claim that a *specific* productive system requires a *specific* property-owning system.

In order to understand the problem we should first note how loosely Marx expresses the relations he takes to exist between his key variables. The *Preface* offers us a useful example. We are told first, that production relations *correspond* to a definite stage of the productive forces; second, that the economic structure *conditions* the superstructure; third, that the social existence of men *determines* their consciousness.[74] All three terms are used indiscriminately by Marx, but express different degrees of stringency. To say 'A corresponds with B' is to impute a regular relation of co-existence, with no necessary implication of the dependence of either upon the other.[75] To say 'A determines B', or 'A conditions B', is to impute a regular relation of co-existence and dependence of B upon A, in the first in a strong sense, in the second in a weak sense. Indeed, for A to condition B would not preclude B conditioning A in turn. Further, we should note that Marx often uses *determine* when in context he means at the most *condition*. In fact, as we shall see, he sometimes uses *determine* when he is seeking to describe relations of reciprocity.[76] These generalisations can be amply documented from both the *German Ideology* and the *Introduction* to the *CPE*.[77] As the former is the earliest version of Marx's approach, it would be wrong to expect complete clarity of meaning. For instance, while the notion of productive force already has the protean character of the later concept, instead of *production relations* Marx uses the even looser term, *form of intercourse* (*Verkehrsform*) to mean the general social intercourse of individuals and groups. We shall use some examples from the *Introduction*.

In the first section of the Introduction it is stated that 'All production is appropriation . . . within and through a definite form of society'. Hence it is a tautology to say that 'property (appropriation) is a condition of production'. All societies have some kind of property system. There are 'social conditions corresponding to a certain stage of production'. Finally, 'every form of production creates its own legal relations, forms of government. . . .' [78] This is the strong form of the claim. Production relations are said to be determined by the productive forces in such a way that a specific productive system requires a specific kind of property-owning system.

However, there is a different view in the second section. Here Marx discusses the connections between production and distribution, exchange and consumption. These are all aspects of a single process. 'Production and consumption . . . appear . . . as phases of one process whose actual point of departure is production which is accordingly the decisive factor' (*übergreifende Moment*). At the same time, consumption, 'as a necessity and need, is itself an intrinsic aspect of productive activity'.[79] More than a reciprocal relationship is implied here: consumption is seen as a moment of production. At this point, Marx introduces distribution, which in all societies 'on the basis of social laws determines the individual's share in the world of products'. Yet distribution is not, apparently, independent of production: 'The particular mode of men's participation in production determines the specific form of distribution, the form in which they share in distribution.' Marx considers some apparently contrary cases: conquest, in which the conqueror establishes a certain division and form of landed property, or turns the conquered into slaves and makes slave labour the basis of production; revolution, in which large landed estates are broken up into small parcels of land, thus giving 'production a new character';

or of legislation which 'perpetuates land ownership in large families or distributes labour as a hereditary privilege and thus fixes it in castes'. But, Marx argues, distribution means more than merely a distribution of products. It is

1. Distribution of instruments of production, and
2. Which is another determination of the same relationship, it is a distribution of the members of society among the various kinds of production (the subjection of individuals under specific relations of production). The distribution of products is . . . only a result of this distribution which is bound up with the process of production and determines the organisation of production. To examine production divorced from this distribution which is a constituent part of it, is obviously idle abstraction. . . .

Thus Marx gives an answer to the conquest example. The conquerors have three alternatives: they can impose their mode of production on the conquered; they can leave things as they are and exact tribute; they can allow a mutual synthesis to emerge from an interaction of the two modes. In all three possibilities 'it is the mode of production . . . that determines the new mode of distribution employed'. In order to plunder there must be production: 'Even the method of plunder is determined by the method of production. A stock-jobbing nation, for example, cannot be robbed in the same way as a nation of cowherds.' If slavery is to be adopted, it remains necessary 'that the structure of production in the country to which the slave is abducted admits of slave labour, or (as in South America etc.) a mode of production appropriate to slave labour has to be evolved'.[80] Marx allows that laws can perpetuate land in certain families, or encourage subdivision into small parcels. But only if such laws were in harmony with the prevailing system of production would they be of economic importance.

After specifying that exchange is also a constituent moment of production, Marx sums up his position:

The conclusion which follows from this is, not that production, distribution, exchange and consumption are identical, but that they are links of a single whole, different aspects of one unity. Production is the decisive phase. . . . The process always starts afresh with production. That exchange and consumption cannot be the decisive elements is obvious; and the same applies to distribution in the sense of distribution of products. As for distribution in the sense of distribution of the agents of production, it is itself a moment of production. A specific form of production thus determines the specific forms of consumption, distribution, exchange, and *the specific relations between these various moments*. Of course, production in its one-sided form is in its turn determined by the other moments; e.g. with the expansion of the market, i.e. of the sphere of exchange, production grows in volume and is subdivided to a greater extent. With a change in distribution, production undergoes a change; for example, with concentration of capital, different distribution of population in town and country, etc. Finally, the demands of consumption also determine production. A mutual interaction takes place between the various moments. Such is the case with every organic body.[81]

It should be noted that in this passage Marx is not putting forward a version of reciprocal interactionism in which all the designated variables mutually influence each other to the same extent. Production is the decisive variable, the *übergreifende Moment*, but the other elements also influence the total process. To express this more clearly Marx should have used *bedingen* instead of *bestimmen* where he means *condition* rather than *determine*.

A number of points arise out of Marx's account. First, he tends to oscillate between loose and stringent versions of the relation said to exist between production and the other three moments. Even in his conclusion he still uses *determine* where *condition* would better express his meaning. Yet he is aware of the difficulties presented for the strong version of his approach by such social items as art and law. A note later in the *Introduction* makes this clear:

6. The unequal development of material production and, e.g. that of art. . . . However the really difficult point to be discussed here is how the production relations as legal relations take part in this uneven development. For example, the relation of Roman civil law . . . to modern production.[82]

An attempt to face this problem is made in the *Grundrisse*. Marx notes that although the legal system of Roman law

corresponds to a social state in which exchange was by no means developed, nevertheless, in so far as it was developed in a limited sphere, it was able to develop the *attributes of the juridical person, precisely of the person engaged in exchange*, and thus anticipate (in its basic aspects) the legal relations of industrial society, and in particular the right which rising bourgeois society had necessarily to assert against medieval society.[83]

His answer seems to be that a certain element of the modern economic system (exchange) can be found in a primitive form in other modes, and that it is therefore possible for the corresponding legal relation to develop. But it could equally well be said that the legal rules governing the basic exchange relation are of such an abstract character as to be applicable to any mode of production. The same difficulty applies to attempts to show that a particular philosophic system has a specific relation to a particular mode of production.

Marx also notes that the assessment of artistic achievement leads to results which bear no relation to the development of society as a whole:

for example, the place occupied by Shakespeare, or some of the ancient Greek artists and poets. He argues that 'the difficulty does not lie in understanding that Greek art and Greek epic poetry are bound up with certain forms of social development'. They presuppose Greek social organisation and mythology. The problem lies elsewhere: 'The difficulty is that they still give us aesthetic pleasure and are in certain respects regarded as a standard and unattainable ideal.' It is a difficulty because in the days of Roberts & Co., the *Crédit mobilier* and Printing House Square we should not, if our consciousness is 'determined' by the society in which we live, feel such satisfaction. But Marx's answer is to appeal to some kind of universal psychological truth: 'The Greeks were normal children . . . its charm is a consequence of this.'[84] In effect, Marx is saying that the Greeks were normal children – and we all like children. He may be right when he says of his views: 'The difficulty lies only in the general formulation of these contradictions. As soon as they are reduced to specific questions they are explained.'[85] But his own specific examples only make the general formulation the more implausible.

A second point concerns Marx's attempt to show how the mode of production determines production relations in the sense of property relations. His arguments do not prove his point. For instance, his analysis of the alternatives open to the conquerors is (nearly) logically exhaustive:[86] the fact that they have to choose one of them does not determine which one. They have a choice because they won the battle, not because they have a particular mode of production. It is true that a stock-jobbing nation cannot be robbed in the same way as a nation of cowherds. But distribution is conditioned by such factors, not determined by them. Marx's very next point should have alerted him to the weakness of his case. He says that if slave labour were chosen as a method of appropriation by the conquerors, 'a mode of production appropriate to slave labour has to be evolved'.[87] If Marx admits the possibility of choice, then existing methods of production can at the most condition, not determine choice.

This brings us to the third point, namely, the crucial ambiguity in Marx's concept of production. We must agree with Habermas that Marx only salvages production as the dominant moment by terminological equivocation.[88] When consumption and exchange are said to be moments of productive activity, and 'production divorced from . . . distribution which is a constituent part of it . . . is . . . idle abstraction', this is definitionally to subsume the other moments under the concept of production. Here we shall comment only on Marx's discussion of the relation between production and distribution.

Marx states that the labour process is always carried on within and through a specific social form, by which he chiefly means a property system. Participation in production involves production relations, which involve both work relations and ownership relations. But Marx goes further, and claims that production determines the property system which is part of production. If production is used in a wide sense (involving the technical work process *plus* property relations), then the claim is of the form P(A+B) determines B, which is unenlightening, not to say tautological. If production is used in a narrow sense (involving the technical work process only), then the claim is of the form P(A) determines B, which is not tautological and entails a technological determinism. The latter claim makes sense and is false. That some property system is always associated with production in the narrow sense does not entail that either is determined by the other. Or, to put it another way, that production requires *some* system of rules regulating persons and property does not entail that a *specific* kind of property system is required.[89] One example will suffice. The USSR and the USA are countries whose methods and level of production are approximately the same in all relevant respects, but their property systems are quite different. The claim that production determines the property system cannot therefore be sustained. It appears most plausible in extreme cases. For instance, it is unlikely that a nation of shepherds could invent the limited liability joint-stock company independently of influence from an economically more advanced nation. As Marx says, 'Don Quixote long ago paid the penalty for wrongly imagining that knight errantry was compatible with all economical forms of society.'[90] But to make a claim of the form 'A determines B' is to make a claim which admits of no exceptions unless a carefully defined *ceteris paribus* clause is added.

It is this prevarication between 'A+B determines B' and 'A determines B' that has led to different views being taken about the concept of *mode of production (Produktionsweise)*. If we include the property system, then there are different modes of production in the USA and the USSR; if we exclude the property system, then the modes are the same. A middle line is to emphasise the mode of production as a property system. In this way we distinguish modes of production from each other by noting the respective positions of workers in relation to the means of production. 'The essential difference between the various economic formations of society . . . lies only in the form in which . . . surplus labour is in each case extracted from the direct producer, the labourer.'[91] Thus the worker could be working with the same tools, but for himself; as a slave, a serf, or a proletarian; or for the community in some form of socialised production. His economic position and degree of freedom are a consequence of the specific kind of property system which exists in a particular society.[92] Marx is saying at least this, but he means to say more. This formulation leaves open the question of specific links between particular economies and particular property systems. The following passage exhibits this difficulty, as well as the others we have mentioned:

The specific economic form, in which unpaid surplus labour is pumped out of the direct producers, determines (*bestimmt*) the relationship of ruler and ruled, as it grows directly out of production itself and, in turn, reacts upon it as a determining element. . . . It is always the direct relation of the owners of the conditions of production to the direct producers – a relation always naturally corresponding (*entspricht*) to a definite stage in the development of the methods of labour and thus its social productivity – which reveals the innermost secret, the hidden basis of the whole social structure and with it . . . the corresponding specific form of the State.[93]

Thus the basis of society is the relation of those who own the means of production to the direct producers: but this relation always has a 'natural correspondence' with a specific stage in technological development; and there is in each case a specific form of the state.

Acton, on the other hand, is quite clear that Marx's view is basically a technological theory of history. His main motive for seeing Marx's views in this way 'is that it does at least purport to provide a definite theory of history whereas the alternatives are almost too vague to discuss'.[94] In his later account Acton agrees that we can draw from Marx's writings both of the first two claims we have mentioned: that history is ultimately determined, either by the level of the productive forces alone, or by the level of the productive forces plus the production relations. As Marx was unclear, we cannot definitively say what his view was, but Acton opts for the first alternative. For Marx, man is essentially a toolmaker, and his social relations are ultimately determined by this fact.[95] Acton discerns a development in Marx's views. In 1846, individuals are said to express their lives in their production, both 'in *what* they produce and with *how* they produce'.[96] In 1867, a far more restrictive view appears:

> It is not the articles made, but how they are made, and by what instruments, that enables us to distinguish different economic epochs. Instruments of labour not only supply a standard of the degree of development to which human labour has attained, but they are also indicators of the social conditions under which that labour is carried on.

Marx has moved from a broad 'material view of history' in 1846 to a narrow technological theory of history in 1867.

> Technology discloses man's mode of dealing with Nature, the process of production whereby he sustains his life, and thereby also lays bare the mode of formation of his social relations, and of the mental conceptions which flow from them.[97]

We can therefore quarry out of Marx's writings general passages which state or imply that technology is the ultimately determining factor in all social change. There are also many passages, particularly in *Capital*, which attest the importance Marx attaches to particular technological changes in changing social relations in capitalist society. Thus 'changes in the material mode of production', that is, the revolutionising of industry by water power, steam and machinery, leads to 'corresponding changes in the social relations of the producers', attempts by factory owners to establish an unlimited working day, and finally a reaction by 'society which legally limits, regulates and makes uniform the working day'. Another example is Marx's claim that 'in manufacture, the revolution in the mode of production begins with the instruments of labour'. Indeed, 'a radical change in the mode of production in one sphere of industry involves a similar change in other spheres': thus 'the revolution in the modes of production of industry and agriculture made necessary a revolution . . . in the means of communication'.[98] The introduction of machinery also effected changes in the law. 'The revolution effected by machinery in the juridical relations between the buyer and seller of labour power', through the employment of child labour, led to state interference and the Factory Acts.[99]

But that Marx places considerable weight on the role of technological change in bringing about social change, does not commit him to a technological theory of history. Such change is a necessary, but not sufficient, condition for the abolition of private property, in that it paves the way for the abolition of scarcity. The owners of capital will exclude 'all rational improvement beyond a certain point': for instance, it is technically feasible in the conditions of Modern Industry to operate 'a rapid and constant change of the individuals' tending machinery. The capitalist does not do so, thus reducing labour costs and rendering the labourer totally dependent.[100] The introduction of the Factory Acts is seen as a result of certain values in society at large concerning the treatment of minors as well as the political pressure of the working class. The definition of a *normal* working day has nothing to do with technology, and everything to do with politics.[101] Marx was well aware of the role of the state in creating conditions in which technological change could come about.[102] He was also aware that the same economic structure could harbour quite different political systems.[103] Finally, there is no hint in Marx's writings that the four major modes of production differ from each other by virtue of different levels of technological development; or that, for instance, a slave economy gave way to a feudal serf economy because of some significant change in technology. The major technological change in the capitalist mode does not come until the end of the eighteenth century: the introduction of machinery.

Marx is himself to blame for the different constructions placed on the term *mode of production*. In the passages we have quoted two distinct meanings can be assigned: (1) MP as a technical process; (2) MP as a technology plus social relations. The first is in fact used, as we have seen, not of productive epochs (e.g. capitalism), but of stages *within* a productive epoch (e.g. Manufacture and Modern Industry).[104] If the term is to bear a technical meaning, then it should be used consistently. It is clear, too, from what we have said that Marx's overall view is much wider than a technological or even 'technologico-economic' theory of history. Again this is often obscured by Marx's use of language. Sometimes he appears to assimilate any causal factor to the economic. Thus 'force is the midwife of every old society pregnant with a new one. It is itself an economic power'.[105]

b. *Historical Periodisation*

We turn now to the problem of historical periodisation. In 1846, stages in the social division of labour are said to correspond to various property forms. After the pre-class form of communal property, three kinds of class formations based on private property are noted: the ancient, feudal and capitalist, based on slave, serf and wage-labour respectively.[106] A second attempt at periodisation occurs in the *Grundrisse* (January 1858), and the concept of an Asiatic mode is included.[107] Marx's list of the modes of production in the *Preface* (Asiatic, ancient, feudal, modern bourgeois) clearly has the *Grundrisse* discussion in mind. In the 1870s Marx was increasingly preoccupied with the forms of primitive communalism and the relation of the village commune to social development in Russia.

It has been widely assumed that the *Preface* gives us a framework of world history, to be understood as a series of successive, progressive modes of production, stages through which all societies must necessarily pass, that these stages are fixed in a specific sequence, and that each mode of production has an internal dynamism of its own which leads to its collapse and at the same time the generation of its successor.

With respect to the succession question, it seems evident that in Western Europe at least, the ancient, feudal and modern bourgeois modes succeed each other. We should not be misled by the geographical appellation of the Asiatic mode: 'The Asiatic or Indian forms of property constitute everywhere in Europe the beginning. . . .'[108] But Marx does not consider that the succession is one which applies to world history. In his articles on India, Marx portrays a backward communal system being replaced by Western capitalism rather than the ancient or feudal modes. Similarly, American capitalism is seen to have attained a more dominating form in the USA partly because of the lack of any feudal past. In his drafts on Russian developments, Marx envisages the possibility of the village commune providing a starting-point for a communist development.

Marx states that the four modes are in some sense *progressive*: capitalism is a 'higher' mode than feudalism, and so on. Two criteria of progress seem to be involved here. The first is economic: capitalism is a more effective utiliser of resources than feudalism. But this is not so clear of the feudal mode in relation to the ancient. How far Marx was committed to this criterion is difficult to say: all the pre-capitalist modes are insignificant in this respect when compared as productive machines with capitalism. A second criterion may be the degree of freedom enjoyed by non-possessing groups. Thus a serf is more free than the slave. Although he is tied to the land, he is not a chattel and has some kind of independent economic status. A proletarian is wholly free legally, for capitalism requires a free and mobile labour market. He has no economic independence, but capitalism paves the way for all to have economic freedom. The notion of *progressive* does not, however, involve any claim about a particular order of succession of the modes. At any time or place, the capitalist mode would be more progressive than the feudal mode.

It is true that the prefaces to *Capital* I lend themselves to a 'fixed stages' interpretation. Marx argues that 'the country that is more developed industrially only shows, to the less developed, the image of its own future'. Industrialism and capitalism are logically related (they go together) and constitute an inevitable stage for all countries. A society 'can neither clear by bold leaps, nor remove by legal enactments, the obstacles offered by the successive phases of its normal development'. All that can be hoped for is that, profiting from the experience of nations like Britain who have gone through the process, 'one nation can and must learn from others' and 'shorten and lessen the birth pangs'.[109]

In 1873 Marx quoted approvingly a characterisation of his intentions:

... to show, by rigid scientific investigation, the necessity of successive determinate orders of social conditions ... both the necessity of the present order of things, and the necessity of another order into which the first must inevitably pass over ... every historical period has laws of its own. ... As soon as society has outlived a given period of development, and is passing over from one given stage to another, it begins to be subject also to other laws. ...[110]

This seems explicit enough: yet even here there is no hint that there is any overall law of historical development which determines any particular succession of historical modes.

The notion of necessity in Marx's writings is used in a variety of ways: as logical entailment, dialectical necessity, need, desirability; as what is predictable; as historical necessity, and so on.[111] Two meanings are especially important to our discussion. First, there is the overall necessity of events according to the structural relations of a mode of production: 'It is a question of these laws ... these tendencies working with iron necessity towards inevitable results.'[112] We shall discuss this when we have outlined Marx's model of capitalism.

Second, there is the concept of historical necessity.[113] There is an important passage in the *Grundrisse*:

This process of inversion is a merely historical necessity, a necessity for the development of the forces of production solely from a specific

73

historic point of departure, or basis, but in no way an absolute necessity of production.[114]

Industrial development in Western Europe occurred in a certain context, which included private property ownership, and therefore began and developed on that basis. The development of the productive forces is the result of human activity. But men are limited in what they do by their circumstances, 'by the productive forces already acquired, by the social form which exists before they do, which they do not create, which is the product of preceding generations'.[115] In this sense, capitalism is historically necessary, but not absolutely necessary: if communal property forms had been dominant in the sixteenth century, things might have fallen out differently.

Within a mode of production, once it has crystallised and become dominant, there is the kind of necessity depicted by Marx in *Capital*. By the 1870s he confines such necessity to the countries of Western Europe. This is made quite clear in his letters and manuscripts on developments in Russia. In 1877 the Russian populist writer Mikhailovsky posed the dilemma he believed confronted the Marxist in Russia, 'a collision between moral feeling and historical inevitability'. The Marxist believes that Russia must go through the horrors of the capitalist phase in order to attain socialism. His belief reduced him to the role of an onlooker, unable to take part in a wicked process which he nevertheless regards as inevitable and 'in the final result, beneficial'.[116]

Marx wrote a reply, in which he stated that the chapter on primitive accumulation in *Capital* is no more than a 'historical sketch' tracing 'the path by which, in Western Europe, the capitalist order of economy emerged from the feudal order of economy'. The expropriation of the agricultural producer 'has been accomplished in radical fashion only in England ... but all the countries of Western Europe are going through the same movement'.[117] The sketch has only two lessons for Russia. First, if she is to become a capitalist nation she must transform 'a good part of her peasants into proletarians'. This follows by definition. Second, once the capitalist mode is dominant, Russia 'will experience its pitiless laws like other profane peoples'. Marx refused to be saddled with a 'general historico-philosophical theory, the supreme virtue of which consists in being super-historical'. History is to be understood by an empirical examination of each form of social evolution and a comparison of the results.[118]

The letter was never sent, but the issue was reopened by Vera Zasulich in 1881. The Russian populists believed that the old Russian village commune could become the basis for socialism without the necessity of going through a capitalist stage. They therefore rejected the implications they saw in *Capital*. As Zasulich put it, if the village community is fated to perish,

the socialist as such has no alternative open, but to devote himself to more or less ill-founded calculations in order to find out in how many decades the land of the Russian peasant will pass from his hands into those of the bourgeoisie, and in how many centuries Russian capitalism will attain perhaps a development similar to that of Western Europe. . . . Thus, you understand, Comrade . . . what a great service you would render us, if you expounded your ideas on the possible destiny of our village community, and on the theory of the historical necessity for all countries of the world to pass through all phases of capitalist development.[119]

Marx's reply drew attention to the passage in the French edition of *Capital* I, and pointed out that in Western Europe the development had entailed a transfer from one kind of private property to another, and not, as in Russia, the (possible) transfer from communal to private property. The analysis in *Capital* therefore adduces 'no reasons for or against the vitality of the rural community'. Indeed, this community could be 'the mainspring of Russia's social regeneration' if weakening influences could be removed.[120]

But Marx also wrote a number of drafts, in which he developed his ideas on the primitive communities.[121] He discerned elements both of communal and of private property. The agricultural land is held inalienably in common, subject to periodic redistribution. The peasant, on the other hand, owns his house and farmyard. Thus private appropriation and accumulation can take place, 'for example money, domestic animals, and sometimes even slaves or serfs'. Such movable property is 'the decomposing factor of primitive social and economic equality'. Historically the village community has often represented a transitional phase between a society founded on communal property and one founded on private property. But this is not inevitable. The 'innate dualism' of the village community allows us an alternative development, in which collectivism predominates. Indeed, Russia

occupies a unique position, without precedent in history. . . . The communal ownership of the soil offers it a natural base for collective appropriation, and its historical environment, the contemporaneous existence of capitalist production lends it all the ready-made material conditions of co-operative labour. . . . The community can thus adopt the positive achievements elaborated by the capitalist system without having to undergo its hardships.[122]

But Marx also notes many negative factors. Since the 1861 serf emancipation, which created a free labour market, private ownership of movable assets has grown, leading to social differentiation among the peasantry. Above all, there are the activities of the Russian state:

What menaces the life of the Russian community is neither historical necessity, nor a social theory: it is the oppression by the State and the exploitation by capitalist intruders who have been made powerful at the expense and cost of the peasants by the very same State.[123]

In the last analysis, only a revolution can save the Russian village community. A few months later Marx added that salvation would only come 'if the Russian revolution sounds the signal for a proletarian revolution in the West, so that each complements the other'. Only then could the commune form 'the starting-point for a communist development'.[124]

We must conclude that for Marx there is no law of historical development which determines any specific sequence of successive and necessary stages. Indeed, in transitional periods, when the old mode of production has ceased to dominate but the new one has yet to take root, effective choice of mode may be made by political means if state power can be brought to bear. The implications for revolutionary politics are considerable. There seems to have been a development in Marx's thinking here. In 1846 he believed that private property was necessary for 'certain stages of development of the productive forces' and could not be dispensed with until it had become 'a restricting fetter'.[125] By the 1870s he envisages situations in which this need not be the case. The change can already be seen in the *Grundrisse*, where the forms which can be taken by property in pre-capitalist societies are seen to depend on many factors: the natural inclinations of the tribe, the economic conditions in which it appropriates nature (climate, soil, raw materials), relations with other communities, modifications introduced by migration or other historical experience.[126] Such factors may jointly entail historical necessity in the sense in which we have defined it, but no more.

We must now examine the role played by internal change. The general claim made in the *Preface* is that social change is caused by internal contradictions and tensions within the existing system of production. This is echoed in *Capital*: 'The historical development of the antagonisms, immanent in a given form of production, is the only way in which that form of production can be dissolved and a new form established.' [127] Marx often uses an organic analogy to express this belief: 'The present society is . . . an organism capable of change, and constantly changing.' [128] But this is a limited analogy. Organic processes typically occur *within* a given structural pattern, but for Marx the entire structural arrangements of society can change. 'But capitalist production begets, with the inexorability of a law of Nature, its own negation. . . .' [129] Similarly, 'the economic structure of capitalist society has grown out of the economic structure of feudal society. The dissolution of the latter set free the elements of the former'.[130]

A central problem of Marxist historiography is to show in a particular case exactly how, for example, internal changes in English feudalism led to capitalism. There are two issues here. First, why feudalism disintegrated in Western Europe, bearing in mind the unevenness of the process, the second serfdom in parts of Europe in the sixteenth and seventeenth centuries, and so on. Second, there is the time scale: why did it take so long? In the classic English case, two centuries had elapsed between the decline of labour services and the 'bourgeois revolution' claimed to have occurred in the seventeenth century; and nearly as long until the Industrial Revolution. The so-called Pirenne thesis is one answer to the first question: the dissolving effects of trade upon an otherwise stable feudal system.[131] Most Marxist historians appear reluctant to accept this answer. All avenues of empirical investigation must be explored before a central principle of method can be discarded.[132]

However, Marx is not consistently of the view that all significant social change is a result of internal tensions within the previous mode of production. He sought to show this in great detail with respect to capitalism and the transition to communism. But there is little argument of an analogous kind concerning the other modes. He claims that it is true of the emergence of capitalism from feudalism. But what his account amounts to is the claim that capitalism emerged from the womb of a socio-economic formation in which feudalism was the dominant mode. Marx never sketched the internal contradictions of feudalism as a mode of production. He talks rather of the disintegrative effects of urban developments on agrarian feudalism, but gives no reasons why it should be so soluble.

> If the countryside exploits the town politically in the Middle Ages, wherever feudalism has not broken down by exceptional urban developments – as in Italy – the town, on the other hand, exploits the land economically everywhere and without exception. . . .[133]

There are arguments for an internal collapse of the ancient mode, but no hint that feudalism had necessarily to succeed it.[134] Equally, there is no hint that the Asiatic mode lays the foundation for the ancient mode. Indeed, Marx's view seems to be that early communal organisation is the source of a subsequent fourfold differentiation into Asiatic, Greco-Roman, Germanic, and Slavonic forms.[135]

At a more particular level, Marx was convinced that revolution in Russia could occur only if a complementary revolution occurred in another productive order. Similarly, the Russian autocracy was 'the unbroken bulwark and reserve army of counter-revolution' whose destruction was a necessary condition of any successful proletarian revolution in Germany.[136] As a final example we may cite Marx's explanation of the American Civil War as one between a bourgeois North and a slave South, in which once again the challenge to the latter comes, not from its own internal strains, but from another productive system.[137]

These are all cases where Marx admits that significant alterations in the productive system have been caused by external factors. But he went further: one mode of production, the Asiatic, has no internal dynamism whatever. When Marx first noted this mode in the early 1850s, the crucial feature appeared to be the absence of private property in land,[138] as well as the typical combination of home industry and small-scale agriculture in a system of self-sufficient villages, a feature widespread in both India and China. In both countries, there were no significant mechanisms of internal change.[139] Marx ascribed considerable importance to the structure of these communities.

> The simplicity of the organisation for production in these self-sufficing communities . . . supplies the key to the unchangeableness of Asiatic societies. . . . The structure of the economical elements of society remains untouched by the storm-clouds of the political sky.[140]

Such communities 'had always been the solid foundation of Oriental despotism'. It follows that Marx saw European colonial rule as a brutal but, in the given conditions, necessary step towards socialism: only outside dissolvents could change the system. In this light the Indian Mutiny and the T'ai P'ing Rebellion are regressive movements.[141] England has a twin mission in India, annihilating the old Asiatic mode and laying the economic foundations for a new society.[142]

In the early 1850s the concept of the Asiatic mode is applied to China, where there was in fact private land holding. This is a possible reason for a later shift in focus. The basic feature of the mode is now tied to the unity of small-scale agriculture and home industry as the basis of the self-sustaining village community, with common ownership of land in some cases only.[143] We now hear that it is found 'among all civilised nations at the dawn of their history',[144] and thus in early Western Europe as well as in the contemporary East. Indeed, 'Mexico, and especially Peru, among the ancient Celts, and some tribes of India' all possess characteristics of the Asiatic mode.[145]

We can conclude that Marx's general formulations about history were more flexible than they appeared to his contemporaries: first, because they are loosely and often ambiguously phrased; second, because Marx himself was prepared to modify his views when confronted by particular cases. Such modifications occur, not only in his polemics on French politics, where less rigorous formulations are to be expected, but also in writings where Marx is addressing himself to specific methodological problems. Marx's successive formulations, only one of which was published in his lifetime, may be regarded as characterisations of a perspective rather than fully articulated theoretical statements. Why was it, then, that a rigid determinist theory of history was attributed to Marx? In part this may have been a misreading of the 1859 *Preface*. More importantly, Engels often emphasised more heavily than Marx the element of determinism, for instance, in his attack on Tkachev's view that there could be a revolution in Russia leading to socialism before it is attained in the West.[146] Plekhanov developed a full-fledged stages theory out of such suggestions. It is ironic that Engels should have been partly responsible for such interpretations, for late in his life he made many efforts to emphasise Marx's approach as a method of investigation rather than a rigid dogma; [147] and in the 1890s sought to redress the one-sided emphasis on economic determinism.[148] Briefly, Engels posits a relationship of reciprocal interdependence among the variables in which in 'the last instance' economic factors are ultimately decisive. Thus the economic element is 'in the *last instance* the determining element', not 'the *only* determining element', yet in the final analysis it 'asserts itself as necessary'. These formulations have often been criticised by many followers of Marx (Korsch, Sartre and Althusser among them), but are not noticeably inferior to the Marxian formulations we have examined, and share the same weaknesses.

c. *Class and Ideology*

The concepts discussed so far are applicable to all societies. To conclude our survey of the *Preface* and allied texts, we need to introduce two concepts not applicable to non-class societies, namely class and ideology. Historically there has been a differentiation of societies into social groups occupying different 'social positions' and hence developing outlooks on the society in which they live. Social classes are for Marx of crucial importance among such groups. 'The history of all hitherto existing society is the history of class struggle.' [149] Conflict is an essential dimension of all class societies. Not only has economic development been *accompanied* by class conflict but the far stronger claim is made that the latter has been in some way instrumental in *generating* economic development. 'Without conflict, no progress: that is the law which civilisation has followed to the present day. Until now the forces of production have developed by virtue of the dominance of class conflict.' [150] The concepts of class and ideology receive only fragmentary treatment in Marx's writings, and we have to disentangle a number of uses in polemical contexts. Both Aron and Jordan are led by this fact to distinguish between the sociological concept of class as employed in *Capital*, and the concept as employed in Marx's 'historical writings' (the polemics on French politics).[151] But in fact we are better able to understand Marx's use of class from his polemical writings. The only attempt to define class in *Capital* breaks off unfinished.

In *Capital* III Marx began by presenting a trichotomic schema of the 'three big classes of modern society based on the capitalist mode of production'. These are the owners, respectively, of labour power, capital and land, who are differentiated by their source of income: wages, profit and ground rent. This is the 'pure' or 'classic' form of class stratification. Even in England it is obscured by 'middle and intermediate strata'. But ultimately this is irrelevant, for capitalist development will ensure the polarisation of all labour into wage-labour and all means of production into capital. Marx then asks: 'What constitutes a class?' At first sight, the criterion appears to be the source of revenue. But this would enable physicians and officials to be seen as classes. With this objection the manuscript breaks off.[152] We can assume that Marx would have rejected the threefold distinction: landownership will be increasingly subsumed under capital. He would also have rejected a definition which would have allowed physicians or officials as distinct groups to be called classes. Class is never defined only by reference to source of income, or indeed to any single criterion, whether income, birth, status, education or occupation, though these features would undoubtedly enter any full account of a specific class structure and the economic inequalities it entrails.

Two major criteria seem to have governed Marx's use of class. First, the group so designated must share more or less permanent economic interests, in terms of the ownership or non-ownership of the means of production, a criterion which clearly divides any society into two, usually unequal, parts.[153] This is not by itself sufficient, for it would place capitalists, peasants and master-craftsmen in the same class. A further distinguishing economic characteristic might be the employment or otherwise of a labour force. Marx also saw the political as well as the economic importance of distinguishing between owners of landed property, loan capital and industrial capital.

A common economic situation, however closely defined, constitutes a necessary, not a sufficient condition for a social class. The second major criterion of class is class-consciousness. The members of a class are deemed to share a common life-style, beliefs and values. Further, they have a perception of their own class position. Such perceptions are vital because they affect the ways in which the class members act politically. However, a class is only fully class-conscious when it is organised politically to promote its objective economic interests. Marx puts the point with respect to the French small-holding peasantry:

> In so far as millions of families live under economic conditions of existence that separate their mode of life, their interests and their culture (*Bildung*) from those of other classes, and put them into a hostile opposition to the latter, they form a class. In so far as there is merely a local interconnection among these small-holding peasants, and the identity of their interests begets no community, no political organisation among them, they do not form a class.[154]

We could distinguish non-possessing classes (slaves, serfs, proletarians) from each other on the basis of their degree of freedom. But this characteristic can be deduced from the way in which surplus labour is pumped from the direct producer in each case.

Marx's actual use of *class* is more complex than this summary suggests. In *Class Struggles in France*, five classes are mentioned: big bourgeoisie, petty bourgeoisie, peasantry, proletariat and lumpen-proletariat. In *The Eighteenth Brumaire* the same classes are noted, together with the landed aristocracy. This is not all. The big bourgeoisie is said to comprise three *fractions*: the industrial bourgeoisie, the finance aristocracy and the large landowners, each with a distinct interest as against the other two fractions and a distinct political voice. The lumpenproletariat has both urban and rural elements. The terms merchant class, burgher class, lower middle class (meaning petty bourgeoisie), middle classes (referring sometimes to petty bourgeoisie, but also to bourgeoisie as such, for instance in the final chapter of *The Eighteenth Brumaire*), and so on, are also used. The term *class* is therefore used of social groups who do not fulfil the basic criteria. They all fulfil the first criterion (except perhaps for the lumpenproletariat, which seems to be a rag-bag of assorted elements [155]), but not the second. The peasantry, though it is said to have both revolutionary and conservative elements, has no full class-consciousness, nor has the lumpenproletariat. Concerning the petty bourgeoisie, Marx prevaricates: in the *Manifesto* it has not; in the *March Address* and *Class Struggles in France* it has. In the latter instance it has a distinct political organisation under the leadership of Ledru-Rollin. In the former the democratic petty bourgeoisie is even credited with the potential of revolutionary initiative.

For Marx, each class goes through a period of class formation in which its organisation and ideology are developed on the basis of shared economic interests, a process in which a class in itself (*Klasse an sich*) becomes a class for itself (*Klasse für sich*). The bourgeoise has arisen in Western Europe, bringing about major socio-economic changes, explaining and justifying such changes and its own dominant social position by reference to certain political and economic theories. As a result of industrial development, a new class, the proletariat, has grown up, whose interest is said to be irreconcilable with that of the bourgeoisie. The demands of the two classes are said to be incompatible: in the long run no accommodation is possible. Tactical requirements may mean class alliances, but only in pursuit of the long-term goal. The revolutionary class 'finds directly in its own situation the context and the material of its revolutionary activity: foes to be laid low; measures, to be dictated by the needs of the struggle, to be taken – the consequences of its own deeds drive it on'.[156] Thus the objective interest of the class as defined by the Marxian theory, its actual situation, and what it does, will all coincide in the fully conscious class. Here and in other similar passages Marx makes the assumption that the economic characteristics of a class will determine the socio-political outlook of its members. But there are also many places in his writings where it is clear that Marx realises modifications are necessary to such an assumption. Individuals within a class can have interests opposed to each other, or to the class as a whole.[157] Fractions of a class can have opposed interests: for instance, owners of loan capital as opposed to industrial capital.[158] Above all, the members of a class may fail to realise their class interest. Hence the need for the political education of the proletariat. Indeed,

Marx is aware that political leaders and ideologists of the class not only need not be of the class themselves, but may well have a better conception of the class interest than the members of the class.[159] This has the further implication that the consciousness of individuals is not necessarily bound by their class situation, and that transfer between classes is possible. Marx and Engels must have counted themselves among that portion of 'the bourgeois ideologists who have raised themselves to the level of comprehending theoretically the historical movement as a whole', and who have passed with this knowledge to the side of the proletariat.[160] The reverse can also happen: indeed, 'the more a ruling class is able to assimilate the foremost men of a ruled class, the more solid and dangerous becomes its rule'.[161] Marx seems to have believed that a high degree of social mobility is likely only in periods of rapid transition. Thus he says of the USA that 'though classes already exist, they have not yet become fixed, but continually change and interchange their elements in a constant flux'.[162] If this should be the norm rather than the exception under capitalism, then class divisions will become blurred and education in class-consciousness correspondingly difficult.

For Marx, class and ideology are linked: all ideology is *class* ideology. In the *Preface* he lists the 'ideological forms' through which men become aware of class conflict: legal, political, religious, artistic, or philosophical. These ideas change through time: 'Man's ideas, views, and conceptions, in one word, man's consciousness, changes with every change in the conditions of his material existence, in his social relations, and in his social life.'[163] This is near-tautological, for concepts are involved in all human activity. Social relations are relations between language users: indeed, concepts partially constitute the relationships. Marx means more than this. Not only are all social concepts, and therefore theories, subject to change, but they change in accordance with changes in class relationships.

Marx never explicitly defined *ideology*. In general, he used it to refer to a more or less coherent system of ideas which purported to explain and justify the social position of class. Here the notion of a social position is analogous to that of a physical position.[164] A social class has a 'place' within a society. Its point of view determines the angle from which it 'sees' in society and thereby what it sees. Engels related ideology to a complex division of labour: 'Society gives rise to certain common functions. . . . The persons appointed for this purpose form a new branch of the division of labour within society. This gives them particular interests. . . .'[165] Each branch appears independent to those acting within it, and to operate according to its own rules. For the actors within a sphere of activity, it is difficult to have an overall view of society. Ideological thinking is not deliberately hypocritical: the process 'goes on without the person who is acting being aware of it'.[166] Indeed, 'in all ideology men and their circumstances appear upside down as in a *camera obscura*'.[167] This phenomenon is termed inversion (*Verkehrung*).

Marx's emphasis on the ideological character of much social thought does not imply a total social relativism. Total relativism of any kind is logically self-contradictory. So far as a given society is concerned, all actors within it must share *some* ideas which do not depend for their meaning and validity on any particular social position. Otherwise communication between them would be impossible. Marx distinguished between ideology and science: 'Where speculation ends – in real life – there real, positive science begins.' For social science to be possible, minimally we must be able to distinguish knowledge from belief, and accept that some concepts are indispensable in any coherent language. The claim that certain kinds of social conditions are necessary for certain kinds of theoretical development does not imply relativism. Certain social conditions were propitious for the development of modern physical science, but the content of that science does not depend for its validity on any kind of social context. Marx reminds us that it is often important to ask of a social theory: what interest is supported by this theory? But it remains the case that if the empirical claims of the theory can in principle be tested, then the empirical validity of its claims can be established or refuted without reference to the origins of the theory, which are logically irrelevant to its truth value. It should also be noted that a true theory may support, by implication, certain interests and not others. Marx certainly believed that his economic theory was true, and that it supported the interests of the proletariat.

Ideological thinking is said to reflect a *false* consciousness about society. This notion involves more than mistakes about matters of fact: an ideology may include many true claims. But a class may believe certain things to be the case because of its interests, thus causing it to have an inadequate view of how society functions. Marx argues that at the point at which knowledge of the truth about society becomes a danger to the interests of the possessing class, the ideologist stops his investigations. The main function of ideology is justification, not explanation. Ideology supports class interests. The interest of a ruling class is the maintenance of its political and economic power. As we have seen, a class may be unconscious of its objective interest. Indeed, it may entertain beliefs inimical to its interests: 'The advance of capitalist production develops a working class, which by tradition, education, habit, looks upon the conditions of that mode of production as self-evident laws of nature.' [168] The dominant class is able to impose its ideas upon society. 'The ideas of the ruling class are in every epoch the ruling ideas': the possessing class 'has control . . . over the means of mental production'. Marx conceived it as his task to develop a theory which would situate the class position of the proletariat and account for its future development. In this sense the objective interest of the proletariat is what it is to become in the future. A major function of the theory is to combat the work of ruling class ideologists, 'who make the perfecting of the illusion of the class about itself their chief source of livelihood'.[169]

In bourgeois society the political economist is seen to have a major ideological role. Several levels of consciousness are involved here. First, there are 'the conceptions by which the bearers and agents' of economic relations seek to understand those relations, as well as the concepts actually involved in their performance.[170] Marx considers that even the most everyday linguistic conventions may reinforce and legitimate existing social relations:

> For the bourgeois it is so much the easier to prove on the basis of his language, the identity of commercial and individual, or even universal, human relations, since this language itself is a product of the bourgeoisie, and therefore in actuality as in the language the relations of buying and selling have been made the basis of all the others.[171]

From one point of view the pattern of relationships perceived by the actors themselves has a real existence. Economic relations are as they seem to be, and are reinforced by the fact that these appearances 'determine the actions of individual capitalists etc., and provide the motives, which are reflected in their consciousness'.[172]

There are, secondly, reflections upon such ideas by social theorists. Here we can discern three levels, in the thought of vulgar, classical and Marxian political economy respectively. For Marx, vulgar economy 'does no more than interpret, systematise and defend in doctrinaire fashion the conceptions of the agents of production who are entrapped in bourgeois production relations'.[173] By classical economics, Marx understands 'that economy, which since the time of William Petty, has investigated the real relations of production in bourgeois society'.[174] Marx sees his own economics as the inheritor of that tradition, going beyond it with the theories of surplus value and of the wage cycle, cast in a historical perspective, and being at once an economics, a sociology and a politics. We have placed these three levels in an ascending order of adequacy from Marx's point of view, but they have a different historical order.

Classical political economy developed in a period when the industrial bourgeoisie was rising to prominence. Both Smith and Ricardo sought a scientific explanation of how wealth is produced, although their work contains ideological elements. Smith's *Wealth of Nations* speaks 'the language of the still revolutionary bourgeoisie, which had not yet subjected to itself the whole of society, the state, etc.'.[175] At this point, however, the interests of the rising class coincide with the interests of the human species, for capitalism is 'the most advantageous for the production of wealth'. Ricardo's ruthless advocacy of production for the sake of production entailed a scientific honesty which served the objective interest of his class. Both he and Smith were prepared to attack the bourgeoisie. Marx observes that when the short-term interests of the bourgeoisie conflict with the long-term interests of production, Ricardo is 'just as *ruthless* towards it as he is at other times towards the proletariat and the aristocracy'.[176] It remains open to an economist to be purely ideological in his approach. According to Marx, Malthus drew only those conclusions useful to the aristocracy against the bourgeoisie and to both against the proletariat. 'When a man seeks to accommodate science to a viewpoint which is not derived from science itself (however erroneous it may be) but from outside, from alive, external interests, I call him "*base*".'[177]

Marx notes a number of sources of error in classical political economy, but few derive from the ideological standpoint of the economist. First, there are errors of fact and logical contradictions of a formal nature within the analysis. Second, and more important, Marx discerns some major theoretical weaknesses. Smith, for instance, moves 'in a perpetual contradiction', for without realising it he is constantly moving between two conceptual levels: on the one hand, 'the intrinsic connections between economic categories . . . the inner connection, so to speak, of the bourgeois system'; on the other hand, 'the connection as it appears . . . to the unscientific observer just as to him who is actually involved and interested in the process of bourgeois production'.[178] This oscillation is followed by Smith's successors. It is Ricardo's enduring scientific merit to have stated the basic scientific premise, from which all else must (hopefully) be deduced: 'The starting-point for the physiology of the bourgeois system . . . is the determination of *value by labour-time*.' Bound up with this 'is the fact that Ricardo exposes and describes the economic contradictions between the classes'.[179] As time passes, however, the scientific deficiencies of his own procedures will become more visible.

A third source of error stems from the fact that the capitalist mode is one which is developing through time. Smith and Ricardo were not acquainted with many of the phenomena apparent in mature capitalism.[180] Economic concepts themselves change with changes in society.[181] But the major error was the failure of the classical economists to realise that their premises were the product of a historical process, not natural premises true of all societies.[182] Indeed, there are contradictions in their analysis which reflect the development of contradictions in society. Political economy 'is confronted with its own contradictions simultaneously with the development of the actual contradiction in the economic life of society'.[183]

Marx singles out three kinds of reaction to the classical economists. Of least importance were the continental critics of Smith and Ricardo, who only revealed 'the lower stage in the conditions of production from which these "sages" start out'. The views of a Rodbertus were perfectly suited to Pomerania but hardly to the advanced English economy.[184] Much more significant were the critics of the historical school. Richard Jones is singled out here.[185] Third, there were the early socialists, who proceeded from Ricardian assumptions and argued that the correct conclusion had not been drawn from the premise that labour is the source of all value. Ricardo's phrase 'labour *or* capital' reveals the prevarication at the heart of the system. The Ricardian socialists had seized on this phrase. 'Capital is nothing but defrauding of the workers. Labour is everything'. Yet they did not understand the theoretical problems involved and retained the ahistorical views of the classical school.[186]

The establishment of the bourgeoisie as a ruling class, which Marx dates as occurring in France and England around 1830, 'sounded the knell of scientific bourgeois economy':

> It was henceforth, no longer a question, whether this theorem or that was true, but whether it was useful to capital. . . . In place of disinterested inquiries, there were hired prize fighters; in place of genuine scientific research, the bad conscience and the evil intent of apologetic.[187]

The theoretical disintegration of the Ricardian school had already begun with James Mill's *Elements of Political Economy* (1821), an attempt at formal logical consistency seeking to dissolve the theoretical contradictions which in Ricardo had neglected the 'contradictory phenomena'.[188] Political ascendancy of the bourgeoisie coupled with the theoretical disintegration of classical economics led to a vulgar economy apologetic in character and capable only of a sterile academic eclecticism.[189] Methodologically, it remains ahistorical: either it identifies aspects of the capitalist economy with phenomena which occur in *all* economic systems; or it assumes that the capitalist forms themselves occur in all economic systems. Both cases reflect the belief in 'the eternal, nature-ordained necessity for capitalist production'.[190]

3 THE THEORY OF CAPITALISM

There are three main reasons why Marx devoted so much of his time to the critique and reconstruction of political economy. In the work of Smith and Ricardo it can be seen as a scientific discipline which sought to explain the economic structure of society and which was therefore worthy of close study. But secondly, in the hands of the vulgar economists, political economy became an ideology, an apology for the existing social order. There was a consequent need to attack this tendency. Above all, Marx's task was to lay a secure theoretical foundation for political action by the working class within the capitalist society, and it was to this end that he sought to 'lay bare the economic law of motion of modern society'.

a. *Exchange, the Division of Labour, and Alienation*

The institutions of exchange and the division of labour are central to Marx's conception of the alienated capitalist society. They constituted 'perceptibly alienated (*entäusserten*) expressions of human activity'.[191] The two are seen as mutually conditioning:

> Exchange, negotiated through exchange value and money, implies a universal interdependence between the producers, but at the same time the complete isolation of their private interests and a social division of labour, whose unity and mutual fulfilment exists as an external, natural relationship, independent of the producers.[192]

Both contribute significantly to the atomistic character of a society in which there appear to exist independent spheres of activity each with its own norms: 'It stems from the very nature of alienation (*Entfremdung*) that each sphere applies to me a different and opposite yardstick – ethics one and political economy another. . . .' [193] The division of labour separates men, who are reconnected only through the exchange system. Political economists are right to see society as a system of commercial exchanges: but for Marx their insight is an alienated one, for it assumes such a society is normal. The consciousness of the actors in the system, as well as of many who week to explain or justify its working leads to *reification* and *inversion*. For example, money ceases to be a mere medium of exchange.

> The human and social act in which men's products reciprocally complement one another – becomes alienated and takes on the quality of a *material thing*, money, external to man. . . . Through this *alien mediation* man regards his will, his activity, and his relationships to others as a power independent of himself and of them.[194]

A relation between persons is seen as a relation between things (reification); and becomes inverted, in that money is valuable because it represents objects of value, but now objects have value because they represent money.

A major feature of historical development has been the elaboration of social organisation and especially the differentiation of functions and roles comprehended by the term 'the division of labour'. A leading theme of the Scottish school of Smith and Ferguson concerned the disparity between the success of the division of labour in increasing labour productivity of the human species as a whole (and thus its vital role in combating scarcity), and the failure to pass on its benefits to the individual, whose all-round development is stunted and confined. This view was also a leitmotive of German cultural critics, chief among them Herder and Schiller.[195] Marx fully shared these views, and agreed with Adam Smith in laying most differences of failure and achievement among men at the door of the division of labour: 'In principle, a porter differs less from a philosopher than a mastiff from a greyhound. It is the division of labour that has set a gulf between them.' [196]

Marx distinguished between the social division of labour, involving the separation and differentiation of functions in society as a whole, and the division of labour in the workshop. Under capitalism the latter takes two forms: an earlier division of labour in manufacture and a more modern division of labour in the factory (the automatic machine-shop). In 1846 the term 'division of labour' is used indiscriminately, being identified with many forms of social organisation, including the feudal, patriarchal, caste and guild systems.[197] Many consequences are attributed to the division of labour: the formation of the state, the rise of ideology, private property and social classes. Hence, 'the abolition of the division of labour' comprehends, especially in *The German Ideology*, the abolition of the state, private property, social classes and ideology, as well as the division of labour in the narrow sense.[198] Marx puts it less confusingly when he says that private property and class relationships are inevitable consequences of the division of labour.[199] Ideology is seen as one consequence of the division of mental and manual labour, which also involves the separation of town and country and the distinction between agricultural, commercial and industrial labour.[200]

In *Capital*, Marx's usage is restricted to the distinction between the social division of labour and the division of labour in the workshop. Throughout history, men have co-operated in order to produce a particular product, for such co-operation produces more use value for the same amount of labour time than the work of the same number of unassociated workers. 'When the labourer co-operates systematically with others, he strips off the fetters of his individuality and develops the capabilities of his species.' [201] The first advanced form of co-operation is the division of labour in manufacture (*c.* 1550–1780), which arises both from the union of several independent handicrafts, and from co-operation between artificers of one handicraft. The result is the same – 'a productive mechanism whose parts are human beings'. The basic division here is 'the resolution of a handicraft into its successive manual operations'. Each workman is 'exclusively assigned to a particular function'.[202] Division saves time; simplifies, improves and multiplies the instruments of labour; and isolates each stage of production. The effect on the workers is to deprive him of variability of function. A class of unskilled labourers is also created. A speciality is made 'of the absence of all development'.

The division of labour in manufacture (DLM) is built upon a well-developed social division of labour (SDL), which entails the 'tying down of individuals to a particular calling'.[203] Analogies can be drawn between the SDL and the DLM, but they 'differ not only in degree, but in kind.' [204] In the SDL the only bond between independent producers is the exchange relation. In the DLM despotism replaces anarchy. The detail worker has no independence and cannot produce a commodity by himself. The capitalist directs production according to an 'iron law of proportionality' which subjects 'definite numbers of workmen to definite functions'.[205] Both kinds of division have disadvantages:

> Some crippling of mind and body is inseparable even from division of labour in society as a whole . . . manufacture carries this social separation of branches of labour much further, and attacks the individual at the very roots of his life.' [206]

The latter division is both 'a necessary phase in the economic development of society' and, in capitalist hands, 'a refined and civilised method of exploitation'.[207]

Finally the narrow technical basis of handicrafts and rural domestic industries must come 'into conflict with requirements of production . . . created by manufacture itself'. The machine removes the need for handicraft skills, and thereby 'the technical reason for the lifelong annexation of the workman to a detail function'.[208] The second period of capitalism, Modern Industry, begins. Here 'the revolution of the mode of production' is not in the kind of labour power used but in new instruments, namely machines and machine tools.[209] The effect on the worker is to make him an appendage of the machine, to allow the employment of women and children, and to enable the capitalist to prolong the working day and to intensify labour. The division of labour in the factory is primarily 'a distribution of the workmen among the various machines . . . the automaton . . . is the subject, and the workmen are merely conscious organs'.[210]

> The independent and alienated character which the capitalist mode of production . . . gives to the instruments of labour and to the product, as against the workman, is developed by means of machinery into a thorough antagonism.[211]

The unemployed may be swallowed up by the new branches of production or by work involving canals, bridges, tunnels and so on; or by being unproductively employed as members of a servant class (*dienenden Klasse*) [212] or as commercial workers; [213] or by becoming part of the industrial reserve army. Another way out is emigration and colonisation. There finally arises an international division of labour, which 'converts one part of the globe into a chiefly agricultural field of production, for supplying the other part which remains a chiefly industrial field'.[214] In this way the system becomes world-wide.

The exchange system developed in the same measure as the division of labour. It involves 'the exchangeability of all products, activities, relations with a third *objective* entity which can be re-exchanged for everything *without distinction*. . . .' [215] A system of independent producers exchanging their products gives way to the exchange of products mediated by money as the universal equivalent. A complex division of labour means that individuals no longer directly produce their subsistence and receive it in money. Reciprocally, exchange 'provides the possibility of an absolute division of labour'.[216] It implies, as we have seen, the dissolution of traditional ties and dependency relations. The interdependence of individuals is expressed through the social bond of exchange value, the only connection of individuals whose behaviour is purely atomic. To them exchange appears 'as something alien to them, autonomous, like a thing. In exchange value the social connection between persons is transformed into a social relation between things.' [217]

The exchange model of the economists involves the act in which equal exchangers freely exchange equivalents expressed in exchange values (money). It involves a reciprocal relation between 'proprietors, as persons whose will penetrates their commodities'.[218] Their property is the product of their own labour. In the exchange model we have the ideal realm of a free, competitive market.

According to Marx the exchange system constitutes the presupposition of bourgeois democratic theory. As early as 1843, when Marx analysed the French Constitutions of 1791, 1793 and 1795, he concluded that

> none of the so-called rights of man goes beyond egoistic man, man as he is in civil society, namely withdrawn behind the private interests and whims and separated from the community. . . . The only bond that holds them together is natural necessity, need and private interests, the maintenance of their property and egoistic persons.[219]

By the late 1850s Marx's analysis is linked to an economic theory. The exchange system is 'the productive, real basis of all *equality* and *freedom* . . . [which] . . . presuppose relations of production as yet unrealised in the ancient world and in the Middle Ages. . . .' [220] But exchange is only a surface process: 'In the depths, entirely different processes go on, in which this apparent individual equality and liberty disappear.' The French socialists are wrong 'to depict socialism as the realisation of the ideals of *bourgeois* society articulated by the French Revolution'.[221] In *Capital* I Marx concludes his discussion of exchange, 'a very Eden of the innate rights of man', in the following way:

> There alone rule Freedom, Equality, Property and Bentham. Freedom, because both buyer and seller are constrained only by their own free will . . . as free agents. Equality, because each enters into relation with the other, as with a simple owner of commodities, and they exchange equivalent for equivalent. Property, because each disposes only of what is his own. And Bentham, because each looks only to himself . . . and just because they do so, do they all, in accordance with the pre-established harmony of things, or under the auspices of an all-shrewd providence, work together to their mutual advantage, for the common weal and in the interests of all.[222]

But there is one type of exchange in which the equality of the exchanges is purely formal: the sale of his labour power by the worker to the capitalist for its exchange value. Not only does the worker alienate 'his life expression (*Lebensäussserung*) only as a means towards his own life',[223] but the capitalist has obtained the only use value which can be used to create surplus value. The creative power of the worker's labour 'establishes itself as the power of capital, as an *alien power* confronting him'.[224] Marx's reasons for this claim are best dealt with in the context of his mature economic theory. First we must consider the concept of alienation.

Exchange and the division of labour are said to be forms of alienation. This concept has to be understood in the light of Marx's early account of a true communal society (*Gemeinwesen*), and his claim that man's central life activity is productive life.

> To say that *man* alienates himself is the same as saying that the society of this alienated man is the caricature of his *actual common life*, of his true generic life. His activity, therefore, appears as torment, his own creation as a force alien to him, his wealth as poverty, the essential bond connecting him with other men as something unessential so that his separation from other men appears as his true existence.[225]

The basic claim being made is that capitalist society consists of closely interrelated forms of social organisation (private property in the means of production, exchange, the division of labour) which, while laying the material basis of a truly human society, prevent men from pursuing their life activity and engender certain psychological states in them.[226] In such a society, theories such as those of political economy can at most show only an 'estranged insight' into the real conditions of modern society. Marx distinguishes various forms of alienation: religious, philosophical, political and economic. Nevertheless, 'the whole of human servitude is involved in the relation of the worker to production'.[227] Religious alienation, for instance, is a matter of consciousness, but economic alienation is the basis of '*real life*'.[228] Marx's *Economic and Philosophic Manuscripts* of 1844 (*EPM*), which constitute his first attempt at a critique of political economy, also contain his first full account of alienation.[229]

We should note that Marx uses two words which are often, though not always, interchangeable in their use: *Entfremdung* (from *entfremden*, to estrange, make alien, rob) and *Entäusserung* (from *entäussern*, to alienate, part with, sell, externalise). The latter conveys the sense of a transfer of ownership which also is a renunciation; or, in context, a sense of making something external.[230] Marx may also have seen polemical possibilities in using a word which could refer both to 'alienation from species-being' and to the practices of a commercial society. A closely related term is *Veräusserung*, also in common use as 'selling' and as a technical term for the legal transfer of property. Thus Marx notes that '*Veräusserung* is the practice of *Entäusserung*'.[231] The term *Entfremdung* does not carry the double meaning of selling as well as

alienation, but where used in connection with property carries over-
tones of robbery rather than a legal transfer. It is also interesting to note
that Marx does make a distinction in the course of a discussion of Hegel,
between 'indifferent foreignness' (*Fremdheit*) and 'antagonistic alienation' (*Entfremdung*).[232] Thus the latter term is used to suggest that what
is alienated becomes not only strange and alien, but also hostile.[233]

The first three (parallel) sections of the first manuscripts deal with
Wages of Labour, Profit of Capital and Rent of Land. They analyse in a
skeletal fashion parts of the work of some political economists (notably
Adam Smith; but also J. B. Say, Schulz, Pecqueur, Loudoun, Buret),
and sketch the implications of their theorising. Apart from Smith, these
writers are largely hostile to the system they are describing. Hence it is
not surprising that Marx is able to say that 'on the basis of political
economy, in its own words, we have shown that the worker sinks to the
level . . . of the most wretched of commodities'.[234] Even under the most
favourable conditions possible within the system, 'the inevitable result
for the worker is overwork and premature death'.[235]

Yet because political economy accepts the fact and necessity of private
property it is unable to explain why the system works as it does. 'The
only wheels which political economy sets in motion are *avarice* and the
war amongst the avaricious – competition.' The explanation offered is
psychological: the universal egoism of human nature, or, in Adam
Smith's case, the universal human propensity to exchange. But greed is,
for Marx, a contingent, not a necessary feature of human psychology.
It is one among a set of interrelated aspects which together constitute
an alienated society. What requires explanation is the connection
'between this whole *Entfremdung* and the *money* system'.[236]

Marx's discussion of work alienation is introduced in the context of
his attempt to give an explanation of society where the political economists have failed. Work should be the objectification of a man's
capacities:

> Labour's realisation is its objectification. In the sphere of political
> economy this realisation of labour appears as *loss of realisation* for the
> worker; objectification as *loss of the object* and *bondage* to it; appropria-
> tion as *Entfremdung*, as *Entäusserung*.[237]

Under capitalism, the work process invariably leads to alienation. Two
main characteristics of work alienation are cited. First, the worker, who
has sold his labour power to the capitalist, is related to the product of his
labour 'as to an alien object . . . it exists outside him independently, as
something alien to him'.[238] His labour creates the alien and hostile social
power of capitalism. Second, alienation is found in 'the act of production
within the labour process'.[239] The worker is unable to work creatively.
His work is 'not the satisfaction of a need; it is merely a *means* to satisfy
needs external to it'.[240] On the one hand, ownership and control of the
work process are vested in the capitalist, who decides what is to be pro-

duced, how much, and in what way, as well as the disposal of the product. On the other hand, the technical exigencies of the work process, the subordination of the worker to the machine and the division of labour, mean that he cannot engage in his life activity. In both ways, man is alienated from his species-being, his essential nature. This itself logically entails that each man is alienated from every other man, and this for Marx is reflected in the political economist's conception of civil society 'in which every individual is a totality of needs and only exists for the other person, as the other exists for him, in so far as each becomes a means for the other'.[241]

What is the relationship between work alienation and private property? Marx states that 'private property is . . . the product, the result, the necessary consequence of alienated labour. . . . Later this relationship becomes reciprocal.' Private property is the product of alienated labour; and the means whereby labour alienates itself.[242] If Marx means that alienation is the historical cause of private property ownership, then the latter must be regarded as an effect of a more deeply rooted problem which would not necessarily be eliminated after the abolition of private property. But what Marx probably has in mind is that the worker, in alienating his labour power for wages, himself aids the continuance of the system, but that this is all he can do, as ownership and control of the means of production and investment decisions are the prerogatives of a minority. Marx is emphatic that 'the positive transcendance (*Aufhebung*) of private property . . . is . . . the positive transcendance of all alienation (*Entfremdung*)'.[243]

All men in an alienated society suffer from alienation, though in various ways. 'Everything which appears in the worker as an activity of *Entäusserung*, of *Entfremdung*, appears in the non-worker as an activity of *Entäusserung*, of *Entfremdung*.'[244] The alienation shared by capitalist and worker cannot, of course, be work alienation. The capitalist can enjoy at least 'a *semblance* of human existence', whereas the proletarian is utterly powerless.[245] But both are under 'the sway of inhuman power'.[246] The laws of capitalism rule the capitalist as much as the proletarian.

The concept of alienation is one which in the *EPM* is put to many analytically distinct uses. The claim that societies dominated by capitalism are alienated seems to involve three separable kinds of empirically observable conditions. First, there is alienation from the conditions of production. This phrase, or allied ones, is used throughout Marx's mature work. The worker is said to be separated from the conditions of the work process: he does not own his tools, the materials or the product, and he has no control over production or investment conditions. The social power constructed through his own labour has an independent, alien and hostile character.

The objective conditions of labour assume an ever more colossal independence . . . opposite living labour; social wealth confronts labour as an alien and dominant power . . . which social labour itself erected.[247]

Second, there is the claim that the work process prevents independent or creative work, inducing dissatisfaction in the worker. Third, there is the claim that agents of production, as well as those theorists who seek to explain and justify the system, are enmeshed in the conceptual confusions of reification in particular and false consciousness in general.[248] In all three cases, the empirical claims involved can, in principle, be tested against relevant evidence. But the significance of these claims is their relation to a standard external to them. In order to identify certain conditions as alienating, or as involving alienation, we require a standard of what men are capable of under different circumstances. The concept of alienation from species-being in the *EPM*, or, in later writings, from one's life activity, provides the standard by which the empirical claims have significance. We need such a concept in order to understand what Marx means when he says the worker is a 'spiritually and physically dehumanised being'.

It is often claimed that the conception of human nature developed in the *EPM* has no relevance to the mature Marxian theory. It is true that the Feuerbachian term species-being (*Gattungswesen*) is often used in the *EPM*, and that this concept is subjected to fierce criticism in the *The German Ideology* for its ahistorical and asocial character.[249] Marx's position is put in the following way. Feuerbach's work on religion as 'alienated human essence', though it had paved the way to a critical view of society based on empirical observation, had said nothing about society. The essays in the *Deutsch-Französische Jahrbücher* heralded the new outlook, but it remained misunderstood because of the continued use of phrases like *menschliches Wesen* (human essence) or *Gattung* (species).[250] The following passage shows how much Marx was prepared to jettison:

Equipped with an unquestioning faith in the conclusions of German philosophy as formulated by Feuerbach, viz., that '*Man*', 'pure essential man', is the ultimate purpose of world history, that religion is estranged human essence . . . believing further in the German socialist truths that money, wage-labours, etc., are also an estrangement of human essence, that German socialism is the realisation of German philosophy and the theoretical truth of foreign socialism and communism, etc., Herr Grun travels to Paris with all the complacency of a true socialist.[251]

But Marx is not attacking every conception of human nature, only the specific one of an asocial static human essence. Any concept of alienation must imply *some* view of what it is that men are alienated from, but this is not necessarily to be committed to a view of a Feuerbachian kind.

Even in the *EPM*, Marx's conception of human nature has a historical dimension. For a man to realise all the capacities that are his as a human being 'is only possible through the totality of men's actions, as the result of history'.[252] It is true that there are many major theoretical developments in Marx's thought subsequent to the *EPM*. For instance, the structural concepts we have already discussed first make their appearance in *The German Ideology*.[253] Again, when Marx talks in the *EPM* of the worker alienating his life activity he is thinking primarily in moral terms, and it is only much later that he sees a vital theoretical discovery in the fact that the worker sells his creative power, and this becomes a central theme in Marx's mature account of capitalist economics. But these developments do not mean that there is no concept of alienation in the mature writings. We have seen that both the term and some at least of the meanings of the term are present in both the *Grundrisse* and *Capital*. Some of these meanings are, of course, purely descriptive. For instance, the notion of alienation from the conditions of production has a clear empirical meaning, and it is possible to state what it would be for the worker not to be alienated in this sense without reference to any conception of human nature. But ultimately it is difficult to understand why Marx should see alienation from the conditions of production as a problem at all unless he entertains some logically prior normative conception of human personality and its capacities not given in experience. We shall return to this problem when we have dealt with Marx's mature economic theory.

b. *The Mature Economic Theory*

Marx distinguishes capitalism from previous modes of production not simply by commodity production, which existed at earlier periods, nor by the use of machinery, which played only a minor role before the nineteenth century. Two types of commodity possessor come face to face in the open market: the owner of capital, who wants to buy labour power, and the free labourer, who must sell his labour power in order to live. 'With this polarisation of the market for commodities, the fundamental conditions of capitalist production are given.'[254] The historical process of 'primitive accumulation' is the expropriation, the freeing of the peasant and the independent artisan from property in the means of production. Such means become capital when used by the owners to pump surplus value out of free wage-labour. Marx saw this process as both inevitable and desirable, though carried out by morally obnoxious methods.[255] Primitive accumulation involved a complex political and legal process. 'The power of the State, the concentrated and organised force of society', was employed, 'to hasten, hothouse fashion, the process of transformation'.[256]

Accumulation is the mainspring of the capitalist system: 'Accumulate! Accumulate! That is Moses and the prophets!'[257] Simple reproduction is the replacement of worn-out capital; accumulation is the extension of capital. Capitalism involves the pursuit of profit, much of which is reinvested. How is this profit made? The theory of surplus value, constructed on the basis of a labour theory of value, is an attempt to answer this question. The labour theory claims that the value of any commodity is determined by the labour time required to produce it. A commodity is something produced for exchange in the market. It has a use value; and it has an exchange value. Commodities are commensurable in that they all share one common property: they are all products of abstract human labour. Value is equal to the labour time 'socially necessary for production', the time required for producing a use value under the extant social and average conditions of production and with the average degree of skill and intensity of labour.[258] Value is equal to 'simple average labour', and skilled labour is equal to so many units of 'multiplied, unskilled labour'. The ratio is fixed, not by technical means, but 'by a social process which goes on behind the backs of the producers, and to them, therefore, appears to be established by custom'.[259] Marx also notes that 'nothing can have value, without being an object of utility'.[260] Finally, Marx distinguishes productive and non-productive labour: not *all* labour creates value. The labour of the agents of circulation; domestic servants; kings; priests, soldiers, police, and the professions, does not create value, though some of it may be necessary. They are non-productive labourers, paid out of the surplus created by the productive labourers.[261]

The capitalist buys in a free market the various items required for the production of a commodity, and he then sells the article for more than he paid. This is represented by the formula $M - C - M^1$. No one is robbed in the process. Commodities are purchased at their exchange value, and the product is sold at its exchange value. Yet there is an increment of value. This cannot come from M (money), for money is only 'value petrified'; nor from the sale (M^1), for this is merely the money form of the commodity. Marx argues that the change must come about in the use value of one of the bought commodities. Labour power is the only commodity whose use value 'possesses the peculiar property of being a source of value'.[262] The value of labour power is equivalent to the value spent on its production, namely, the customary subsistence of the labourer, what training he requires, and the expense of rearing children as substitutes. It contains 'a historical and moral element'.[263] The exchange value of labour power is less than the value of its potential use, from which the capitalist derives surplus value.

To emphasise that labour power is the source of surplus value, Marx divides capital into *constant* capital, which consists of machinery plus materials used up in the course of production (C); and *variable* capital (V), which is labour power. Constant capital merely transfers its value to the product, whereas variable capital 'both reproduces the equivalence of its own value, and also produces an excess, a surplus value'.[264]

The proportion of constant to variable capital (C:V) is called 'the organic composition of capital'. We can now expand the primary formula. An article costs C+V to produce; it is sold for C+V+S, where S represents surplus value.

Absolute surplus value, which involves the lengthening of the working day, is distinguished from relative surplus value, which involves raising the proportion of constant to variable capital and thus increasing the productivity of labour. The rate of surplus value is also distinguished from the rate of profit. The former is calculated on the variable part of capital alone, and is obtained by dividing surplus labour by necessary labour.[265] If a labourer works for 12 hours when his subsistence requires only 6 hours, then $\frac{S}{V} = \frac{6}{6}$, a rate of surplus value of 100 per cent. It is assumed that the labourer always works for longer than is necessary for his subsistence. The rate of surplus value indicates the degree to which labour power is exploited. The rate of profit is calculated on C+V combined: the capitalist has paid for both, and expects a return on both. His calculation is therefore $\frac{S}{C+V}$. The rate of profit will always appear lower than the rate of surplus value. Yet it is the latter which is 'the immediate purpose and compelling motive of capitalist production'.[266]

Marx deduces three laws from what he has said so far. The first is that the mass of surplus value (S) is equivalent to the total variable capital (V), multiplied by the rate of surplus value. Thus $S = V \times \frac{S}{V}$. This implies secondly that 'if the variable capital decreases, and at the same time the rate of surplus value increases in the same ratio, the mass of surplus value produced remains unaltered'. The third law follows: 'The rate of surplus value . . . being given, it is self-evident that the greater the variable capital, the greater would be the mass of the value produced and of the surplus value.' Thus 'the masses of value and of surplus value produced by different capitals . . . vary directly as the amounts of the variable constituents of their capitals'.[267] The implication here is that the more labour used in proportion to constant capital, the larger the rates of surplus value and of profit. Yet the very reverse process occurs in the capitalist accumulation process. Nor do the rates of profit in different branches of industry vary directly with the amounts of the variable constituent, for in a competitive economy rates of profit do not vary very much.[268] As Marx comments, 'This law clearly contradicts all experience based upon appearance. . . . For the solution of this apparent contradiction, many intermediate terms are as yet wanted. . . .'[269] Marx's own solution, though first published in 1894, was arrived at well before the publication of *Capital* I.[270]

The solution is that the amount of surplus value appropriated will depend upon the proportion of variable capital to constant capital only if we calculate for the total volume of capital in the economy. Competition forces an *average* rate of profit. The price of production is calculated at $C+V+S$, where S is an *average* surplus value for the whole economy. Some commodities are sold above, and some below, their true value. The true value is the average of all the prices of production. We need, therefore, to know the prices before we can know the values. Thus 'the sum of the prices of production of all commodities produced in society . . . is equal to the sum of their value'. The law of value 'acts as the prevailing tendency only in a very complicated and approximate manner, as a never ascertainable average of ceaseless fluctuations'.[271] Though we can know values only when we know prices, it would be to see only appearances and to disregard their 'internal and disguised essence' if we were to think that therefore the theory of value is redundant. Yet Marx tells us that the exchange of commodities at their values 'requires a much lower stage than their exchange at their prices of production' and that therefore the values of commodities are 'not only theoretically but also historically *prius* to the prices of production'. He adds that this applies to conditions in which the worker owns his means of production.[272]

We turn now to the accumulation process. The circulation process involves the repetition of the $M-C-M^1$ cycle, in which the capital-labour relationship is constantly re-created. The surplus labour of the worker forges the chains that bind him. Accumulation involves expanded reproduction, the conversion of 'the largest possible portion of surplus value . . . into capital'.[273] Marx singles out three laws here: the increase in the organic composition of capital; the increase in the centralisation of capitals; and the progressive production of an industrial reserve army.

The effect of capital growth on the position of the working class is considered in the famous chapter on 'the general law of capitalist accumulation'. Marx first considers the case where total capital grows but the proportion of C:V remains constant. The demand for labour will increase proportionately to the increase in capital. If demand exceeds supply, real wages may rise. Such conditions 'are those most favourable to the labourers . . . they can extend the circle of their enjoyments'. But this means only 'that the length and weight of the golden chain the wage-worker has already forged for himself, allow of a relaxation of the tension of it'. [274] The rate of wages is always dependent on the rate of accumulation.

But these favourable conditions are not characteristic of the system. The development of labour productivity through the use of machines and other techniques 'becomes the most powerful lever of accumulation'.[275] The demand for labour decreases relative to the social capital. Even if more workers are employed, which should be the case if total social capital grows, the proportion of constant to variable capital (C:V) will increase. Further, competition means that large capitals swallow small ones, and accumulation itself entails that the minimum amount of capital required to carry on business increases. The development of the credit system becomes 'the specific machine for the centralisation of capitals'.[276] These tendencies accelerate the decline in the variable constituent of capital. Capitalist accumulation tends to produce 'a population of greater extent than suffices for the average needs of the self-expansion of capital, and therefore a surplus population'.[277] This is a law of population peculiar to capitalism. Marx points out that the number of labourers employed may remain the same, or even fall, with an increase in variable capital: for it is 'an index of more labour, but not of more labourers employed'.[278] This production of a relative surplus population is said to develop more rapidly than the technical revolution in production. Marx sums up as follows:

> The greater the social wealth, the functioning capital . . . and, therefore, also the absolute mass of the proletariat and the productiveness of its labour, the greater is the industrial reserve army. . . . But the greater this reserve army in proportion to the active labour army, the greater is the mass of a consolidated surplus population, whose misery is in inverse ratio to its torment of labour. The more extensive, finally, the lazarus layers of the working class, and the industrial reserve army, the greater is official pauperism. *This is the absolute general law of capitalist accumulation.* Like all other laws it is modified in its working by many circumstances. . . .' [279]

But the system contains self-destructive tendencies. Increasingly, social production exists alongside private control of production and distribution, a control whose motive is private profit rather than the satisfaction of general human requirements. Marx sees an irreconcilable contradiction between the *social* power of capital, and the fact that this power is privately owned: 'Capital . . . becomes an alienated, independent social power, which stands opposed to society.' Yet the contradiction implies, for Marx, that the conditions of production will be transformed into 'general, common, social conditions'.[280] Finally,

> The real barrier of capital is capital itself. . . . The means – unconditional development of the productive forces of society – comes continually into conflict with the limited purpose, the self-expansion of the existing capital.[281]

The limits of capitalism can be seen in two ways. First, there is the moral limitation that expansion or contraction of production is determined, not by 'the relation of production to human requirements', but by the expected rate of profit. Second, Marx argued that a rising organic composition of capital entails a falling rate of profit: for if with capitalist accumulation, the proportion of constant to variable capital rises, and

the rate of exploitation remains the same, then the rate of profit $\left(\dfrac{S}{C+V}\right)$

must fall. In a profit-based economy the action typical of the capitalist paradoxically but inevitably lowers his rate of profit. Indeed, the real difficulty is to explain why the fall has not occurred much more rapidly than it has, and Marx suggested a number of factors which 'cross and annul the effect of the general law' and ensure that there is only 'a tendency to fall'.[282] He cited the lengthening of the working day and the intensification of labour; the use of the industrial reserve army to increase surplus value without increasing constant capital; increase of constant capital which increases the value of variable capital at the same time; and the effect of foreign trade, which may cheapen elements of both constant and variable capital.[283]

In the *Grundrisse* the fall in the rate of profit is seen as 'the most important law of modern political economy', and central to any understanding of why the capitalist system must collapse.[284] But it is generally agreed among economists that Marx's account is analytically defective, in that the phenomenon of a falling profit rate is not logically derivable from his premises.[285] Further, it is doubtful whether the phenomenon which so worried Ricardo and his fellow economists ever existed historically.[286] Nor does Marx explain how a slow tendency of a declining profit rate is related to the cyclical crises of capitalism.

One explanation of cyclical crises given by Marx is that over-production is fundamentally owing to under-consumption, because production expands faster than the market:

> The ultimate reason for all real crises always remains the poverty and restricted consumption of the masses as opposed to the drive of capitalist production to develop the productive forces as though only the absolute consuming power of society constituted their limit.[287]

Such a feature leads to crises of over-production which get worse as the system develops. This situation would itself be a spur to political action by the working class.

It must also be noted that Marx observes various positive trends within the capitalist mode of production itself. The growth of modern technology requires a new kind of worker, given an all-round technological education. 'Modern Industry . . . imposes the necessity of recognising, as a fundamental law of production, variation of work, consequently the fitness of the labourer for varied work, consequently the greatest possible development of his varied aptitudes.' [288] Marx cites the setting up of technical and agricultural schools as a step in this direction. He also views co-operative factories as manifestations of the new form within the old.[289] The formation of joint-stock companies, involving the divorce of ownership from the managerial function, seemed to him fresh evidence of the 'abolition of the capitalist mode of production within the capitalist mode of production itself, and hence a self-dissolving contradiction which *prima facie* represents a mere phase of transition to a new form of production'.[290]

It has often been argued that the tendencies depicted in the model constructed in *Capital* bear little resemblance to actual historical developments. The concentration and centralisation of capitals has occurred, though not always as pervasively or as quickly as Marx was inclined to suggest. But he failed to establish a theoretical explanation of the general tendency, in the long run, of the profit rate to fall, and in any case indicated cases (for instance, a rising rate of exploitation as a consequence of a rising C:V) where the laws of the system itself, as well as extraneous factors, would act as counteracting tendencies.

It has also been much debated whether we should understand the immiseration of the working class depicted in *Capital* in an *absolute* or a *relative* sense. The latter sense is consistent with cases where the proportion of C:V remains constant, or where V rises relative to C. In both these cases, total social capital rises by more than the rise in the worker's share. Real wages rise, but the class is relatively worse off, and suffers social or psychological deprivation rather than physical misery. The absolute sense involves real physical deprivation.

Those who choose the absolute sense argue that Marx's account implies that cases of relative immiseration are only brief interludes in a worsening scene. Indeed, the demand for labour 'falls progressively with the increase of the total capital, instead of, as previously assumed, in proportion to it'.[291] The output of consumer goods outstrips the demand for them, for most of the population have inadequate purchasing power. Marx emphasises that the industrial reserve army grows with the advance of capitalism and can exist only in a pauperised state. He concludes:

> Accumulation of wealth at one pole is, therefore, at the same time, accumulation of misery, agony of toil, slavery, ignorance, brutality, mental degradation, at the opposite pole, that is, on the side of the class that produces its own product in the form of capital.[292]

This passage certainly implies absolute immiseration, and it is possible for those who interpret Marx's meaning in this sense to point to such passages and argue that, as the living standards of the working class have in fact improved considerably, Marx was wrong in one of his basic claims concerning the effects of the capitalist system upon the working class.

However, Marx's theory commits him only to relative immiseration. He said of *Capital* I that limitations of space had led him to concentrate his attention on 'the worst-paid part of the industrial proletariat, and . . . the agricultural labourer, who together form the majority of the working class'.[293] But to do so meant a much gloomier picture than is entailed by the theory. True, in his earlier writings the price of labour is said to be equal to its production cost, which is almost wholly the physical subsistence minimum for the worker and his family. Below this 'millions of workers do not get enough . . . to exist and reproduce themselves'.[294] But in *Capital*, the value of labour power contains 'a historical and moral element'. What is taken to be subsistence is relative to the level of production. Thus the claim that there comes a time in every industrial cycle 'when forcible reduction of wages beneath the value of labour power is attempted for the purpose of cheapening commodities',[295] does not necessarily mean a reduction below physical subsistence. There are in fact plenty of passages where Marx emphasises the relative nature of the worsening position of the working class.[296]

There are also to be found, though chiefly in manuscripts left unpublished by Marx, the elements of a view of the character of capitalist development which, if not incompatible, seem hard to reconcile with the version given in *Capital* I. A growth is noted in the numbers and kinds of social groups who live on the surplus created by the productive worker. There are many unproductive labourers, whose services are exchanged against revenue.[297] The labour of some of these is necessary if unproductive in the capitalist sense. On the whole, however, in proportion to the total population the numbers of such people will not rise significantly. More importantly, Marx tells us that the growth of productivity in modern industry 'allows of the unproductive employment of a larger and larger part of the working class, and the consequent reproduction . . . of a servant class'.[298] In addition, he recognises the rise of the commercial worker, who produces no surplus value directly but 'belongs to the better-paid class of wage-workers'. But the wages of both groups will fall with the development of capitalist accumulation.[299]

In these passages a differentiation rather than homogenisation of the working class is implied. But there are also passages where Marx goes further and envisages the rise of new middle groupings. Ricardo failed to emphasise

> the constantly growing number of the middle classes, those who stand between the workmen on the one hand and the capitalist and the landlord on the other. The middle classes maintain themselves to an ever increasing extent directly out of revenue, they are a burden weighing heavily on the working base and increase the social security and power of the upper ten thousand.[300]

Indeed, 'the course taken by bourgeois society' involves a growth in the mass of the middle class and a decline in the proletariat as a proportion of the population as a whole.[301]

Nicolaus has seen in these passages an embryonic 'law of the tendential rise of a new middle class', which is deduced from Marx's conclusion that, although there is a tendency for the *rate* of profit to fall, nevertheless both the rate and mass of surplus value, and therefore the mass of profit, will rise.[302] Nicolaus assumes that by 'middle class' Marx is referring to technical and managerial groups, but there is no evidence for this in the context of the quotations. So far as the servant class and the commercial worker class are concerned, they increase in number and share in the surplus revenue, but their wages will fall with the advance of the capitalist mode. How much consuming power they present remains problematic. Nicolaus' view is suggestive but hardly conclusive. We can, however, state certain things with confidence. Marx's later views envisage a relative immiseration of the working class, which is differentiated rather than homogeneous in composition; a decline in the numbers of the industrial proletariat in relation to the total population; and, therefore, a much more complex picture than the class polarisation picture of the *Manifesto*. Whether, if Marx had lived, these hints would have been properly integrated into a consistent theoretical structure remains a matter of speculation. The political implications of Marx's economic theorising will be examined later. Here we conclude by considering the role played by the notion of law in Marx's account of capitalist society.

We have seen that capitalism is a historical phenomenon, regulated by historical laws which are not to be equated with natural laws.[303] The behaviour of men within capitalism is purely atomic. 'Hence their relations to each other in the process of production assume a material character independent of their control and conscious individual action.' [304] The regular relationships of exchange and production act as 'external, coercive laws' which appear to the agents as 'overwhelming natural laws that irresistibly enforce their will over them, and confront them as blind necessity'.[305] In fact, they are internal, social laws which are the resultants of the unco-ordinated actions of many purposive individuals.

There are passages where Marx compares social laws with those of physics and biology.[306] But the analogies he draws are limited to certain specific characteristics that are clear enough in their context. Of most interest is Marx's comparison of his method with that of the physicist, who 'either observes physical phenomena where they occur in their most typical form, and most free from disturbing influence, or, where ever possible, . . . makes experiments . . .'.[307] Marx cannot, of course, experiment. What he does is to take England as the 'classic ground' of capitalism. His model of capitalism is the mode in its 'typical form'.

England is chosen as the empirical case because it is the society furthest advanced towards full capitalism. Thus Marx's model is more than an analytical abstraction. It is a model of what, in Marx's view, any society will become once dominated by the capitalist mode.

In scientific terms, to explain an event requires the stipulation of a determinate set of initial conditions plus a universal law (or laws) which state that certain events are regularly connected, either deductively (if X, then Y) or probabilistically (if X, then 0.7 probability Y). Gregor considers that whereas in the *Manifesto* the laws of capitalism lead to inevitable results, being deterministic, irreversible, sequential, necessary and sufficient for the collapse of the system, in *Capital* there is 'little talk of "inevitabilities"' . . . Marx made regular recourse to "tendencies"'; the invariants are stochastic (if X, then probably Y) and contingent (if X, then Y, but only if Z).[308] There is certainly more talk of tendencies in *Capital* than in Marx's earlier (and more polemical) writings. Thus Marx decided to refer to the fall of the rate of profit 'as a tendency to fall' because there were 'counteracting influences at work, which cross and annul the effect of the general law'.[309] But Marx was never wholly clear. In the preface to *Capital* I we read that 'it is a question of these laws themselves, these tendencies working with iron necessity towards inevitable results'.[310] Here *tendency* and *inevitability* are equated.

It is true that Marx makes many statements of a statistical nature. The inner law of value is 'visible only when these accidents are grouped together in large numbers'; the laws of commodity production operate as 'a prevailing tendency', 'a never ascertainable average of ceaseless fluctuations', as 'the ideal average, i.e. an average which does not really exist'.[311] But Marx seems to have agreed with Quetelet concerning the nature of statistical regularities. The latter had demonstrated 'how even the apparent accidents of social life, in their periodic recurrence and their periodic averages, possess an inner necessity'.[312] Indeed, 'as Mr Quetelet remarks, "It would be difficult to decide in respect of the two" (the physical world and the social system) "which of the acting causes produce their effect with the greater regularity"'.[313] Marx says of the regulation of market price by prices of production that 'the same domination of the regulating averages will be found here that Quetelet pointed out in the case of social phenomena'.[314] It is evident that Marx tended to assimilate the notion of statistical probability to that of some social equivalent of physical necessity, despite the fact that he and Quetelet agreed that no statistical generalisation implies any logical necessity for all members of the class to which the generalisation relates to behave in the same way.

A possible resolution of this difficulty lies in the distinction between the *model* of capitalism, in which the variables in the model interact in such a way as to bring about a logically inevitable result, and the *reality* to which it applies in only an approximate manner. This distinction enables us to say that the model reveals the 'inner necessity', the internal logic of an essentially unstable capitalist system which must collapse through the free working out of that logic, but that the system to which it applies is operating within a society which can in many ways impose limits upon its mode of operation, through legislation and the political and economic action of the working class. Thus, though from the viewpoint of the model the laws of its operation do not 'depend upon the good or ill will of the individual capitalist', yet it is possible for the individual to do something to moderate the effects of the system.[315]

This position fits some of what Marx has to say, but it remains only a partial resolution of the problem. He always believed that the capitalist mode, in Western Europe at least, would finally become the dominant mode. Reality would ultimately conform to the model:

> In theory, it is assumed that the laws of capitalist production operate in their pure form. In reality, there is only approximation; but, this approximation is the greater, the more developed the capitalist mode of production and the less it is adulterated and amalgamated with survivals of former economic conditions.[316]

Finally, the immanent laws of capitalist production will 'enter completely into reality'.[317]

4 ETHICS AND POLITICS

Marx and Engels prided themselves on their freedom from illusion and upon their ability to explain the material basis of existing society and at the same time show how such circumstances could be changed. They renounced moralising about the state of society:

> The communists do not preach morality at all. . . . They do not put to people the moral demand: love one another, do not be egoists, etc.; on the contrary, they are well aware that egoism, just as much as self-sacrifice, *is* in definite circumstances a necessary form of the self-assertion of individuals.

Moralising merely reflects the illusion that to change social circumstances requires only good will and the changing of hearts.[318] But to act effectively necessarily requires a knowledge of circumstance together with the power to act. Causal knowledge about the way in which society works is necessary to the making of intelligent choices between real alternatives. Marx's theory is above all an attempt to define the limits within which action to change society will be effective. The proletarian must be rid of the illusion that there are impersonal natural forces dominating his life, but at the same time be brought to realise the real constraints upon the range of choices he can make within capitalist society as well as the real possibilities opened up to him through the development of the capitalistic system.

Marx considered that moral demands, for instance, those concerning some kind of redistribution of wealth to accord with some principle of human equality, have point only within the range of possibilities offered by the socio-economic system within which they are made. 'Right can never be higher than the economic formation and the cultural development of society conditioned thereby.'[319] Even within a specific society where class interests conflict, the passing of moral judgements has no point. Thus Marx argued that within capitalism, 'the nature of the exchange of commodities itself imposes no limits on the working day', and that there can be no such thing as a fair or normal working day. The 'normal' working day is a result of a struggle between capital and labour. 'Between equal rights force decides.' [320] Marx is, of course, aware of the persuasive use of moral language, as his use of it in the *Inaugural Address* and elsewhere indicates. But moral assessments do not constitute a substantive element in his own political calculations.

Moreover, Marx considered that in an analysis of society, theoretical and moral concerns should be kept strictly separate. He commented on a passage in Ricardo that the view expressed was 'quite meaningless from a theoretical standpoint. Moral considerations have nothing to do with the matter'. [321] In principle it was misplaced to attribute moral praise or blame. In his preface to *Capital* Marx emphasised that

> individuals are dealt with only in so far as they are the personification of economic categories, embodiments of particular class relations and class interests. My standpoint, from which the evolution of the economic formation of society is viewed as a process of natural history, can less than any other make the individual responsible for relations whose creature he socially remains. . . .[322]

A scientific analysis of the capitalist system is distinct from an ethical critique of that system; and in general individuals within the system cannot be held blameworthy for its overall effects, whatever benefits they may themselves enjoy from their situation. The results of the system do not 'depend on the good or ill will of the individual capitalist.[323] However, Marx, in quoting this comment in a letter to Kugelmann, continued:

> That, nevertheless, the individual can do something has been clearly demonstrated by such manufacturers as Fielden, Owen, etc. Their main effectiveness must of course be of a public nature.' [324]

It is, for instance, possible for the good will of a capitalist to be effective if he is influential enough to persuade the state to pass a law of benefit to the working class, for then the costs of such a measure are borne by the capitalist class as a whole. With this modification, it remains possible for Marx to attribute blame to individuals as well as to the system as a whole. A moral stance is clearly discernible in *Capital*. But the explanation of the system is intended to be independent of the moral stance. For Marx, only the truth can benefit the proletariat.

This is not to say that Marx is always successful in keeping empirical description and ethical evaluation separate. For instance, we are told that when the 'communist materialist' sees

> instead of healthy men a crowd of scrofulous, over-worked and consumptive starvelings . . . [he] . . . sees the necessity, and at the same time the condition, of a transformation both of industry and of the social structure.[325]

106

The necessity here concerns a strong desirability in terms of moral criteria concerning the treatment of human beings. Such criteria are linked to the empirical 'facts' in the sense that the circumstances must be such as to allow of a change in their treatment. Thus moral evaluation is incorporated in the description. Marx's fierce concern for the exploited needs no emphasis, either here or elsewhere. To be a revolutionary must imply a negative moral evaluation of existing society. This may, but logically need not, blind him to the facts of the case.

In the *EPM* there is a clear moral stance in much of what Marx says about human nature. An account is given of 'real, corporeal *man* . . . exhaling and inhaling all the forces of nature', who establishes his 'real, objective, essential powers as alien objects by his externalisation' of those powers. Man is dependent on the external world, not only for the satisfaction of his physical needs, but also because 'he can only *express* his life in real, sensuous objects' which are 'indispensable to the manifestation and confirmation of his essential powers'. Man's life activity is 'productive life . . . the life of the species. It is life-engendering life . . . free, conscious activity is man's species-character.' [326] Thus the labour process is one which involves free, purposive activity. Yet Marx is well aware that this is far from being a paradigm of human activity in any historically existing society. His description is an account of what ought to be the case, rather than of what is the case. Similarly, if we accept the claim made in the *EPM*, that man is the only animal to produce when free from physical need, then if we find that the wage-labourer produces only to satisfy his physical needs, we are led to accept that his condition is subhuman. As we have seen, the notion of alienation in the *EPM* involves empirical claims, but the significance of these claims involves reference to a standard external to them, namely a theory of human capacity which goes beyond the empirical evidence and ultimately rests upon moral judgements concerning the way in which human beings should be treated.

There is no controversy about the moral stance taken in the *EPM*: but what of Marx's mature work? Here the position is more complex. Marx sought to keep moral and theoretical considerations apart, yet there is a moral stance apparent in *Capital*. The term alienation is used both in the *Grundrisse* (frequently) and in *Capital* (much less frequently). It no longer refers to the *EPM* notion of species-being, but it still implies some view concerning the capacities of men in different socio-economic circumstances, a view which goes beyond the available evidence and ultimately rests upon a moral evaluation. A brief examination of the notion of the labour process in *Capital* may be useful here.

In *Capital* the model of the abstract labour process is put forward as a rational abstraction, stressing features common to all social formations known in history. It involves three elements: (1) labour power, (2) material, (3) instruments of production. The worker purposefully works on his material with the aid of his instruments. But the model of the *capitalist* labour process looks more like this:

(1) Labour Power.

    (a) Necessary ⎱ The capitalist owns the use value, the worker
    (b) Surplus   ⎰ the exchange value.

    The use of labour power is 'none of the worker's business'.

(2) Material.

(3) Instruments of production: machinery.[327]

Because of the changed nature of elements (1) and (3), in the capitalist labour process, (3) purposefully works on (2) with the aid of (1). The process constitutes an inversion of the abstract model. In *Capital* the account of the abstract labour process is followed by the 'characteristic phenomena' of capitalist production, namely the ownership and control of the worker's labour and its product by the capitalist.[328]

As theoretical abstractions employed for specific methodological reasons, the models of both the abstract labour process and the capitalist labour process are neutral. No moral recommendations are implied. On the one hand, we have the claim that if one examines all past societies, then certain general features of the labour process common to them all will be found; while on the other hand, we have the claim that if one examines the capitalistic labour process, then certain specific features of that process will be found. However, moral implications can be drawn from a comparison between these models, if, like Marx, we are committed to a position which stresses the desirability and, in a kind of society not yet known in history, the possibility of the free, purposive activity of human beings. With this moral premise, we can compare the elements of the abstract model, which stresses the purposeful character of the worker's activity, with those of the capitalist model, and find the latter wanting. In a communist society, Marx hopes and believes, men will for the first time regulate their interchange with external nature on a rational basis and achieve this 'under conditions most favourable to, and worthy of, their human nature'.[329] There is, after all, no point in being a revolutionary unless one believes, not only that a new society is possible, but also that it is desirable. In this sense, one can accept Colletti's conclusion that the Marxian theory is both science, in being an attempt to provide an analysis of the way in which the capitalist system actually works, and revolutionary theory, in that the analysis is undertaken from what in Marx's belief is the objective viewpoint of the working class.[330]

III

Politics

Politics in the Marxian sense can be defined as a sphere of social activity in which at least two social classes, whose objective interests are mutually antagonistic, engage in a struggle for control of the state, the organised force of society. 'Political power, properly so-called, is merely the organised power of one class for oppressing another.'[1] Distribution of property in the means of production, which involves control over the labour power of those who own little or no means of production, ultimately determines the distribution of political power. In this sense, property ownership involves both control over production and political control, if a further condition is satisfied. Only a class whose members are aware of their objective class interest, who have a will to forward that interest, and who possess a political organisation, can be said to act politically. This is the link between class and politics. Thus 'out of the separate economic movements of the workers there grows up everywhere a *political* movement, that is to say, a movement of the *class*, with the object of enforcing its interests . . . in a form possessing general, socially coercive force.'[2] Politics in this sense is, however, a transient phenomenon, confined to class societies. In a full communist society private property will be abolished, and this entails the disappearance of classes and hence of class conflict. And 'when class rule has disappeared . . . no state will exist in the *current political sense*'.[3] The 'public power' will lose its 'political character'.[4]

For Marx any political situations must be defined, described and interpreted primarily in terms of a specific socio-economic structure conditioning a particular configuration of social classes. This does not mean, however, that political action is unimportant, or that control of state power is merely a resultant of a determination by economic structure. On the contrary, the winning of political power is vital to the ultimate success of the working class. The balance between economic and political action is given an emphasis as early as 1844. Marx argues that if the proletariat thinks only in political terms, then its actions are likely to be futile. 'Because it thinks politically, it sees the causes of all evils in *will* and all remedies in *force* and the overthrow of a particular form of the state.' Nevertheless, 'revolution in general . . . is a political act. Without revolution . . . socialism cannot come about'. [5] There must therefore be no abstention from politics.

1 THE STATE

Marx and Engels have little to say about the origins of the state. In general, the argument is that with population increase, society became larger, its organisation more complex and consequently there arose the need for control through enforceable rules. Thus the state arose as part of a functional division of labour in society, in which specific functions are carried out by specific people. The state is differentiated from other institutions by its possession of the means of organised coercion, which can be used to back up the adjudication of disputes. Such disputes are not only personal, but class disputes. Indeed, Engels argues that the functional division of labour itself involved the creation of 'antagonistic classes with conflicting economic interests', and claims that 'the state arose from the need to hold class antagonisms in check'. At the same time, as the state arose in the midst of class conflict it becomes 'as a rule, the state of the most powerful, economically dominant class, which, through the medium of the state, becomes also the politically dominant class'. [6] Engels in this account assumes, though it does not logically follow, that a functional division of labour must lead to a division into economic classes. In *Anti-Dühring* he offers two reasons for this. First, he describes 'the setting up of organs to safeguard common interests and combat conflicting interests'. These organs become independent and finally dominant in society. Thus 'the exercise of a social function was everywhere the basis of a political supremacy'. Second, Engels emphasised the fact of war, the taking of prisoners, and slavery. [7]

The theme of the separation of the state from civil society can first be found in Marx's 1843 critique of Hegel's political thought. Hegel distinguished between the state and civil society (*bürgerliche Gesellschaft*). The latter is a sphere governed by a 'mixture of caprice and physical necessity', in which, 'in the course of the actual attainment of selfish ends . . . there is formed a system of complete interdependence'. Civil society involves the system of needs, the system of justice, and provision against contingencies still lurking in these systems by means of the Police and Corporation. It is a sphere in which economic laws operate automatically and the satisfaction of need is accidental 'because it breeds new desires without end . . . civil society affords a spectacle of extravagance and want as well as of the physical and ethical degeneration common to them both'. [8] The state, however, is the sphere of universality, in which the ethical will is consciously exercised to moderate the conflicts and miseries of civil society.

A major contention of Marx's manuscript is that the speculative philosophy of Hegel presents the empirical facts as appearances or phenomena emanating from the Idea. The modern phenomenon of the state/civil society separation is presupposed and developed 'as a *necessary moment of the Idea*, as an absolute truth of Reason'.[9] Hegel's differentiation and reconciliation of the two spheres is itself symptomatic of the deep rift in modern society. Civil society is indeed the sphere in which men are regarded as private, egoistic, atomised individuals with inalienable rights. But the state is the 'illusory community', the ideal universal sphere where man is a member of the community with duties as a citizen.[10] The separation is the result of a historical development in which all private spheres have attained an independent existence and even politics is made 'pure', that is, divorced from actual civil society.[11]

The spheres are not only separate but also hostile. The state is alien to the nature of civil society. The police, the judiciary and the administration are not agents of civil society: 'They are office-holders of the state, whose purpose is to manage the state in opposition to civil society.'[12] The effect of the separation upon the individual is profound.

> The individual must thus undertake an essential schism within himself. As actual citizen he finds himself in a twofold organisation: (a) the bureaucratic . . . the executive power . . .; (b) the social, the organisation of civil society, within which he stands outside the State as a private man. . . .

Marx traces the atomism of civil society to this division. It results necessarily from the fact that the commonwealth (*Gemeinwesen*), the communal being (*Kommunistische Wesen*) within which the individual exists, is reduced to civil society separated, from the state.[13]

Hegel's 'universal class', bureaucracy, is the only group whose roles in the state and civil society are said to coincide. Yet bureaucracy itself arises out of the separation of the two spheres. According to Marx, Hegel's account is partly empirical, and partly the account bureaucracy would give of itself. The state is said to mediate the contradictions of civil society. The civil servant, educated in 'thought and ethical conduct' as well as in the mechanics of administration, forgoes his own subjective interests and finds satisfaction in the dutiful discharge of his public functions. The bureaucracy is prevented by the combined pressures of the sovereign and the corporations from 'acquiring the isolated position of an aristocracy and using its education and skill as means to an arbitrary tyranny'.[14] Marx gives short shrift to these claims. The bureaucracy is 'a particular closed society within the State' which defends the 'imagined universality' of state interest.[15] It is merely another kind of closed and hierarchical corporation. The bureaucrat has a private interest: to build a career and climb the hierarchy.[16] The chance every citizen has of becoming a civil servant through competitive examination is simply a 'legal recognition of the privileged knowledge of State citizenship' which should be the knowledge of all. In a rational state, politics are public affars, *res publica*, an affair of society as a whole and not merely a single individual (as in Asiatic despotism); or of an elite group, whether aristocratic, admitted by birth, or bureaucratic, initiated by the equivalent of a masonic rite. A man will not need to take an examination in *Staatswissenschaft* in order to become 'a good citizen of the State, a social man'.[18] In the rational state, the universal class must be the class of every citizen. The true state, or democracy, involves (at least) the disappearance of the dichotomy between the state and civil society, and indeed of them as separate and opposed entities, and also the transcendence (*Aufhebung*) of bureaucracy.[18] Marx is confident that as executive functions have been routinised they can be 'executed perfectly by civil society itself'. At this point Marx believes that the attainment of universal suffrage would lead to the dissolution of the state and civil society as separate spheres and the end of a bureaucracy treating public affairs as its own private business.

The vote is the chief political interest of actual civil society. In unrestricted suffrage . . . civil society has actually raised itself . . . to political existence as its true universal and essential existence . . . the *reform of voting* advances the *dissolution* of this political state, but also the *dissolution of civil society*.[19]

Marx claims that 'the drive for the most fully possible universal participation in legislative power' is a tendency present in society.[20] It remains unclear what this involves, though his opposition to representation and some approving remarks about delegation, suggest that Marx already sees a possible solution in mandated delegates, revocable at the will of their electors.

Although the basic theme of the *Critique* is the state/civil society separation, Marx is beginning to see this separation as an illusion. 'The political state everywhere need the guarantee of spheres lying outside it. It is not actualised power, but supported impotence.' [21] The historical development which led to the separation is said to be dependent upon non-political factors. 'Where commerce and property in land are not free, not yet autonomous there is also not yet political constitution.' [22] Formal political rights, where they exist, do so alongside economic inequalities: 'People are equal in the heaven of their political world but unequal in the earthly existence of society.' [23] But though this theme is introduced, it is not linked to any clear conception of social class. Marx is concerned with what the *Stand* (estate) of contemporary German society is not, compared with the *Stand* of medieval society. Unlike the latter, civil and political positions no longer coincide in the contemporary *Stand*, which is an accidental, even arbitrary social grouping of men into which particular individuals fall by chance, and not a deliberately organised community like the medieval guild. Formerly the profession or function of the individual gave him a function and a status in society. Now 'it is partly chance, partly labour, etc. . . . which determines whether he remains in his *Stand* or not'. Thus 'the medical man . . . forms no particular class in civil society. One businessman belongs to a class different from that of another businessman, i.e., he belongs to another social position.' This would define *Stand* in terms of status rather than function.[24] Marx's comments are tentative and exploratory.

It has recently been argued that what Marx terms democracy in the *Critique* is not fundamentally different from what he later calls communism, and that 'true democracy' involves not only the end of the state/civil society separation, but also the abolition of class differences and of private property. Marx's 'ultimate conclusion regarding the *Aufhebung des Staats*' had been thought out as early as 1843.[25] But Marx says nothing in the *Critique* about the abolition of private property and he has yet to work out a coherent concept of class. In September 1843 he refers to communism as a 'dogmatic abstraction'.[26] The solution offered to the problem of the state/civil society separation is a purely *political* solution, namely, universal suffrage. Avineri is correct in thinking that the politics of the *Critique* are not those of a Jacobin democrat, as Lichtheim had thought, but nor are they those of a communist. We have seen that Marx's mature conception of the state involves claims that it arises predominantly in class societies, that its major function is as an instrument of class rule, and that the end of classes and of private property entails the end of the state. This will occur as a result of the economic development of the capitalist system and through the agency of the proletariat. Not one of these characteristic claims appears in the *Critique*. Avineri is therefore wrong to argue that the *Manifesto* of 1848 is 'immanent' in the *Critique* of 1843.[27] Two elements of the *Critique* can be found in Marx's later political writings, though not in the *Manifesto*: the criticism of state bureaucracy; and the theme of the state/civil society separation, stated as an apparent separation and firmly tied to class analysis.[28] This is already clear by 1846: 'The State has become a separate entity, beside and outside civil society, but it is nothing more than the form of organisation which the bourgeois necessarily adopt . . . for the mutual guarantee of their property and interests.'[29]

According to Marx, therefore, fundamentally the state is not 'an independent entity with its own "intellectual, ethical and libertarian bases"', as the Gotha Programme would have it.[30] The power and independence of the state itself depend on the prevailing configuration of class interests, and these in the last instance rest upon economic conditions.[31] In this sense it is subordinate to society. The state is separate from society in that the class controlling it does so in the interests of a minority. It is therefore an instrument of class rule. Marx distinguished between the state as 'the government machine, or the state in so far as it forms a special organism separated from society through division of labour'; and the state as the political system of a nation, for instance, the Wilhelmine Empire as 'a military despotism embellished by parliamentary forms'.[32] We need to consider Marx's view on both aspects, namely, state forms on the one hand, and governmental machines on the other. Finally, we must note his distinction between the performance by the state of 'the specific functions arising from the antithesis between the government and the mass of the people' and those 'common activities arising from the nature of all communities'.[33] By implication the end of class rule does not entail the end of the latter functions.

These are the main elements of Marx's general and extremely simplistic account of the state. In his analysis of concrete examples he was forced to introduce modifications.

First, Marx's scattered but largely consistent remarks on the Asiatic mode suggest that a state can exist which does not involve the rule of a class. Within this mode there can be 'either a more despotic or more democratic form of the community', and it is only when a system of small, self-sufficient communities with communal landownership is associated with the need for large-scale irrigation works that the solid foundation for oriental despotism arises.[34] Marx seems to envisage the Asiatic mode as marking a transition from classless to class society.[35] There may be urban elements within a socio-economic formation containing the Asiatic mode, but whatever the class configurations generated as a result, these are not related to the dominant mode. It is evident from Marx's account that oriental despotism cannot be the instrument of a class owning the means of production. The power of the state arises from the exercise of a necessary social function, but it remains independent. This state form, however, is given little analysis, nor is any consideration devoted to the large bureaucracy such a despotism requires in order to function adequately.[36] We are left with generalities about the state as 'landlord and tax-gatherer'.[37] Mandel talks here of a ruling class 'which appropriates the social surplus product'.[38] But that the state appropriates a surplus product does not make the ruling group a class in the usual Marxian sense. The land remains the major means of production, and this is held in common by the individual village communities. The case is more one of ruling elite, rather than class, domination.

Further, the claim that within class societies the state is the product of class antagonisms does not entail the claim that it is always the instrument of a dominant class. Marx introduced a modification to this latter position well before the *Manifesto*, when he noted that many a political situation reflected a period of transition between the passing of one dominant mode of production and the establishment of another. He attributed the strength of the bureaucratic state in Germany to the fact that in the seventeenth and eighteenth centuries,

> The impotence of each separate sphere of life . . . did not allow any one of them to gain exclusive domination. The inevitable consequence was that during the epoch of absolute monarchy . . . the State built itself up into an apparently independent force.[39]

We shall discuss Marx's classic account of politics in a situation of class balance, *The Eighteenth Brumaire of Louis Napoleon*, in which the coming of the Second Empire in France is interpreted as the outcome of a class struggle which did not establish a new organised class rule.

Louis Napoleon's *coup d'état* (2 December 1851) seems to have taken Marx by surprise. Engels wrote:

> It really seems as if old Hegel in his grave were acting as World Spirit and directing history, ordaining most conscientiously that it should all be unrolled twice over, once as a great tragedy and once as a wretched farce . . . such silly nonsense cannot last.[40]

Marx did not reply for a week. 'Quite bewildered by these tragi-comic events in Paris, I have kept you waiting for an answer.' [41] In his pamphlet Marx sought to show 'how the class struggle in France created circumstances . . . that made it possible for a grotesque mediocrity to play a hero's part'. By the end of his analysis Marx was able to say that 'if ever an event has, well in advance of its coming, cast its shadow before, it was Bonaparte's *coup d'état*'. It was, he said, 'a necessary, inevitable result of antecedent developments', although, like Hegel, he was unable to realise this until after the event.[42]

Marx's account relates the political events of the second French Republic (1848–51) to the conflict of class interests. Between 1815 and 1848 the French state had been controlled by fractions of the bourgeoisie. During the Bourbon monarchy (1815–30), 'big landed property had governed, with its priests and lackeys'. During the Orleanist monarchy (1830–48), 'high finance, large-scale capital, large-scale trade, that is, *Capital*' had ruled, though in effect rule had been in the hands of the finance aristocracy.[43] The Second Republic was the bourgeois republic, in which the whole class had ruled. In June 1848 the defeat of the Paris proletariat had revealed that the '*bourgeois republic* signifies the unlimited despotism of one class' over the rest. Yet Marx has to admit that during the June Days 'all classes and parties had united in the Party of Order against the proletarian class'.[44]

The history of the Constituent Assembly following the June insurrection saw the domination but eventual collapse of the republican faction of the bourgeoisie, a clique that had attacked the finance aristocracy under the July monarchy and had enlisted the support of the industrial bourgeoisie.[45] For six months, led by Cavaignac, the republicans ruled alone, pushing through a constitution involving universal male suffrage, liberties of the person, press, speech, association and assembly, together with measures concerning education and religion. Far from ignoring this new political form, Marx sought to show how it helped to crystallise class issues through the incipient conflict between the single-chamber National Assembly and a President elected not by an electoral college but by universal suffrage, and in control of a large bureaucratic apparatus. Three constitutional Articles in particular were to prove of great importance: Article 45 prevented the re-election of a President; Article 111 required a vote of three-quarters of the Assembly for any constitutional revision; while Article 44 stipulated that 'the President . . . must never have lost his status of French citizen'. The last Article was deliberately aimed at Louis Napoleon. Yet on 10 December 1848 he was overwhelmingly elected to the presidency: '*a reaction of the peasants* . . . against the remaining classes of the nation'.[46]

Marx argues that throughout the life of the Second Republic there was a retrogressive shift in the alliances of social groups. Unlike the first French Revolution, each successive dominant group retreated from the aims with which the February revolution began. On the surface this appears as a simple conflict between republicans and royalists. But 'this superficial appearance, which veils the *class struggle*', disappears on closer examination. Whatever the participants may believe, they are in fact divided by 'the rivalry between capital and landed property'.[47] They can unite only within the parliamentary republic. But complete political rule under conditions of universal suffrage makes their social power insecure. Pure, undisguised class rule is always a danger to the ruling class, as it attracts rather than diverts the antagonism of the subject classes.[48] Soon a challenge was to arise from a coalition of 'petty bourgeois and workers', who believed that an appeal to the nation would be sufficient to ensure victory. Fortunately for the bourgeoisie, the coalition had no insight into the way in which the balance of class interests determined political events, and was provoked into a caricatured repetition of the June Days. A street procession was swept away by Changarnier's troops (13 June 1849). The event had no importance in itself, but convinced elements of the bourgeoisie that 'all the so-called bourgeois liberties . . . attacked and menaced its *class rule* at its social foundation'.[49] In reaction came the Law of 31 May 1850, which abolished universal suffrage and reduced the electorate from 10 to 7 millions.

The political manœuvres of Louis Napoleon took place within the context of this class situation and are seen as a series of attempts to win political advantage from class divisions by playing off one group against another. Inch by inch, he began to assert the authority of his office. He could now pose as the champion of universal suffrage. In the society of 10 December the Parisian lumpenproletariat were organised in his support. 'This scum, offal, refuse of all classes [is] the only class on which he can base himself unconditionally.'[50] The National Assembly had meanwhile wasted its time and reputation in seemingly petty disputes with the President, the significance of which went unrecognised in the country at large. The final crisis arose with a move to revise the Constitution and in particular Article 45. All the class issues surfaced once again. For Legitimists and Orleanists alike,

> *The parliamentary republic* . . . was the unavoidable condition of their *common* rule, the sole form of State in which their general class interest subjected to itself . . . both the claims of their particular factions and all the remaining classes of society.[51]

Some believed that a revision might open the way for the two royalist factions to agree on a common monarch. For Marx, this was to ignore the importance of ideological considerations to both sides. Despite their material interest in such an agreement, their respective ideological positions made it impossible, either for a Legitimist monarchy to become the monarchy of the industrial bourgeoisie, or for a bourgeois monarchy to become the monarchy of the hereditary landed aristocracy. The failure to achieve agreement was reflected in the collapse of the parliamentary alliance of the two groups. Revision was defeated in the Assembly by 278 to 246 (19 July 1851). Rejection meant that Louis Napoleon must either submit or attempt a *coup d'état*. Three months later, he demanded the restoration of universal suffrage: a demand expecting, and getting, the answer No (348–355). On 2 December came the *coup*. Parliament succumbed, 'left in the lurch by its own class, the army and all the remaining classes'.[52] Political liberties appeared irrelevant to the bourgeoisie, so long as business was good and social order maintained.

With the *coup d'état*, the French state appeared to have become completely independent. 'And yet the state power is not suspended in mid-air. Bonaparte represents a class, and the most numerous class of French society at that, the *small-holding peasants*.' As we have seen, the latter do not possess class-consciousness, 'are consequently incapable of enforcing their class interests in their own name', and need another to act for them politically.[53] The ideological power of the Napoleonic legend won the peasantry to Louis Napoleon. Small-holding property is itself 'a suitable basis for an all-powerful and innumerable bureaucracy', while the army is 'the swamp-flower of the peasant lumpen-proletariat'.[54] Yet Louis Napoleon is in a difficulty. At the time of Napoleon I the interest of peasant and bourgeois *vis-à-vis* the landed aristocracy had been the same. But economic development has 'radically changed the relation of the peasants to the other classes of society'.[55] Moneylenders, mortgagers and capitalists have replaced the old landmarks. The peasant has only an illusion of peasant proprietorship. Sixteen million peasants are 'troglodytes' who live in hovels. The peasant economy is being gradually eroded by parcellation and the growth of capitalist farming. The interest of peasant and bourgeois is now sharply opposed, and the natural ally of the peasant is the urban proletarian.

Yet at the same time, despite his appeal to the peasant, Bonaparte remains the guardian of the bourgeois order, whose strength lies in the 'middle class' of whom he is the representative despite the fact that he has broken its political power. Industry and trade will 'prosper hot-house fashion under a strong government', Napoleon wants to appear as the universal benefactor, but 'he cannot give to one class without taking from another'.[56] French capitalist development ensures that the bourgeoisie will benefit and the peasantry suffer. Marx ended by a prophecy that when small-holding property collapsed, so would the state structure on which it was based.

Marx appears to have been correct in his general view that French capitalism would develop within the framework of authoritarian government resting on the control of the army and the state bureaucracy, and the acquiescence if not active support of the propertied classes and the peasantry. The rule of Napoleon III can be seen as depending on the support of shifting coalitions of interests, support which was steadily eroded as the years passed by. However, Marx's account has been criticised on a number of points. We have seen that the Paris working classes did not constitute a proletariat in the sense of a class of industrial workers. The peasantry constituted a far more complex phenomenon than is accounted for by a reference to 16 million 'troglodytes', with many local and regional variations in economic position and political attitudes. Nor did the features like parcellation of land-holdings necessarily have the significance attributed to them by Marx.[57] The pace of industrial development in France proved to be far slower than he had assumed. State economic investment was largely in railways and public works, while direct productive investment remained financed from the traditional limited sources. Seventeen years later the transitional regime of Napoleon III still existed, small-holding property had not collapsed, and Marx excised his prophecy from the second edition of *The Eighteenth Brumaire*. A year later the Empire had collapsed, but this was owing to defeat in an unnecessary war, and not to internal economic developments in France.

More importantly for our present subject, there is, despite Marx's belief that a situation of class balance is inherently unstable and of short duration, an admission that 'pure' class rule is a danger to the class that attempts such a policy. In 1848 Marx had written:

> The best form of polity is that in which the social contradictions are not blurred, are arbitrarily – that is, merely artificially, and therefore only seemingly – kept down. The best form of polity is that in which these contradictions reach a state of open struggle in the course of which they are resolved.[58]

It does not seem to have occurred to Marx at the time he wrote *The Eighteenth Brumaire* that a conclusion to be drawn from this kind of consideration is that the class situation in the French Second Republic may be far more common than the two-class model of the *Manifesto* would indicate. That this is so may also be gathered from Marx's view that polarisation into two major classes will take place at some point in the future. It is a model whose *raison d'être* is, if anything, to imply a prediction about the future class configuration of capitalism. There is, therefore, little reason for Marx to subsume under the term *bourgeoisie* owners of land, loan capital and industrial capital, so far as events in France in 1848–51 are concerned.

Indeed, as the nineteenth century wore on, Marx himself became more aware that the class situation depicted in his pamphlet was more of a *normal* than a *transitional* form. The state as the instrument of a dominant class was seen much more as the exception rather than the rule. Thus Marx explained the nature of the state in the United States of America by reference to the absence of earlier modes of production, and in particular the feudal mode. Because of this, capitalism develops in a purer form, and 'the State, in contrast to all earlier national formations, was from the beginning subordinate to bourgeois society . . . and never could make the pretence of being an end in itself'.[59] Such a situation is exceptional, and occurs only when the economic mode has established a position of dominance within the socio-economic formation with no competition from other modes.

A further reason may be gleaned from Marx's scanty remarks on the subject in the *Grundrisse*. This is the idea that the bourgeoisie can allow political power to rest elsewhere because political force is not necessary to the extraction of surplus value in a capitalist economy. Thus 'with kidnapping, slavery, the slave trade and forced labour, the increase of these labouring machines . . . is posited directly by force; with capital, it is mediated through exchange'. [60]

Thus the perspective of the *Manifesto*, which sees the state as purely the instrument of a ruling class, tends to recede into the background, to be brought out and dusted down for special occasions of political polemic. Marx was aware of the different possibilities of successful political action by the working class which existed within different state forms. He was always insistent that the state form matters. In general, Marx and Engels considered that a democratic republic with universal suffrage would be the most advantageous state form for the working class. In 1843, before his reading of economics had made him more pessimistic, Marx had even believed that a system of universal suffrage would itself mean that property distinctions had no meaning. His reading of Thomas Hamilton seems to have influenced him here. Rubel argues that Hamilton had seen 'what Tocqueville had failed to notice: the revolutionary implications of American democracy'.[61] Hamilton had argued that property could not withstand the assault of a 'suffering class' in whose hands 'will be practically deposited the whole political power of the State'.[62] This perspective reappears in Engels' argument that the political rule of the proletariat will be established by a democratic constitution, and that democracy itself will serve as a launching pad for a direct assault on private property.[63] In the *Manifesto*, the first major aim is stated to be the raising of 'the proletariat to ruling class, to win the battle of democracy'.[64]

In the early period of the 1848 revolution, the term *democrat* is still used in a favourable sense. In Brussels the Marx circle had described themselves as 'democrat-communists'. In Cologne, the *NRZ* was labelled an 'organ of democracy', partly as a means of attracting maximum support from bourgeois democrats in accordance with the *Manifesto* policy of alliance between communists and the bourgeois radicals. But by the end of 1848, the democrats were referred to as a group with views separable from those of Marx, and indeed the term is more and more associated with a particular social group, the petty bourgeoisie. Thus the 'democratic party' is the party of the *Kleinbürgerschaft* in Germany, and similarly, Ledru-Rollin's democratic party in France is seen as one advancing petty bourgeois views. In essence, a democrat is one who wants '*la république démocratique*' but shrinks from '*la république démocratique et sociale*'. In 1851 Marx referred to the *March Address* as 'none other than a battle plan against democracy'.[65]

Nevertheless, in the early 1850s Marx still held the view that universal suffrage is a danger to bourgeois rule. He commented of the constitution of the French Second Republic:

> The classes whose social slavery the constitution is to perpetuate, proletariat, peasant, petty bourgeois, it puts in possession of political power through universal suffrage. And from the classes whose old social power it sanctions, it withdraws the political guarantees of their power.

Thus universal suffrage 'jeopardises the very foundations of bourgeois society'.[66] Hence Marx remained unsurprised when in May 1850 universal suffrage was abolished. By October 1850 it is seen only as a 'school of development' through which the majority of society had to pass in a period of revolution.[67]

In 1852 Marx seems to have modified his view, possibly to take into account the different kinds of circumstances in which universal suffrage might be introduced. He now saw universal suffrage as a danger to the bourgeoisie only if at least two sets of conditions were satisfied. First, that universal suffrage must be accompanied by conditions without which it would be an illusory gain, such as the secret ballot, payment of members and annual general elections. Second, that certain socio-economic conditions must be satisfied:

> Where the proletariat forms the large majority of the population,

where . . . it has gained a clear consciousness of its position as a class, and where even the rural districts know no longer any peasants, but only landlords, industrial capitalists (farmers) and hired labourers.

Only in the presence of these conditions would the introduction of universal suffrage in England lead to '*the political supremacy of the working class*'.[68] Marx, like many other radicals at the time, was well aware of the effect of the peasant vote upon the composition of the French Constituent Assembly following the election of April 1848. He was soon to note the restoration and use made of universal suffrage by Napoleon III, which he saw as 'the best machinery in the world by which to establish a despotism upon a firm and comely basis'.[69] Marx was later to criticise Lassalle for failing to learn the lesson.

With Buchez's state aid for associations he combined the Chartist cry of universal suffrage. He overlooked the fact that conditions in Germany and England were different. He overlooked the lessons of the Second Empire with regard to universal suffrage in France.[70]

Thus democracy is seen as a means to the end of communism, as 'an instrument of emancipation'.[71] Within capitalist society democratic institutions are to be viewed with reserve to the extent that they are capable of being manipulated by the ruling groups, or place voting power in social groups with outlooks reactionary in Marxian terms, but they can be used to the advantage of the working class. As we shall see, the democratic institutions of the Paris Commune were seen by Marx as the proper political means to the ultimate goal. The attack on 'the old, democratic litany' in Marx's critique of the Gotha Programme must be seen in this light. There is no point in the litany if the form of the state is that of a military despotism.[72]

Marx left unresolved a major theoretical problem concerning the state. He felt that he had said sufficient about political economy for others to complete what he had begun. But the same was not true of the problem of 'the relations of different state forms to different economic structures of society'.[73] We have seen that in Marx's general statements, at least a 'natural correspondence' is postulated between a specific state form and a specific economic structure. Yet Marx notes many cases where the state, far from being dependent on pre-existing economic conditions, can be used to bring about economic changes desired by the holders of political power.[74] Further, there is little in Marx's writings to suggest in precisely what sense differences in economic structure entail that Great Britain is a constitutional monarchy; the United States a federal republic; France in the nineteenth century a kaleidoscope of Legitimist monarchy, Orleanist monarchy, democratic republic, Bonaparte semi-dictatorship, and then a republic again; and Germany, once united, 'a military despotism embellished by parliamentary forms'. Marx admits that the same economic structure may show 'infinite variations and gradations in appearance . . . due to innumerable different empirical circumstances, natural environment, racial relations, external historical influences, etc.' in different societies.[75] By parity of reasoning the same may be true of state forms. But such considerations surely entail that we are not able to deduce from the basic economic structure either what that structure will look like in specific societies, or which state form is likely to prevail.

2 POLITICS IN CAPITALIST SOCIETY

For Marx, there must be no abstention from political action. This involves both revolutionary politics, the destruction of the capitalist order, and politics carried on within the framework of capitalist society and hence involving a provisional acceptance of at least some of the values and assumptions inherent in that framework. We shall discuss the latter now, reserving the subject of revolution until the next section. But first we must note that Marx's views about what is possible and effective political action changed in the course of his life, partly because of changes in his economic views, and partly because of changes in political circumstances.

a. *The Lessons of 1848*

The perspective of the *Manifesto* involved a belief in a rapidly maturing world revolution, based on the assumption that the creation of the world market by capitalism entailed an interdependence which was already rapidly breaking down national barriers and leading to similar conditions in all civilised countries. Marx envisaged united action by the proletariats of 'the leading civilised countries at least', in which the German proletariat would play its part.[76] England was seen as the country where economic development and hence class antagonisms were the most advanced, and the Chartist movement the mass working-class organisation which was about to overthrow the system. In Germany the bourgeoisie would carry out the tasks completed by the French bourgeoisie in 1789; the creation of a liberal constitution, the ending of feudal obligations in the countryside, and the creation of a free, independent landowning peasantry. But the proletariat would be close on the heels of the bourgeoisie, ready to utilise the freedoms of the new order and bring about a communist revolution. The unreality of this position requires no comment.

Marx drew a number of parallels between France in 1789 and Germany in 1848. But these were misleading. Three major issues confronted German society in 1848: the political issue of liberal institutions;

the social issue of a rapidly changing socio-economic structure, involving the remnants of feudalism, a declining but radical artisanate, and growing numbers of bourgeois and factory workers; and the national issue of unification. Only the political issue allows of a comparison between 1789 and 1848. Marx did, of course, see certain differences between the two periods. Germany was at a higher level of socio-economic development than either England in 1642 or France in 1789. The proletariat was already present, able to follow the example of the French proletariat and challenge the established order. But Marx concluded, wrongly, that this feature meant that the bourgeois revolution would be a prelude to the immediately following proletarian revolution. In the event, the national question, which was itself left unresolved, proved to be of major importance in the failure to achieve either liberal institutions or social reform. In *The Eighteenth Brumaire* Marx poured scorn on those who engaged in re-enacting the scenes of the 1789 revolution. Yet this was his own stance in the early months of 1848. By the end of July, however, Marx sees the revolution as merely '*a parody of the French Revolution of 1789*'.[77] Marx was far more cautious in future about the drawing of superficial parallels. Apart from this general lesson, he seems to have drawn a number of conclusions from the experiences gained in the 1848–9 revolutions.

First, there is the question of nationalism. The *Manifesto* had argued that the cosmopolitan character imparted to production by the bourgeoisie meant a 'universal interdependence of nations', and that all nations would finally become bourgeois. As for the working class, they had no country, not having a role in society. When the proletariat of each nation became supreme, then the tendency already present for national differences and antagonisms between people to become fewer and fewer, would, with the end of class conflict within each nation, lead also to the ending of 'the hostility of one nation to another'. Nations would still exist as separate units, but within an increasing interdependence in the world market.[78]

The policy of the *NRZ* towards nationalism involved a distinction between the great 'historical nations' of Germany, Hungary and Poland; and the 'unhistorical peoples'. Marx and Engels never accepted the principle of the national self-determination of *any* subject people. Thus, apart from the Poles, the Russians and perhaps the Slavs in Turkey, the Slavs had no future, 'for the simple reason that all other Slavs have not the primary historical, geographical, political and industrial conditions for independent and viable life'.[79] National self-determination is justified in Marxian terms only if it helps to promote the kind of socio-economic change that means the development of an industrial working class. Small national groups are seen as strengthening the forces of reaction. Thus the attempt to seize Schleswig from Denmark and incorporate it into Germany was justified by Engels as 'the right of civilisation against barbarism'.[80] In Austria, the Magyars represented the revolution, the south Slavs the counter-revolution. 'All the south Slav peoples placed themselves at the disposal of the Austrian reaction.'[81]

Marx and Engels therefore recognised that nationalism was a stronger force in the revolutions of 1848–9 than the position of the *Manifesto* could account for. But this recognition was filtered through some extremely chauvinist attitudes of their own, and as expressed in Engels' articles did not necessarily arise out of a typical Marxian analysis. For instance, Hungary appeared to be *the* revolutionary nation, but in fact the structure of Magyar society was backward and feudal, and would not have been altered by a successful national revolt. Magyar propaganda proclaimed that 'Slavs are not human beings'. Thus when the abolition of the feudal corvée had met the most important grievance of the peasant Slavs, they were ready to fight in the armies of Windischgratz and Radetsky, having no reason to prefer Magyar domination to Habsburg rule.[82] Further, Engels made no attempt to distinguish between the various classes in Czech society. The Czech nation was seen as counter-revolutionary as a whole.[83] The analyses of the *NRZ* reflected a basic belief that nationalism was, in most cases, a phenomenon which helps to blur the real conflict, that between worker and capitalist. We shall see that Marx later noted the great political importance of English working class feeling against the Irish working class, but only as a phenomenon which blurs class conflict.

There is a major contrast between the treatment of the Slavs in general, and of the Poles. In August 1848 there was a debate at the Frankfurt Assembly. The issue was whether or not to admit certain Polish districts administered by Prussia as voting units in the German Confederation. Engels held that the Polish state should be reconstituted within the boundaries of 1772, which involved handing back territory now German. He wrongly assumed that 'the struggle for an independent Poland is at the same time the struggle of *agrarian democracy* – the only possibility in Eastern Europe – against *patriarchal feudal absolutism*'.[84] A democratic Poland was essential to a democratic Germany.

Associated with the argument for an independent Poland, was Marx's realisation that the Czarist regime in Russia posed a major threat to any European revolution.[85] Russian troops were used to restore the authority of the traditional ruling groups in the Austrian Empire. The need for a revolutionary war in the East to shore up the sagging fortunes of the German revolution became a major theme of *NRZ* editorial policy. Just as in 1792 the assaults of the coalition had led to the cry of '*la patrie en danger*' and Carnot's victorious offensive against the old regimes of Europe, so equally war with Russia would place the German fatherland in danger, the revolution and the nation would become identified, the masses would become revolutionary and the revolution would be saved. 'Only a war with Russia is a war of a revolutionary Germany. . . .'[86]

Fortunately for Europe, Marx's advice went unheeded. As Lassalle was later to point out, because war against Russia would be unpopular in Germany, it would be foolish to call upon the Hohenzollerns to wage it, for a victory would secure the monarchy, not the revolution. The unification of Germany under Bismarck in fact achieved precisely this. Marx in 1870 saw the victory of Prussia over France as in a sense providing the basic conditions for the development of the German working class. '*The war has shifted the centre of gravity of the working class movement on the Continent from France to Germany.*' [87] Political unity did indeed aid the unity of the German labour movement, but at a very high price. Marx's experience in 1848 gave him a greater awareness of the national factor than before, but his understanding of the issue remained limited.

The second major problem concerned the role of the bourgeoisie. Before the February revolution Marx had seen its role as one in which, as a condition of its own rule, the bourgeoisie had to introduce basic political and civil freedoms, which could then be used by the proletariat. But now Marx believed that the French bourgeoisie had been openly revolutionary in 1789 because there was no proletariat to challenge them. The Parisian sansculottes had been used and then pushed aside. Similarly, the Parisian artisanate had made the July revolution of 1830, but the fruits of victory had gone to the finance aristocracy. But in 1848 the leaders of the German bourgeoisie had realised that it was no longer in their interest to sanction illegal acts. The growing menace of an urban proletariat signified that violence could be turned against private property as such. The Prussian governments of Camphausen and Hansemann had sanctioned only indirect elections, had failed to abolish the old legal system, and had done nothing for the peasantry. The March revolution was merely the weak repercussion of a European revolution in a backward country, where the bourgeoisie was not the confident leader but only the timid beneficiary of the work of others and conscious of a rising proletariat. Hansemann had sought to strengthen the state against both anarchy and reaction, but had succeeded only in strengthening the police, the judiciary, the bureaucracy and the army. Indeed, all the supports of the *ancien régime* had been given time to organise themselves and reassert their authority.[88]

Marx drew two conclusions here. The first was that it would be a mistake for the proletariat, when its turn came, merely to take over the state machine, as suggested in the *Manifesto*. The taking of political power without genuine control of the organs of power (police, army and bureaucracy), would be a futile exercise. Hence the later emphasis on the need to smash the state machine and reconstitute it along more suitable lines. This essential difference between a bourgeois and a proletarian revolution will be given further consideration later.

125

The second conclusion concerned the bourgeoisie itself. In 1852 Engels offered Marx a definition of bourgeois society as

a phase of social development, in which the Bourgeoisie, the Middle Class, the class of industrial and commercial capitalists is, socially and politically, the ruling class; which is now the case more or less in all the civilised countries of Europe and America.[89]

But for Marx the failure of the bourgeoisie to act as a ruling class, to give their economic power political substance, was one of the major features of the post-1848 situation, as true of England and France as of Germany. At first he regarded this feature as a short-term one. In 1849 Marx commented upon the Prussian constitution imposed by Frederick-William IV. He asked whether the bourgeoisie had won 'a political form enabling it freely to run matters concerning its class as a whole'? This involved the pursuit of industrial and commercial policies designed to produce a freely competitive economy while managing the state apparatus as cheaply as possible. But an absolute monarchy means that power is in the hands of the feudal estates, 'whose interests are profoundly antagonistic to those of the bourgeoisie'. The result must therefore be 'an industry fettered by bureaucracy and an agriculture fettered by feudal privileges'. Thus the government is 'entirely consistent, when it attempts to replace free competition with the guild system, mechanical spinning by the spinning-wheel and the steam plough by the hoe'.[90] Nevertheless, economic development must inevitably break the chains of absolutism and feudalism, despite the fact that the bourgeoisie had preferred to ally with the old order rather than face the proletarian challenge.

A similar argument can be found in an early comment by Marx on British politics, where government rested in the hands of the Whig oligarchy. He commented of the bourgeoisie: 'If the aristocracy is their vanishing opponent the working class is their arising enemy. They prefer to compromise with the vanishing opponent rather than to strengthen the rising enemy, to whom the future belongs.' But Marx remains certain that 'historical necessity and the Tories' will drive the bourgeoisie into direct political power.[91]

By 1856 Marx had ceased to stress the temporary nature of this phenomenon. He explained the failure of the 1856 revolution in Spain by reference to the fact that if the middle class were to be successful against a regime akin to an oriental despotism, it required working-class aid. But inevitably the working class claim a share of the victory, and so, 'frightened by the consequence of an alliance thus imposed on their unwilling shoulders, the middle classes shrink back again under the protecting batteries of the hated despotism'. This is, Marx concludes, 'a new illustration of the character of most of the European struggles of 1848–9, and of those hereafter to take place in the Western portion of that Continent'.[92]

Thus the link between the level of socio-economic development and the nature of the political institutions is by no means as straightforward as the analysis of the *Manifesto* assumed. There were also other circumstances which may have led Marx in the same direction. In the early 1850s he seems to have thought that the state form best suited to the bourgeoisie was the 'bourgeois republic',

> in which free competition rules supreme in every sphere of life; in which there remains altogether that *minimum* only of Government which is indispensable for the administration, internally and externally, of the common class interest and business of the Bourgeoisie; and where this minimum of government is as soberly, as economically organised as possible.[93]

Marx at this point believed that the full development of capitalism required only a minimal state. An implication of this kind can be found in the *Grundrisse*, where it is argued that

> the highest development of capital exists when the general conditions of the process of social production are not paid out of deductions from the social revenues, the state's taxes, but rather out of capital as capital.[94]

Marx's general view, which rested heavily on developments in Great Britain, seems to have been that in the early stages of capitalist development, the state will be used to hasten the process through legal and political measures of various kinds (the removal of internal barriers to trade, the creation of a free labour market, industrial freedom, protective tariffs, suitable taxation and credit policies, and so on); but that with a society dominated by the capitalist mode, the functions of the state will be reduced more and more to those required to ensure that a free market economy can operate, that is, to a general policing role. In such a situation there would be no need for a large-scale state bureaucracy. Views of this kind constituted the liberal programme of economic reform urged on the Prussian government in the 1850s and 1860s by publicists of the industrial and commercial bourgeoisie.[95] But it became clear that both the Second Empire, and later, the Wilhelmine Empire, not only involved government in which the bourgeoisie had no direct share, but also large state bureaucracies. In 1866 Engels argued that where there was no equivalent of the Whig oligarchy in France and Prussia, then 'a Bonapartist semi-dictatorship is the normal form'.[96] In 1871 Marx went further, and asserted that 'imperialism is . . . the ultimate form of state power' in bourgeois society, and that the Second Empire 'was the only form of government possible at a time when the bourgeoisie had already lost, and the working class had not yet acquired, the faculty of ruling the nation'.[97] The establishment of the French Third Republic, however, required a revision of ideas, and by 1875 Marx once more saw the democratic republic as the last state form of bourgeois society.[98]

127

b. *Economic Theory and Political Practice*

A major aim of Marx's economic theory was to give guidance in political practice. But there were major changes in his economic views. In particular, the differences between the views put forward in the 1840s and those of the late 1850s are so important, despite many overlaps, that Nicolaus is prepared to see them as two distinct economic theories.[99] The *Manifesto* stressed the centrality of competition to the economic system, and forecast an inevitable polarisation of classes into a small, wealthy capitalist class and a large, impoverished proletariat. All other groups – the petty bourgeoisie, the peasantry, the artisanate – will decline into the proletariat. The capitalist class is credited with having immensely increased the productive power of society, but there is no theory of surplus value or, indeed, of accumulation. Labour is a commodity like any other. The system means absolute immiseration for the proletariat, for it is impossible for wages to rise much above the minimum for physical subsistence. The capitalist must resist any combination to raise wages, or legislation to shorten hours of work, for any such measures would be fatal to the system. But the system itself is doomed to collapse through crises of over-production, and the development of the revolutionary proletariat will ensure the end of capitalism. Class polarisation creates a proletarian movement, 'the self-conscious, independent movement of the immense majority, in the interests of the immense majority'. The economic struggle becomes a political struggle: the proletariat must be organised in each country as a national political party. Economic collapse will give the well-prepared proletarian organisation its chance. The proletariat will become the new ruling class, winning 'the battle of democracy' and assuming state power in order to create a communist society.[100]

Marx's early economic views led him to believe that only revolutionary politics stood any chance of success. In 1844 his first reading of political economy convinced him that the proletariat would be driven to revolt because of the insupportable misery of their condition. 'Eventually wages, which have already been reduced to a minimum, must be further reduced, in the face of new competition. This then necessarily leads to revolution.' [101] Two years later Marx wrote that 'the poverty of the proletarian . . . drives him into a life-and-death struggle, makes him a revolutionary'.[102] It is poverty that makes the proletariat a revolutionary class. Thus it is 'through urgent, no longer disguisable absolutely imperative need – that practical expression of necessity' that the proletariat 'is driven directly to revolt'. The daily life situation of the class makes it realise the inhuman character of capitalist society. Consequently

> The question is not what this or that proletarian, or even the whole of the proletariat at the moment considers as its aim. The question is

what the proletariat is, and what, consequent on that being, it will be compelled to do. Its aim and historical action is irrevocably and obviously demonstrated in its own life situation as well as in the whole organisation of bourgeois society today.[103]

This statement appears to have been applied indiscriminately to the situation in England, France and Germany, despite the fact that an industrial proletariat barely existed in the latter two countries. The *Manifesto* assumed that polarisation had already occurred in England and was well advanced in France and Germany. The experience of 1848 modified Marx's views here, but he still maintained that revolution was the only sure political method. 'Every social reform remains a utopia until the proletarian revolution and the feudalistic counter-revolution measure swords in a world war.' [104] The defeat of the Paris workers in June 1848 was a proof 'of the truth that the slightest improvement . . . remains a utopia within the bourgeois republic'.[105] Only in late 1850 did Marx reconcile himself to the fact that many decades of political experience and education would be necessary before the working class could engage in revolution.

The *Manifesto* model of the capitalist economy was replaced by the more sophisticated account first developed in the *Grundrisse*. The important feature of this account in the present context is that the possibilities of effective political action open to the proletariat within the capitalist order are immeasurably widened. All the qualifications we have found Marx making to the model of capitalist accumulation occur at this time: the redefinition of subsistence to include a 'historical element'; the realisation that parts at least of the working class are better off; and the noting of the growth of social groups living on the surplus labour of the productive worker. The *Inaugural Address* reflects these changes in Marx's economic views.[106]

In 1865 Marx had the opportunity to put his views, in a simplified form, before the General Council of the IWA. An Owenite, John Weston, had urged that a general rise in wages was valueless to the worker as it led only to a rise in prices, and that therefore trade unions have a harmful effect. Though this view would not cut much ice among the trade union leaders on the Council, Marx, who considered Weston's ideas to be 'theoretically false and practically dangerous', was concerned lest his views obtained a wide currency and diminished the Council's influence. In rebuttal of Weston, Marx argued that labour power is sold at its value, but that this involves both a physical and a social element, '*a traditional standard of life*'. The maximum profit is limited, so far as wage costs are concerned, by the minimum physical wage and the maximum possible working day. 'It is evident that between the two limits . . . an immense scale of variations is possible.' Within these limits the actual wage is settled by 'the respective powers of the combatants'.[107] As for limitations on hours, this has been achieved by legislation as a result of political agitation by the working class. The tendency of the system is 'to push the *value of labour* more or less to its *minimum limit*' because of the capitalist search for maximum profit. But this does not entail that the working class should cease resistance and 'abandon their attempts at making the best of the occasional chances for their temporary improvement'.[108]

Throughout the life of the IWA Marx never ceased to stress that genuine social reforms could be achieved within capitalist society, that the state could be used to pass and enforce legislative measures of value to the working class; and that trade unions and co-operatives could help towards the ultimate goal. In *Capital*, discussing the law which is said to lead to the growth of the industrial reserve army, Marx argued that 'every combination between the employed and the unemployed can disturb the "pure" play of this law.'[109] The worker must utilise, through appropriate organisational means, both economic and political, all the opportunities afforded him through the development of the capitalist economic system. But it must be stressed that, even in the mature economic theory, a major contradiction lies in the fact that although wage labourers are important as consumers, as sellers of labour power the archetypal capitalist tends to keep them down to the minimum price. This may be well above the physical minimum, but none the less the theory claims that in a capitalist society the worker will always, in the long run, get the worst of any bargain struck with the capitalist. Capitalist development involves a polarisation process, in which all labour becomes wage-labour, and all means of production capital;[110] while, at the same time, it leads 'to a diminishing proportion, compared with the total amount of produce, of that part of it which forms the fund for the reproduction of the labouring class'.[111]

c. *Organisation and Tactics*

For Marx, trade unions had played a limited but vital role in the development of the labour movement, both in preventing the competition of workers among themselves, and in the organisation of collective bargaining concerning wages, hours and conditions of work. But he had reservations:

> Trades Unions work well as centres of resistance against the encroachments of capital. ... They fail ... from limiting themselves to a guerrilla war against the effects of the existing system ... instead of using their organised forces as a lever for the final emancipation of the working class, that is to say, the ultimate abolition of the wages system.[112]

Strikes for economic ends were necessary, but could not serve as 'a means to the complete emancipation of the working class'.[113] Marx castigated 'the Belgian absurdity – *to strike* against war'.[114]

Thus trade unions were inherently limited in their effects. But there were two further criticisms, aimed at the actual policies Marx considered were being pursued by trade union leaders, particularly in Great Britain. First, he was critical of the narrow outlook of the craft based unions, the aristocracy of the English labour movement, whose leaders paid little heed to the interests of non-unionised (largely unskilled) labour. Second, Marx considered that they must enter the political arena:

> They must learn to act deliberately as organising centres of the working class in the broad interests of its complete emancipation. They must aid every social and political movement tending in that direction. . . . They must look carefully after the interests of the worst paid trades, such as the agricultural labourers. . . . They must convince the world at large that their efforts, far from being narrow and selfish, aim at the emancipation of the down-trodden millions.[115]

For Marx, the English trade union leaders were too elitist and too concerned with becoming established within the existing system. It was not so much that no interest was taken in politics, but that the interest was for certain circumscribed purposes, such as the 1867 Reform Act and the 1871 trade union legislation. Further, the leaders preferred to bargain with the Liberal party rather than take an independent political stand.[116] Marx's friend from Communist League days, Eccarius, broke with him in May 1871, partly because the latter could not agree that an independent workers' party should be formed in all countries regardless of local conditions. Eccarius felt that the next step in England was to get working men into Parliament, and for this 'alliances with the advanced men of the middle classes' were necessary.[117] Marx's bitterness at what he took to be the betrayal of their followers by the trade union leaders spilled over at The Hague congress. The English delegates had opposed the seating of Maltman Barry because he was not a known working-class leader. Marx replied that it was 'to Barry's credit not to belong to the so-called leaders of English working men, for they have all more or less sold out to the bourgeoisie and the government'.[118] This ill-considered and widely reported remark ended any hope Marx may still have had of exercising influence within the English labour movement.

With respect to co-operatives, Marx stressed the demonstration effect of 'these great social experiments', the seeds of which had been sown by Owen.[119] He made three main points about them. First, that co-operative production rather than co-operative retailing should be forwarded as far as possible. 'The latter but touch the surface of the present economical system, the former attacks its groundwork.'[120] Second, that the co-operative system could never transform capitalist society. And third, any such system must be controlled by the labour movement as organisations independent of control by other classes or the state. Thus Marx attacked the demand of the Gotha Programme for 'the establishment of producers' co-operative societies with state aid'.[121]

In general, however, Marx emphasised the gains to be made within the existing order. Thus child and juvenile workers would be saved from the effects of the capitalist system 'through general laws, enforced by the power of the state. In enforcing such laws, the working class do not fortify governmental power. On the contrary, they transform that power, now used against them, into their own agency'.[122] Indeed, it is the development of capitalism itself which, by creating the requisite socio-economic conditions, has enabled the working class, for the first time in history, to engage in meaningful, independent political activity. Such activity has been facilitated by the advance of communications, the growth of urban areas, the concentration of the worker in the workplace, and the education of the worker through the demands as much of modern technology as of the working class itself. Marx also laid great stress on the educational value of the political and economic conflicts through which the proletariat would come to a clear consciousness of its position as a class, and on the necessity for the theoretical understanding of the complexities of modern society. In addition, however, the worker must attain a certain level of cultural and technical education before he can engage in politics. 'The working man is no free agent. In too many cases he is even too ignorant to understand the true interest of his child, or the normal conditions of human development.' [123]

Working-class education was therefore a matter of deep concern to Marx. At the Geneva congress of the IWA a resolution was carried concerning child and juvenile labour. It was urged that 'in a rational state of society every child whatever, from the age of nine years, ought to become a productive labourer'.[124] In pursuit of this aim 'a gradual and progressive course of mental, gymnastic and technological training' was advocated. Marx envisaged the technological training as a means of compensating for the deficiencies of the division of labour. He also assumed, as we have seen, that the development of modern industry would require workers with polytechnical training. Marx even believed that the education advocated would 'raise the working class far above the level of the higher and middle classes'.[125] It was, he later claimed, 'one of the most potent forces for the transformation of present-day society'.[126] He admitted to a difficulty here:

> On the one hand a change of social circumstances was required to establish a proper system of education, on the other hand a proper system of education was required to bring about a change of social circumstances.

The Proudhonists had opposed state education. But Marx considered that there could be state education financed through taxation without the content being determined by state officials, if nothing was introduced 'either in primary or in higher schools that admitted of party and class interpretations'.[127] He had in mind the formal and the physical sciences, and the teaching of grammar. Marx reiterated his position in 1875:

> Defining by a general law the expenditures on elementary schools, the qualifications of the teaching staff, the branches of instruction, etc. . . . is a very different thing from appointing the state as the educator of the people.[128]

The naivety of this view contrasts strangely with Marx's more sophisticated comments concerning the pervasive character of ideological thought.

But it is not enough that the working class successfully force or persuade the existing political parties to promote legislation favouring their interests. The proletariat must be organised politically as an independent class party on a mass basis, independent of other class organisations and of sects. Marx distinguished between a *class* movement and *sectarian* movement.

> Sects are justified (historically) so long as the working class is not yet ripe for an independent historical movement. As soon as it has attained this maturity all sects are essentially reactionary.[129]

The role of socialist sects therefore declines with the rise of the labour movement. From the vantage-point of 1860, Marx saw even the Communist League as a sect. To Freiligrath he wrote:

> If you are a poet I am a critic and was really fed up with the things I experienced in 1849–52. The 'League', like the *Société des Saisons* in Paris and like a hundred other societies, was only an episode in the history of the party.[130]

Marx's enthusiasm for the IWA stemmed from his belief that it 'has not been hatched by a sect or a theory', but sprang from the 'real movement'.[131] Any sect with something worthwhile to contribute must finally merge in the class movement 'as an element enriching it'.[132] This is clearly the role Marx saw for himself and his tiny circle of followers: 'The communists do not form a separate party opposed to other working-class parties.' [133] The sect sees itself as inherently exclusive, the repository of the true word, engaging in conspiracy and holding itself aloof from the masses. Mass participation, of course, militates against secrecy. There is no evidence that Marx belonged to any secret society after the dissolution of the League.

At the back of Marx's distinction between sect and class is his belief in the need for the *self-emancipation* of the working class. He sought to distinguish the education of the worker through mass participation from tutelage by a self-appointed elite or by socialist intellectuals. His comments on J. B. Schweitzer's trade union proposals are indicative:

> Centralist organisation, although very useful for the secret societies

and sectarian movements, goes against the nature of trade unions. Even if it were possible . . . it would not be desirable, and least of all in Germany. Here where the workers' life is regulated from childhood on by bureaucracy and he himself believes in the authorities, in the bodies appointed over him, he must be taught above all else to walk by himself.[134]

In 1877 Marx claimed that it had been a condition of his joining the Communist League that 'everything tending to encourage superstitious belief in authority was to be removed from the statutes'.[135] He blamed Lassalle for encouraging the creation of hierarchical authority in the labour movement. In 1879 Marx attacked the elitist tendencies he discerned in the thought of socialist intellectuals from the middle classes.

When the International was formed we expressly formulated the battle-cry: The emancipation of the working classes must be conquered by the working classes themselves. We cannot therefore co-operate with people who openly state that the workers are too uneducated to emancipate themselves and must be freed from above by philanthropic big bourgeois and petty bourgeois.[136]

The workers must fit themselves for power. Partly this will occur as a result of the development of capitalist society itself. Hopefully it might, Marx thought, arise from the kind of educational programme we have outlined. But mainly it is a task the workers must perform themselves and no one else can pretend to do it for them. It is in the very act of participating in labour organisation of both an economic and a political kind that the worker will both educate himself and reveal himself capable of sustaining a new kind of society.

Marx's strategy of political advance for the working class involved a twofold perspective. In the long run class interests are irreconcilable. The interests of bourgeoisie and proletariat offer no prospect of ultimate reconciliation. But this provides a guide only to the outer limit of political possibility. In the short term it is quite possible for classes to have interests in common *vis-à-vis* another class, and for classes to ally if there were advantages to be gained. Thus Marx is able to say even of the Prussian bourgeoisie in 1848 that it should have realised that its only ally was the people (*sic*). 'Not because these two groups have no hostile and contradictory interests, but because they are still welded together by *the same* interests in face of a third power which oppresses them both equally.'[137] Engels stated the position clearly during the Prussian constitutional crisis of the early 1860s. Both bourgeoisie and proletariat are 'children of a new epoch', and it is in the interest of the proletariat to support the bourgeoisie 'in their fight against all reactionary elements'.[138] The *Manifesto* had maintained that it was the duty of the working class to support any force deemed progressive in terms of the development of bourgeois society.[139] This view remained a constant in Marx's attitude to tactics. He castigated the provision of the Gotha Programme in which it was stated that 'the emancipation of labour must be the work of the working class, in contrast to which all other classes are but one reactionary mass'. For Marx this could only be true in a fully capitalist society or at a time of proletarian revolution.[140] Engels returned to this point when he found the same phrase used in the draft of the Erfurt Programme in 1891. 'It enunciates an *historical tendency* correct in itself as an *accomplished fact*.' Until the social revolution begins and the SPD is strong enough to seize state power there can be no certainty at any given moment about who is 'reactionary' and who is not.[141]

Similarly, in the early stages of the working-class movement, the exigencies of organisational unity might require union with incompatible elements from the theoretical point of view. Again, this was seen as a temporary necessity. Thus when the General German Workers' Association declared its adhesion to the IWA, Marx warned a colleague that he must understand that the adhesion 'is necessary only for the beginning, against our enemies here. Later on this organisation must be completely destroyed, because the foundations on which it rests are false'. [142] These foundations included a Lassallean programme, centralised organisation, and a tactical policy of co-operation with Bismarck. Once established on the basis of a Marxian programme, however, an independent working-class party had the duty of maintaining its principles, even if this were to lead to an organizational split. This was presumably the rationale behind the events of 1880–1, when a minimum programme was drafted for a heterogeneous grouping of socialist elements under the title of the *Fédération du Parti des Travailleurs socialistes de France*, with a preamble written by Marx and a set of minimum political and economic demands written by Guesde. The programme was never accepted by the grouping as a whole, and a split soon occurred between the Guesdists and the rest.[143] Engels argued that there are necessary stages of development, but that at each stage there are those who are unable to progress any further. Thus it is

> that actually the 'solidarity of the proletariat' is everywhere being realised in different party groupings, which carry on life-and-death feuds with one another, as the Christian sects in the Roman Empire did amidst the worst persecutions.[144]

The issue of class alliances is a purely tactical one, to be judged by an estimation of the current class configuration and by the long-term trends in capitalist society as designated by Marxian theory.

3 REVOLUTION

a. *Legality and Force*

A social revolution is said to occur when the existing production relations in a society have begun to act as a fetter on the further development of the productive forces. We have noted ambiguities in the terms used in this formulation, but in essence the claim is this: that in any society there is a productive system involving relations which are both work relations and ownership relations, and that there arise points in the history of any society when further economic development is retarded by the limitations of the property system. New property forms are required which allow for the expansion of the productive forces to a new and higher level. For Marx, the major political revolutions of the modern age up to his time are to be explained as the result of long-term social and economic developments, in which new forms of economic exploitation and new forms of property ownership steadily develop. A political revolution is a social revolution when it involves the conflict of social classes. 'It is only in an order of things in which there are no more classes and class antagonisms that *social evolutions* will cease to be *political revolutions*.' [145]

Marx believed that his approach gave him the means to determine the necessary, if not the sufficient, conditions for a revolution in an advanced industrial country. His criticism of the Blanquists focused on their attempts to make revolution without the necessary conditions for revolution. 'For them, the only condition for the revolution is a sufficient organisation of their own conspiracy. They are the alchemists of revolution . . . and look with deepest disdain on a more theoretical clarification of the workers as to their class interest.' [146] Engels summed up the main points of disagreement. The Blanquists believe 'in the principle that revolutions do not make themselves, but are made; that they are made by a comparatively small minority and according to a previously designed plan; and finally, that the time is always ripe. . . .' [147] The attack on Blanquism, the emphasis on the pre-conditions of revolution, and Marx's stress on the creation within capitalist society of some of the necessary conditions of socialism, have led Avineri to suggest that, as early as 1842 (*sic*), Marx had reached the conclusion that 'physical power will either fail or prove to be superfluous'. [148] We need, therefore, to consider the role of violence in Marx's conception of revolution.

In his political writings up to 1850 Marx assumes that the political revolution will inevitably involve the use of force. The image of the French Revolution is never far from his mind. [149] The ruling class possesses a monopoly of legitimate coercive power, and will not give up its position without a struggle. Political methods short of the use of force will not change the system. Thus the communists 'openly declare that their ends can be attained only by the forcible overthrow of all existing social conditions'.[150] Indeed, violent revolution is seen as a desirable method, for two reasons. First, it is argued that for a communist consciousness to develop, 'the alteration of men on a mass scale is necessary, an alteration which can only take place in a practical movement, a revolution'.[151] Second, 'there is only one way in which the murderous death agonies of the old society and the bloody birth throes of the new society can be shortened, simplified and concentrated, and *that way is revolutionary terror*'.[152] Lichtheim has argued that after his 'brief Jacobin-Blanquist aberration' at the time of the *March Address* Marx subsequently developed an evolutionary rather than revolutionary view of political change.[153] Yet in *Capital* Marx remains prepared to stress the historically beneficent use of force: 'Force is the midwife of every old society pregnant with a new one.'[154] Marx identified three major bourgeois revolutions: the Netherlands revolt in the latter half of the sixteenth century; the English Civil War (1642–9); and the French Revolution of 1789. All these involved the extensive use of force.

Marx's Amsterdam speech (8 September 1872) is probably an accurate rendering of his mature view concerning violence, legality and revolution, though it is known to us only through newspaper reports.[155] In *La Liberté*, Marx is said to have emphasised the need for the working class to conquer political power, and stressed that different methods were suited to different countries:

> We know of the allowances we must make for the institutions, customs and traditions of the various countries; and we do not deny that there are countries such as America, England, and I would add Holland if I knew your institutions better, where the working people may achieve their goal by peaceful means. If that is true, we must also recognise that in most of the continental countries it is force that will have to be the lever of our revolutions. . . .[156]

This version is broadly supported by the account of the *Algemeen Handelsblad*:

> The speaker defends the use of violence, where other means fail. In North America the barricades are unnecessary, because there . . . the proletariat can win victory through the polls. The same applies to England and some other countries. . . . But in the great majority of states revolution has to be substituted for legality, because otherwise – by a mistaken sense of generosity, by a falsely directed sense of justice – one will not attain one's ends.[157]

The choice between peaceful, legal means, or the use of force, to achieve political power, remains a tactical matter, to be resolved by careful examination of the particular case. It depends upon the existence or otherwise of favourable socio-economic conditions; upon the attitudes of the existing holders of political and economic power; upon the political form of the state. A peaceful transition is more likely, for instance, in countries where there is a genuine political democracy with institutionalised provision for the transfer of power, a feature never the case in Wilhelmine Germany.[158] With respect to Great Britain Marx considered a revolution to be 'not necessary, but . . . *possible*. If the unavoidable evolution turn into a revolution, it would not only be the fault of the ruling classes, but also of the working class'. [159] He considered that the English working class had so far proved incapable of realising the full potential of its voting power and liberty of action. It would be preferable to achieve the goal without violence, for this would cause the least misery to the proletariat and the least disruption of the economy. But Marx always felt a certain pessimism. He said of the English ruling class, 'Mark me, as soon as it finds itself outvoted on what it considers vital questions, we shall see here a new slave-owner war.' [160]

b. *The Bourgeois Revolution*

Marx's conception of revolution stemmed in the first place from his extensive reading about the French Revolution of 1789. This was, in his view, a political revolution in which the rising bourgeois class was finally able to change the political structures in accordance with antecedent changes in the property structure. In general, the bourgeois revolution involves the displacement of one minority class rule by that of another, 'feudal' rule by 'bourgeois' rule; the use of state power to remodel political and legal structures to suit the interests of the new ruling class; while the ruled majority either aids the rising class or remains passive but acquiescent. The bourgeois class itself normally has its fighting done for it, by the peasantry or the urban artisanate. For a time all classes benefit from the results of the revolution, except the crown and the aristocracy. The revolution is seen as an outcome also of antecedent economic developments. Thus up to a point the regulatory powers of feudalism or of absolute monarchy are essential to the protection of commerce and industry. The founding of trade companies, royal monopolies, or guild organisation is therefore beneficial. But such institutions finally become restrictive on further development, and in England under James I and Charles I, for instance, they became a means of conferring advantages upon the favoured few. Many so favoured were in fact bourgeois in social class, but they were nevertheless opposed to the long-term interest of the society as a whole and their class in particular. Thus the Civil War is said to have occurred because the hold of absolute monarchy over society had to be broken. Christopher Hill once summarised Marx's conception of a bourgeois revolution as one in which 'the feudal state is overthrown by the middle class that has grown up inside it, and a new state created as the instrument of bourgeois rule'.[161]

Marx's review of a book by Guizot is interesting as an example of the kind of criticism he offered of historical writings by Liberal historians. Guizot began his account by emphasising that the conflict was not only political and religious, but also social – 'the struggle between the various classes of society for influence and power'. A great change had occurred 'in the relative strength of the different classes of society', in which the higher aristocracy had suffered a relative economic decline compared with the 'middle classes' (defined as yeomen, merchants, and country gentry). But the latter groups did not possess the political power to which their economic weight entitled them. In this disparity lay the seed of civil war.[162] Marx ungenerously makes no mention of these passages. But there is a certain rough justice in the omission, for Guizot nowhere relates this social conflict to his general theme, which results, as Marx says, largely in 'a most inadequate and banal narration of merely political events'.[163] Largely, but not quite, for Guizot also seeks to show why men like William III and Washington, though of inferior talent to Cromwell's, had succeeded where the latter had failed. His explanation is that 'even in the midst of revolution they never adopted a revolutionary policy'. The success of the 1688 settlement lay in a general class alliance, guided by men 'disciplined in habits of order and experienced in government, and not by . . . revolutionists'.[164] The convulsions of 1640–60 had established a political order in which the Commons played a preponderant role; and a religious order which entailed the definitive ascendancy of Protestantism. But Guizot says nothing about whether or not the social imbalance mentioned at the beginning of his book had been corrected.

Marx explained the conservative character of the English revolution in class terms, involving a 'permanent alliance between the bourgeoisie and the greater part of the large landowners'. The latter group is seen as a new nobility, originating with the sale of church lands during the Henrician Reformation, a bourgeois rather than feudal form of land-ownership. A restoration of Catholicism by the Stuarts would have meant the surrender of their property, while it was a religion unsuited to the interests of the 'trading and industrial middle class', though Marx does not say why. For Marx the result of the revolution was to open the way to 'the grand development and metamorphosis of bourgeois society in England'.[165]

There are (at least) five points from the results of recent historical research which are relevant to Marx's interpretation of the English Civil War as a bourgeois revolution. First, it seems that the Restoration land settlement more or less restored the situation immediately prior to 1642. Second, the results of the Civil War were favourable to many social groups, including bourgeois elements, who had previously been subject to various kinds of arbitrary rule. Before 1789, it was an achievement unmatched elsewhere in Europe, other than the Netherlands, that absolute monarchy was prevented in Great Britain. Third, if by 'feudal landowners' are meant those who drew their income from labour dues of unfree tenants, or personal seigniorial dues, or both, then there was no feudalism to overthrow in 1642, let alone a 'feudal state'. Fourth, the effect of confiscation and sequestration (1640–60) was to prop up declining families for at least another generation. Far from speeding up changes in property ownership, it is probable that the Civil War slowed up the process. And fifth, it has been shown by detailed analysis that there were members of all social classes on both sides during the conflict, which is to be seen as stemming from a split in the ruling elites rather than as a struggle between clearly defined social classes.[166]

It is not necessarily fatal to Marx's views that the Civil War did not disturb property distribution, as it is more the changes in the *kind* of property he was most concerned with. He can also allow that the interests of other social groups coincide with the interests of the rising class for a certain period; indeed, this is an integral part of his account. But that there was no feudalism to overthrow; that the revolution did not speed up the pace of change; and that a *class* line-up cannot be established: these points do damage his overall view. It has recently been argued that we need only to define a bourgeois revolution as one which is generated by long-term economic pressures and whose *result* is 'the clearing of decks for capitalism', but with no implication that it was carried through by a rising bourgeoisie.[167] This was not Marx's view of the matter. More important, we need to know precisely in which respects the revolution 'freed' capitalism, and *why* the transformations of the later eighteenth and early nineteenth centuries required a revolution in the seventeenth century. These issues were raised, but not settled, by Marx's account.

c. *The Proletarian Revolution*

A major concern of Marx's economic theory is to explain those weaknesses in capitalism that will finally lead to its collapse, namely the long-term decline in the rate of profit and the cyclical crises of overproduction and under-consumption. There are delaying tendencies: the growth of monopolies, the extension of the world market, and so on. But the ultimate conclusion remains. Throughout the 1850s, and before he had elaborated his mature economic theory, Marx sought signs of an impending economic collapse, believing a financial and commercial crisis to be the first sign of a new revolution. He was proved wrong on each occasion.[168] Mandel has traced the theoretical inadequacies which help to explain this failure.[169] A crisis of genuine European proportions did arise in 1857: 'I believe that the "mobilisation" of our persons is at hand.' [170] But it was not to be. The severe economic dislocations which occurred in England, France and Germany did not lead to the political repercussions predicted by Marx. In his later years he still harboured hopes of being able 'to determine mathematically the major laws of crises', and only in 1873 did he report that, though theoretically possible, the attempt was impracticable owing to the complexity of the factors involved and the lack of the right statistical materials: 'For the time being, I have stopped working on it.'[171]

Nevertheless, Marx remained convinced that socialism was not only an ideal to be striven for, but something writ large in the actual development of capitalist society. This theme is especially striking in the *Grundrisse*. Capitalism will be transcended through its own developments. Capital civilises: its enforcement of surplus labour not only creates the conditions in which scarcity is no longer a problem, but is said to make 'general industriousness' the property of the human species.[172] The relation between wage-labour and capital, 'the last form of servitude assumed by human activity . . . is . . . cast off like a skin, and this casting off itself is the result of the mode of production corresponding to capital'.[173] Marx sees joint-stock companies and co-operatives as transitional forms, and talks of share capital as a phenomenon 'turning over into communism'.[174] So strongly are these factors emphasised that the role of the proletariat as a revolutionary agency gets no direct mention in the *Grundrisse*. But this must be placed in perspective.

> If we did not find concealed in society as it is the material conditions of production and the corresponding relations of exchange prerequisite for a classless society, then all attempts to explode it would be quixotic.[175]

The agent remains the proletariat marshalled in its political and economic organisations. But attempts to explode capitalism have to be carried out on the basis of the socio-economic prerequisites laid down by the system itself. We need, however, to consider two kinds of proletarian revolution: first, in an advanced industrial society (Great Britain); second, in an advanced society with a large peasant population (France and Germany).

Marx summarised most of the necessary (though not sufficient) economic conditions of revolution in an advanced industrial society in a circular written for the General Council in January 1870.

> Although revolutionary *initiative* will probably come from France, England alone can serve as the level for a serious *economic* revolution. It is the only country where there are no more peasants and where landed property is concentrated in a few hands . . . where the *capitalist form* . . . embraces virtually the whole of production . . . *where the great majority of the population consists of wages labourers* . . . where the class struggle and organisation of the working class by the Trade

Unions have acquired a certain degree of maturity and universality. It is the only country where, because of its domination on the world market, every revolution in economic matters must immediately affect the whole world.

Marx continued: 'The English have all the material necessary for revolution. What they lack is *the spirit of generalisation and revolutionary fervour*.' [176] In addition to organisation, theoretical understanding and a will to revolution are required. There is no question of the proletariat's waiting quiescently for the economic prerequisites to mature.

This circular contains some interesting implications. First, it is admitted that though the economic conditions for revolution in a capitalist society are most developed in England, there is no necessary connection between these and the development of either theoretical understanding or revolutionary consciousness. Indeed, it is argued that because of the deficiencies of the English working class in these matters, the General Council must retain control and not relinquish English issues to a British Federal Council.[177] The position of England is crucial as the 'metropolis of capital'. Only the General Council can provide the English with qualities they lack, and by doing so

> accelerate the truly revolutionary movement here, and in consequence *everywhere*. . . . As the General Council we can initiate measures (e.g. the founding of the *Land and Labour League*) which as a result of their execution will later appear to the public as the spontaneous movements of the English working class.[178]

Second, it is clear from Marx's account that even in an advanced industrial economy it is possible for the revolutionary impetus to come from elsewhere. France is mentioned: but more importantly in the present case, Ireland, an agrarian economy with predominantly large landed property ownership. In several letters written at this period Marx had reported his conclusion that 'the preliminary condition for the proletarian revolution in England' was the overthrow of the English landed oligarchy. But Ireland stood in the way as a major support of the ruling classes in England. For the landed aristocracy Ireland was a major source of income and political prestige. For the bourgeoisie Ireland was also a source of income, cheap meat and wool, and above all cheap surplus labour which depressed English wages. This last point was crucial: 'The ordinary English worker hates the Irish worker as a competitor who lowers his standard of life. . . . This *antagonism is the secret of the impotence of the English working class*, despite its organisation.' [179] Marx's position here is made clear in a letter to Engels:

> *It is in the direct and absolute interest of the English working class to get rid of their present connection with Ireland* . . . for reasons which in part I *cannot* tell the English workers themselves. For a long time I

believed that it would be possible to overthrow the Irish regime by English working class ascendancy. . . . Deeper study has now convinced me of the opposite.' [180]

The 1801 Union should therefore be replaced by 'a free federal relationship'. Once the English army and police were withdrawn, an independent Ireland would find the abolition of the landed aristocracy an easier matter than in England, for it would be a national issue, not merely an economic one.[181] Overthrown in Ireland, the landed aristocracy would 'as a necessary consequence' be overthrown in England, though Marx does not tell us why this should follow. The economic factor – in this case the impact of cheap labour from a backward economy upon an advanced one – remains central to Marx's analysis. But it remains central for political and national reasons which remain valid even if there were no economic differences.

A third point concerns the world-wide nature of the revolution. 'Empirically, communism is only possible as an act of the dominant peoples "all at once", and simultaneously.' [182] Capitalism will ultimately produce a high level of productive forces on a world scale, together with the contradictions Marx saw as implicit in such a development. Such a revolution, he thought in 1850, must begin in England. He related the failure of the French industrial bourgeoisie to win a dominant political position in French society to his view that property relations can be dominated by industrial capital only when the latter dominates the world market. The French industrialists had therefore to serve 'interests which are opposed to the collective interests of their class'.[183] Marx hoped for a situation in which the English proletariat would seize political power in the country which dominated the world market. But by 1870 he seems to have decided that proletarian revolution does not depend as much as he thought it did in 1850 upon the initiative of the proletariat in the most advanced country. Marx suggested a number of reasons for the failure of the English proletariat to fulfil their allotted role in his earlier historical scenario: first, the English proletariat as a whole had shared in the proceeds of England's world economic domination; second, a part of the proletariat, dubbed the 'labour aristocracy', were the best organised but the least revolutionary as their real wages had risen even faster than those of the average worker; third, and least compelling, the English trade union leaders were corrupt.[184]

From the standpoint of the necessary conditions laid down by Marx for a proletarian revolution in an advanced industrial country, the chances of such a revolution in a society with a large peasant population are slim.[185] But Marx was always much concerned with revolutionary possibilities in France and Germany, both advanced societies with capitalist development, a significant proletariat, and for most of the nineteenth century a majority of the population in rural occupations. In both countries, therefore, the peasantry constitute a political problem for working-class leaders, while in Germany there was an additional problem in that whereas France had achieved the bourgeois revolution, Germany had not. In the last decade of his life Marx still maintains that

a radical social revolution is tied to certain historical conditions of economic development; these are its prerequisites. It is hence only possible, where, with capitalist production, the industrial proletariat occupies at least a significant position among the mass of the people.[186]

The latter sentence represents a modification of the position Marx outlined in 1870. The conception of the attainment of political power here involves a situation in which the proletariat lead other social groupings, such as the peasantry, but do not themselves constitute a *majority* of the population. As we shall see, this view arises as early as 1852.

Marx's first attempt to grapple with the problem of a radical revolu- in a country which had yet to achieve its bourgeois revolution comes in the *Manifesto*.[187] He argued that Germany was already part of a world system. The imminent bourgeois revolution would therefore take place within the more advanced conditions of European civilisation, and with a significant industrial proletariat waiting in the wings. Thus 'the bourgeois revolution in Germany will be but the prelude to an immediately following proletarian revolution'. The communists were to support the bourgeoisie in its revolutionary acts against 'the absolute monarchy, the feudal squirearchy and the petty bourgeoisie'. They also had the psychologically difficult task of ensuring that the proletariat realised the full nature of their antagonism to the bourgeoisie. The institutions of liberal constitutionalism which 'the bourgeoisie must necessarily introduce along with its supremacy' were to be used against the bourgeoisie itself.[188] The process would consist of two, telescoped stages, in which the bourgeois revolution is closely followed by the proletarian revolution.

We have seen that Marx failed to realise that the bourgeoisie, confronted with this situation, would ally with the traditional ruling groups against the proletariat. In the *March Address* the 'democratic petty bourgeois party' takes over the role of the liberal bourgeoisie in the impending new revolution. This party

comprises not only the great majority of the bourgeois inhabitants of the towns, the small people in industry and trade and the guild masters; it numbers among its followers also the peasants and the rural proletariat. . . .

The task of the communists would be 'to make the revolution permanent . . . until the proletariat has conquered state power . . . and . . . at least the decisive productive forces are concentrated in the hands of the proletarians'.[189] The attribution of independent revolutionary initiative to an extremely heterogeneous grouping of social elements is unique in Marx's writings, and neither the diagnosis nor the policy had any relevance to political realities at this period.

But on one point Marx remained clear. The bourgeois revolution had failed in Germany, and it would therefore, in the absence of a liberal constitution and national unification, be very difficult for the proletariat to achieve its aims. Hopes were briefly reawakened in 1863–5 with the constitutional struggle of the progressives against the Prussian crown, but Bismarck's political skill was soon to dash them again, though it seemed to both Marx and Engels that the achievement of national unification was in a sense doing their work for them. However, Marx had mentioned another tactical possibility as early as 1856: 'The whole thing in Germany will depend on the possibility of backing the proletarian revolution by some second edition of the Peasant War. Then the affair will be splendid. . . .' [190]

In the *Manifesto* it was assumed that an attempt to destroy small peasant property was unnecessary: 'The development of industry has to a great extent already destroyed it, and is still destroying it daily.' [191] The peasant was thought of as the owner of a piece of land which he worked with his family largely for the sustenance of his family. We have seen how Marx believed that Napoleon III represented the *Parzellenbauern*, the small-holding peasantry. It is on this group that he concentrates his remarks, though he and Engels are aware that a more complex situation exists.[192] Though they share like economic interests, the peasants do not form a conscious class, in that their dispersal creates 'no community, no national bond and no political organisation among them'.[193] In the context of modern industrial development the peasants are a doomed class. Their fate is bound up with the transition from a natural economy to one of scientific and rational exploitation of agriculture. For Marx the ownership of small land parcels

> by its very nature excludes the development of social productive forces of labour, social forms of labour, social concentration of capital, large-scale cattle raising and the progressive application of science. Usury and a taxation system must impoverish it everywhere.[194]

Indeed, the life of the peasant is seen as barbaric: 'Small landed property creates a class of barbarians standing halfway outside of society, a class combining all the crudeness of primitive forms of society with the anguish and misery of civilised countries. . . .' [195] In general, the peasant is seen as conservative both economically and politically.

But Marx also sees the peasantry as a radical force in at least two instances. In the bourgeois revolutions peasant support was essential to revolutionary success. More importantly in the present context, 'the peasants find their natural ally and leader in the *urban proletariat*'.[196] In

1852 Marx hoped that the peasantry would finally lose faith in the small-holding:

> With his despair in the Napoleonic Restoration the French peasant parts with his belief in his small holding, the entire state edifice erected on this small holding collapses, and the *proletarian revolution obtains that chorus without which its solo song becomes its swan song in all peasant nations*.[197]

This view entails that although the peasant is incapable of political initiative, nevertheless he has revolutionary potential; and that with peasant support the proletariat can attempt a revolution in a peasant country.

In order to obtain peasant support an agricultural programme favourable to the peasant was required. The *Manifesto* had assumed capitalism would deal with the peasant problem. But the strength and persistence of the peasantry throughout the nineteenth century in both France and Germany required some new thinking. Marx had exaggerated both the necessity for a decline in the numbers of peasants under economic pressure, and the effects of parcellation, which were not as straightforward as he thought.[198] However, Marx maintained that the peasant's belief in his status as a property owner was an illusion, belied by the fact of his heavy indebtedness.

> The small man is only a nominal proprietor, but he is the more dangerous because he still fancies he is a proprietor. In England the land can be transformed into common property by act of Parliament in the course of a fortnight. In France it must be accomplished by means of the proprietors' indebtedness and liability to taxation.[199]

Marx's answer to the peasant problem was therefore the nationalisation of the land.[200] Apart from this, the only other suggestion was simply to tell the peasant the truth about his ultimately hopeless condition.

The writing of *The Civil War in France* gives some interesting indications of the problems faced by Marx. In the first draft Marx argued that the Paris Commune benefited everyone in France, but above all was in 'the interest of the *French peasantry*', for otherwise it would prove to be the peasant who would pay for the recent national defeat. The Commune would abolish conscription, usher in cheap government and low taxes, reform the legal system, free the peasant of land mortgages, and enlighten him through secular education, restoring him to 'independent social and political life'. If there were free communications between Paris and the provinces for as little as three months, claimed Marx, there would be a general rising of the peasantry against Thiers.[201]

In one form or another these points appear in the published version. What does not appear is Marx's admission that 'there exists of course in France as in most continental countries a deep antagonism between the townish and the rural producers, between the industrial proletariat and the peasantry'. Marx explains this by their different economic interests, on which rest 'a whole world of different social and political views'. He notes, however, that there is a large and increasing rural proletariat; an increase in scientific farming; and decaying peasant proprietorship. 'What separates the peasant from the proletarian is, therefore, no longer his real interest, but his delusive prejudice.' [202] In a political polemic designed to win support, this was lacking in tact, and in the published version these trends are sketched only lightly, with the claim that only the Commune could solve agricultural problems 'in favour of the peasant'.[203]

It is clear from these passages that Marx is keenly aware both of the antagonisms that exist between the peasant and the urban worker, and of the need to design some means of appealing to the former. But his only other extended consideration of the matter, undertaken while attempting to answer Bakunin's strictures concerning the notion of a dictatorship of the proletariat, in fact offers no answer to the problem. Marx agreed that a proletarian government may well have to use coercion to back up its policies but denied that force would be used against the peasant. Agricultural measures would have to meet three criteria: they must immediately improve the position of the peasant, they must not involve a direct attack on the right of inheritance, and yet, at the same time, they must facilitate the transition to collective property. But Marx had only specified the terms of the problem. On the exact contents of the measures he remained silent, except for expressing the belief that the peasant would accept collectivisation if the advantages were clearly put to him. In 1880 Marx was involved in the writing of the Minimum Programme of the French socialists. He wrote the preamble, and Guesde the minimum political and economic demands. A large majority of the French population remained engaged in agricultural pursuits. Yet not a single word concerning the peasant appeared in the whole document.

In general, then, we can conclude that for Marx a radical social revolution in an advanced country with a large peasant population is possible, if the industrial proletariat occupies at least a significant position in the society as a whole, and if a properly articulated policy is designed to win peasant support. This entails that the full range of economic prerequisites specified in connection with revolution in Great Britain are not met, and this presumably involves an even heavier reliance on the organisation and education of the working class itself. It might be that Marx also believed that the world environment of a developing capitalism would also have its effects on possibilities in France and Germany, though he makes no use of this argument in his later writings.

Finally, we should note that in the 1870s Marx's interest turned more and more to the possibilities of revolution in an underdeveloped, pre-capitalist country, Russia. He learnt Russian and delved deeply into the nature of ground rent in an agricultural country. But it is difficult to discern any particular economic theory which could have guided him in his estimates of the chances of revolution in such a country. Indeed, the evidence of the correspondence is such that it seems that political factors were of most significance to Marx when he sought to predict a new revolutionary outbreak, especially in Poland and Russia. We have seen that one reason for his interest in Russia lay in Marx's over-estimate of the power of Tsardom to prevent a proletarian revolution in Western Europe. Hence, his enthusiasm concerning the Russo-Turkish war of 1877, which he saw as 'a *new turning-point* in European history. . . . This time the revolution begins in the East, hitherto the unbroken bulwark and reserve army of the counter-revolution'. [204] In his advice to Zasulich Marx did not make the successful completion of revolution in Russia dependent on a previous victory of the socialist revolution in Western Europe.[205]

4 THE TRANSITION PERIOD

Marx believed that a more or less lengthy transition period must follow the coming to power of the proletariat, and that indeed 'every provisional political set-up following a revolution calls for dictatorship, and an energetic dictatorship at that'.[206] Thus 'the class struggle necessarily leads to the *dictatorship of the proletariat*' and 'this dictatorship itself only constitutes the transition to the *abolition of all classes* and to a *classless society*'. [207] This description of the transition period first occurred in 1850, and appears to be associated with Blanqui:

> The proletariat rallies more and more around revolutionary socialism, around communism, for which the bourgeoisie has itself found the name *Blanqui*. This socialism is the declaration of the permanence of the revolution, the class dictatorship of the proletariat as the inevitable transition point to the abolition of class differences generally, to the abolition of all the productive relations on which they rest, to the abolition of all the social relations that correspond to these relations of production, to the revolutionising of all the ideas that result from these social connections. [208]

But this account contains ideas alien to Blanqui's thought. As Engels was to put it over twenty years later,

> Blanqui's conception of revolution as an attack by a small revolutionary minority logically entails the necessity of dictatorship in the event of victory – a dictatorship, it must be understood, not of the whole revolutionary class, the proletariat, but of just those few who launched the attack.[209]

From the scattered mentions in Marx's writings, there appear to be four major characteristics of a dictatorship of the proletariat. First, it would involve a *class*, not elite dictatorship. In this sense the term is simply a reformulation of the *Manifesto* position that the 'immense majority' would rule, and that the proletariat (identified with the 'immense majority') would be raised 'to the position of ruling class', winning 'the battle of democracy' and replacing the dictatorship or class rule of the bourgeoisie. [210] It has occasionally been argued that the *Manifesto* position does not imply a dictatorship of the proletariat, but Marx's own usage shows this not to be the case. In a letter to the *Neue Deutsche Zeitung* he noted that he had been reproached with having advocated '*the rule and the dictatorship of the working class*, while you as against me urge the *abolition of class differences*'. Marx went on to refute this claim, quoting from the *Manifesto*, the *Poverty of Philosophy* and *Class Struggles in France* in order to show that the dictatorship of the working class was seen as a necessary stage antecedent to the abolition of class differences, which remained the final goal. It is clear from the letter that 'dictatorship of the working class', the notion of the proletariat as a 'working class', and the 'class dictatorship of the proletariat' are equivalent terms for Marx, and inform his views from at least the beginning of 1847.[211]

Second, the dictatorship will employ the coercive power of the state. Just as the bourgeoisie had used the concentrated power of the state to hasten, hothouse fashion, the development of capitalism, so the proletariat, having acquired sufficient power and organisation, would employ coercive measures against the economically privileged classes in order to lay the foundations of a communist society.[212] Thus the third characteristic is implied by the second: such a government will implement a distinctively socialist policy envisaged as ultimately leading to the abolition of class differences and the collectivisation of the means of production. This means that for the liberal the democratic nature of the government is limited, in the sense that the property rights of those who own means of production (capital and land) will in the last resort not be respected. This in turn implies a fourth characteristic: the dictatorship of the proletariat is essentially an *aggressive* phenomenon. In pursuit of its final goal, its policies are highly likely to aggravate rather than diminish class conflict. Indeed, Marx told one audience that before a policy of collectivisation could be successful, 'a proletarian army' would be necessary.[213]

A number of points in this account require elaboration. But first we need to note the claim that Marx's discussion of communism in the *EPM* is relevant to his later views about the transition period and the first phase of communist society. In this discussion Marx distinguished several kinds of communism. Crude communism was the first to be considered. It involved the necessity of all to labour, a levelling down of all talents, and the community of women. This 'approach to *woman* as the spoil and handmaid of communal lust' is for Marx an expression of the degraded nature of such a society, the negation of 'the personality of man in every sphere'. He then notes two kinds of *political* communism, democratic (Cabet?) and despotic (the Babouvists?), as well as one which involved the elimination of the state (Dézamy?).[214] These are seen as historically successive *theories* of communism, each being a little more adequate than the one before it, as the tendencies of capitalist society become clear. Finally, Marx cites his own view, a theory of communism as the *Aufhebung* of private property which includes the empirical claim, which the other theories do not, that the development of modern society leads inevitably to communism.[215]

Both Tucker and Avineri, however, see these successive theories as Marx's scheme of the *actual* stages through which communism will come about. For Tucker, crude communism is equivalent to the transition period of the dictatorship of the proletariat.[216] For Avineri, who denies any relevance to the dictatorship concept, crude communism 'closely resembles' the first stage of future society as outlined in the *CGP*.[217] But there is no textual evidence that Marx was thinking in the *EPM* in terms of future stages. In any case, as we have noted, a number of communisms are mentioned which receive no attention in the accounts of Tucker and Avineri. The latter's parallel between the *EPM* and *CGP* texts is wholly superficial, and ignores the fact that several features of the *EPM* account do not appear in the *CGP* (the holding of woman in common, elimination of talent by force), which in any case talks in meritocratic terms, which is the reverse of crude communism as outlined by Marx.

Apart from the red herring raised by Tucker and Avineri, there remain a number of problems, chief among them that surrounding the use of state power by the proletariat. Bakunin was, of course, hostile to any use of the state. For him, the state was the fount of all evil and had simply to be replaced by communes freely organised and federalised. To Engels, the point was straightforward: the state is an epiphenomenon, not an independent power.

> Do away with capital, the concentration of all means of production in the hands of the few, and the State will fall of itself. The difference is . . . essential . . . without a previous social revolution the abolition of the State is nonsense. . . .[218]

State power must be used to bring about such a social revolution. But Bakunin raised a very important issue by questioning the meaning of 'the proletariat raised into a ruling class', and asking, 'Will the proletariat as a whole be at the head of the government?' He answered his own question by claiming that such a state 'will be nothing else but despotic rule over the toiling masses by a new, numerically small aristocracy of genuine or sham scientists'. Marx is clearly impatient of such questions: 'In a trade union . . . does the whole union form its executive committee? . . . Will all the members of the Commune simultaneously administer the communal interests of the Region?' The questions are clearly rhetorical, expecting the answers 'No'. But he goes on: 'The whole thing begins with the self-government of the Commune.' [219] It is clear from his remarks that even in the transition period Marx does not advocate the kind of centralised state socialism attributed to him by Bakunin. That this is so is implicit in Marx's realisation that the proletariat cannot merely take over the existing state machine, but must smash it and create a new one suited to the situation.

In the *Manifesto* Marx had written as though the state was a neutral instrument for use by whoever controlled it. But one of the major lessons Marx had drawn from the events of 1848–50 was the need to smash the existing state machinery. All revolutions, including those of 1848, had hitherto had the effect of 'perfecting' the state. In metaphysical mood Marx had declared in *The Eighteenth Brumaire* that the Revolution (through the cunning of its own reason?) 'perfects the State power . . . in order to concentrate all its forces of destruction against it'.[220] The new task of the revolution is to smash (*zu zerbrechen*) the state machine, not simply to transfer it to new hands.[221] The political machine which had enslaved the working class could not be 'the political instrument of their emancipation'.[222] The fact that the Paris Commune of 1871 had attempted to smash the state meant that 'whatever the immediate outcome might be a new point of departure of worldwide importance had been gained'.[223] The five major organs of the state had been transformed. The standing army had been replaced by the 'armed people', the church had been disestablished, and free, secular education made available to all. A commune had been elected by universal suffrage, a body of delegates rather than representatives. The delegates, and indeed all public servants, including the police, the administrators and the magistrates, had become the elective, responsible (responsive and accountable) and instantly revocable agents of the people at large. Close communal control would prevent the functionaries from raising themselves above society, and low salaries would discourage place-seeking for motives of profit. Smashing the existing state machine meant not only replacing its personnel, but also creating a new political structure.

In Marx's account of the political structure within the Paris Commune, three points require emphasis. First, the Communal Assembly was portrayed (inaccurately) as a working, not a parliamentary body, being both legislative and executive. In this way the executive functions are no longer 'the hidden attributes of a trained caste' but tasks which can be publicly, effectively and simply undertaken by any workman acting in his role as citizen.[224] Marx's interpretation of the French Second Republic also reflects his belief that the growth of an executive power independent of its social bases, in however illusory a sense, was encouraged by the formal separation of legislative and executive.

Second, we should note Marx's approval of tendencies towards the decentralisation of functions formerly undertaken by the state and the local administration of these. In his view the French state had provided France with a merely artificial unity. This would be supplanted by a genuine 'political union of French society through the Communal organisation'. The old governmental machine would have been super-seded by 'real self-government' and 'local municipal liberty'. Marx stresses that this structure is not a return to the medieval commune, nor a 'reactionary decentralisation' of a France dominated by 'the pro-vincial and local domainial influence of the Châteaux'.[225] He rejected Bismarck's view, which ascribed to the Commune 'aspirations after that caricature of the old French municipal organisation of 1791, the Prussian municipal constitution which degrades the town governments to mere secondary wheels in the police-machinery of the Prussian State'.[226] Nor did such a decentralisation entail a destruction of France as a nation. Those central functions 'necessitated by the general and and common wants of the country' would continue to exist. But they would no longer constitute 'a private property bestowed by a central government upon its tools'. Marx distinguished between the repressive functions of the state, to be finally amputated, and its 'legitimate functions', to be 'restored to the responsible agents of society'.[227] But he tells us nothing of the criteria by which functions would be allocated centrally or locally, and nothing about the organisation of this.

The third point to note is that the local communes would have been connected to the centre by an indirect elective system, the commune principle becoming 'the political form of even the smallest country hamlet'. The rival communes would have been grouped into districts, each with an assembly of delegates. These district assemblies would send delegates to the National Delegation, 'each delegate to be at any time revocable and bound by the *mandat impératif* (formal instructions) of his constituents'. According to Marx, such a system ensured that the peasants would be led by the urban workers, 'the natural trustees of their interests'. Indeed, the events of the Commune constituted 'the first revolution in which the working class was openly acknowledged as the only class capable of revolutionary initiative'.[228] In the first draft of *The Civil War in France*, Marx sketched what he took to be the political organisation of the National Guard in Paris. He tells us that the Central Committee of the National Guard was elected indirectly. Each com-pany elected battalion delegates; these appointed general delegates, each of whom represented an *arrondissement* and co-operated with the delegates of the other nineteen *arrondissements*. These twenty delegates composed the central committee. 'Never were elections more sifted, never delegates fuller representing the masses from which they had sprung.'[229] It seems that for Marx an indirect elective method was genuinely democratic and that the Central Committee gained legitimacy from this fact.

How far was Marx committed to decentralisation of the kind outlined here? It has often been pointed out that Marx's account of the commune is in some ways inaccurate; that a polemic in defence of the commune will contain omissions and inaccuracies motivated by tactical considerations. Marx was not writing a piece of historical research. Most importantly, it has been suggested that Marx's use of the Declaration of 19 April implies acceptance of a political structure advocated in all essentials by Proudhon in *Du principe fédératif*,[230] and that such an acceptance could not be genuine, running counter, as it did, to Marx's views in 1848–50. At this earlier period Marx advocated a single and indivisible German republic. In the *March Address* he went even further:

> The workers . . . must . . . strive . . . within this republic for the most determined centralisation of power in the hands of the state authority. They must not allow themselves to be misguided by the democratic talk of freedom for the communities. . . . As in France in 1789 so today in Germany it is the task of the really revolutionary party to carry through the strictest centralisation.[231]

In *The Eighteenth Brumaire,* where the need to demolish the existing 'military-bureaucratic governmental machinery' is first announced, Marx claims that such a demolition 'will not endanger centralisation. Bureaucracy is only the low and brutal form of centralisation that is still afflicted with its opposite, feudalism. . . .'[232] Finally, we must note Marx's view in 1870 about the significance of a Prussian victory over the French: 'If the Prussians win, the centralisation of state power will be useful to the centralisation of the German working class.'[233]

However, these passages seem perfectly explicable. Marx firmly believed, for reasons as much economic as political, in the need for political unity of the 'historical' nations. So much so, indeed, that he was able to write enthusiastically that in uniting Germany Bismarck was doing 'our work', without paying attention to the possible negative implications. Marx required centralisation, both in 1848–50 and 1870, for a Germany which had yet to achieve political union. Further, as Engels later explained, the allusions to the French example were based on the false belief that administrative centralisation had been established by the Revolution and used by the Convention to defeat the royalist and federalist reaction. In fact, centralisation had been established by Napoleon. Up to the 18th Brumaire elected officials had carried out the local administration. Thus 'local self-government . . . became the most powerful lever of the revolution'. Neither Marx nor Engels saw any contradiction between 'local and provincial self-government' and 'political, national centralisation'.[234] Marx's opposition to Proudhon's political and economic views does not entail opposition to political decentralisation as such. Indeed, Rougerie has suggested, in his discussion of the Declaration of the Commune, that 'all are in agreement (even the Jacobins and Blanquists . . .) on the necessity of breaking down excessive centralisation, grown insupportable under the Second Empire; and at the same time . . . on the necessary maintenance of the national unity accomplished in 1790'.[235] The views in the document are therefore not to be seen as exclusively Proudhonist.

On the basis of universal suffrage, and within a reconstituted political structure, the proletariat dictatorship would pursue a socialist policy. There are only a few places in Marx's writings where any details are given of such a policy, though it is clear that it must lead to the abolition of private property in all means of production. In different countries, and at different periods, different configurations of class relations would mean differences in the exact policies to be followed by a proletarian government. The most explicit formulation appears in the ten demands listed in the *Manifesto*. These demands are seen as a set of necessary though not in themselves sufficient, interim measures. They 'appear economically insufficient and untenable' but will in the course of time prove the thin edge of the wedge, and are thus 'unavoidable as a means of entirely revolutionising the mode of production'. Thus we have:

1. Abolition of property in land and application of all rents of land to public purposes.
2. A heavy progressive or graduated income tax.
3. Abolition of all right of inheritance.
4. Confiscation of the property of emigrants and rebels.
5. Centralisation of credit in the hands of the state, by means of a national bank with state capital and an exclusive monopoly.
6. Centralisation of the means of communication and transport in the hands of the state.
7. Extension of factories and instruments of production owned by the state. . . .
8. Equal liability of all to labour. Establishment of industrial armies, especially for agriculture.
9. Combination of agriculture with manufacturing industries; gradual abolition of the distinction between town and country. . . .
10. Free education for all children in public schools. . . . Combination of education with industrial production. . . .[236]

These measures are seen as 'pretty generally applicable . . . in the most advanced countries'. They will be implemented by a proletarian government based on universal suffrage in an advanced industrial economy. The ultimate aim is the abolition of private property, but this is clearly seen as a long-drawn out process. As we have noted, even Engels' point concerning the gradual expropriation of owners of land, factories, shipping and railways is modified in the *Manifesto* to the abolition of landed property only. Nevertheless, it remains clear that 'by degrees' all instruments of production will be centralised in the hands of the state.[237] Slowly but surely capitalist society will be transformed into a socialist society from within. It has recently been suggested that the measures of the *Manifesto* arise out of Marx's economic analysis. The programme aimed first of all at a fundamental change in the sphere of circulation, and only indirectly in that of production. By controlling banking and credit, the proletarian government would command investment decisions. The owners of circulating capital are organised in a more concentrated way and are therefore easily taken over.[238] It is certainly true that both Marx and Engels saw the incipient conflict of interest between loan capital and industrial capital as something which might be used to the advantage of the working class.[239] Indeed 'there is no doubt that the credit system will serve as a powerful lever during the transition from the capitalist mode of production to the mode of production of associated labour; but only as one element in connection with other great organic revolutions of the mode of production itself'. [240] Whether, however, we should ascribe to the measures of 1848 a theoretical underpinning provided by a theory worked out ten years later is a moot point. Probably *any* economic theory would allow us to conclude that political control of credit and investment was essential to *any* revolutionary government.

The actual outbreak of a revolution in 1848 revealed the difficulties inherent in setting out a list of generally applicable measures.[241] Marx and his friends designed a flysheet, *Demands of the Communist Party in Germany*, containing seventeen points which were presumably considered to be more relevant, and certainly more politic, in the German situation.[242] The measures of the *Manifesto* assumed the attainment of universal suffrage within the framework of the nation-state: the *Demands* included measures (an indivisible republic, universal suffrage, salaried representatives) which would lead to such a framework. The *Manifesto* says nothing of measures affecting the peasantry: indeed, there is no need to destroy petty artisan and peasant property as 'the development of industry has to a great extent already destroyed it'.[243] The request for the abolition of all landed property (*CM*, point 1) disappears from the *Demands*; and the right of inheritance is 'curtailed' rather than abolished (point 14). Four specific measures are included to ease the burdens on the large peasant population in Germany (points 6–9). The *Demands*, rather optimistically, concern an economically and politically backward country about to undergo its bourgeois revolution. Thus even the state monopoly of banking and credit is rather disingenuously represented as necessary 'in order to bind the interests of the conservative bourgeoisie to the cause of the revolution' (point 10).[244]

It is not surprising that when the *Manifesto* was reissued in 1872, it was emphasised that although the general principles remained correct, their practical application depended very much on circumstances, 'and for that reason no special stress is laid on the revolutionary measures proposed at the end of Section II. That passage would, in many respects, be very differently worded today.' The authors cited in particular the 'gigantic strides' made by modern industry and the 'accompanying improved and extended party organisation of the working class', with the experiences of 1848 and 1871 behind them. In particular the need for a reconstituted state machine was indicated. The authors concluded: 'But then, the *Manifesto* has become a historical document which we have no right to alter.' [245]

How should we regard the word 'proletariat' in the term 'the dictatorship of the proletariat'? We have already noted the way *proletarian* expands and contracts according to context in Marx's writings. Earlier, it expands from its basic meaning of 'industrial factory worker' to include the mass of the artisanate. The term 'working class' often helps to conceal this. Later, we find that such groups as the 'servant classes' or the commercial workers are included in a general group of 'wage-labourers' whose interests are opposed to those of the capitalist. Thus the social group called the proletariat which forms the basis of support for a proletarian government can, according to context, contain many heterogeneous elements. Marx's recognition of the rise of new middle groupings also helps to complicate the picture. Further, as his account of the Commune makes clear, Marx was constrained to take note that the peasant in France and Germany was not in significant decline, and that therefore the most that could be hoped for was a working-class government in which the 'proletarian' element would lead other social groups.

This, of course, immensely complicated the task of such a government. If the bourgeoisie has not carried out the task (and incurred the odium) of ending small peasant proprietorship, then the transitional government would have to do it. This was one of Bakunin's main fears, that the dictatorship of the proletariat, however democratic, would be a dictatorship *over* the peasantry. Marx ridiculed such a notion. Revolution could not succeed in a peasant country without peasant support. But he remained unclear about the precise measures a proletarian government could take which would lead to land nationalisation and yet not encroach upon small-holding rights. In the 1860s he had accepted some limitation upon the right of inheritance as a possible measure in a transitional period; [246] but in the later notes on Bakunin he says that the revolution in a peasant country 'must not antagonise the peasant . . . by proclaiming the abolition of the right of inheritance or the abolition of his property'. This would be possible only where the capitalist tenant has ousted the peasant. Presumably Marx hoped to exploit the grievances of the landless agricultural labourer.[247]

Does the Paris Commune fulfil the conditions for a dictatorship of the proletariat? Engels certainly thought so: 'Look at the Paris Commune. That was the dictatorship of the proletariat.' [248] But he refers only to its democratic nature, and to the two 'infallible expedients' (all posts subject to election and recall; all public servants paid workmen's wages) which in his view would have prevented the new state from becoming master of society. Marx never referred to the Commune as such a dictatorship. For him it was 'the political form of the social emancipation. . . . The Commune is not the social movement of the working class . . . but the organised means of action'.[249]

The major feature was that the Commune was a government of the working class working within a reconstituted state structure.[250] But the Commune 'was in no wise socialist, nor could it be'.[251] The drafts of *CWF* show that Marx was well aware of this in 1871. In the first draft, it is true, he claims that 'Republic only possible as avowedly Social Republic'.[252] But as the weeks slipped by Marx began to see that the chances of a socialist policy in the Commune were very slim, and that the Commune itself was essentially a *defensive* posture against those who wanted to destroy the Republic declared in September 1870. If we measure the Commune against the four criteria outlined above, we find that the Commune is said to be a working-class government; and it did smash, for a short time, the existing state machine; but it did not pursue the socialist policy required of a proletarian government; nor was it aggressive in pursuit of such a policy but rather arose from a defensive reaction to the apparent policies of others.[253]

It seems clear from such of Marx's writings as deal with the question that the dictatorship of the proletariat involved some kind of balance between a central state machine and a system of local and regional communes to whom a range of (unspecified) functions would devolve. But he gave no hint as to how the balance would be organised and maintained; or how, in a France where the majority still worked in agriculture and many were still small proprietors, such a decentralised structure could allow the implementation of radical measures. The circumstances would have to be very favourable indeed. Both Marx and Engels agreed that a major reason for the collapse of the Commune was its want of an immediate decisive and authoritarian policy, involving suspension of communal elections and an immediate march on Versailles. 'The Central Committee surrendered its power too soon, to make way for the Commune. Again from a too honourable scrupulosity!'[254] Marx, as we have seen, assumed that the Central Committee already had democratic legitimation.[255] But Bakunin's question, 'Will the proletariat as a whole be at the head of the governments?' remained a crucial one, and Marx's reply that 'the whole thing begins with the self-government of the Commune' fails to carry conviction. If this had occurred in France, no socialist policy could have been implemented, for the communes would have been peasant-dominated. Thus the question concerning the organisation of the dictatorship receives no satisfactory answer from Marx. It is possible that the renewed stress laid by Marx and Engels on the need for mass, national workers' parties from 1870 onwards could be linked to some solution of this question, but here we can only speculate. Lenin's answer was to be the professional revolutionaries' communist party organised along the lines of democratic centralism, a party which after 1917 was soon to turn the dictatorship of the proletariat into a dictatorship of the party over the proletariat and peasantry. But we should not read back later events in order to gauge the significance of what Marx himself was attempting to say.

5 FUTURE SOCIETY

Marx never committed himself to a detailed account of communist society. The principles are reasonably clear, but institutional details are rare. A consideration of the utopias of Cabet, Weitling, Fourier and others had shown him that detailed blueprints were likely to make the originator look foolish. Utopias were typically the product of theorists who 'were compelled to construct the elements of a new society out of their heads because these elements have not yet become generally visible in the old society'. They merely diverted attention from current problems: 'The doctrinaire and necessarily fantastic anticipation of the programme of action for a revolution of the future only diverts one from the struggle of the present.' [256] Late in life Marx noted the growth of new kinds of utopian doctrine, 'playing with fantastic pictures of the future structure of society', but in a more futile form, 'not to be compared with the great English and French utopians but with – Weitling'.

> It is natural that utopianism, which *before* the era of materialist-critical socialism concealed the latter within itself *in nuce*, coming *post festum* can only be silly – silly, stale and fundamentally reactionary.[257]

The working class have no need for 'ready-made utopias'. Marx's own theory shows that 'they have no ideals to realise, but to set free the elements of the new society with which old collapsing bourgeois society itself is pregnant'.[258] Caution is also tactically sound, for many difficult questions arise concerning the details of a communist society. Further, such a society is evolving and dynamic, not static, as Engels makes clear in a comment on a discussion about distribution in future society:

> . . . to everyone . . . 'socialist society' appeared not as something undergoing continuous change and progress but as a stable affair fixed once for all. . . . All one can reasonably do, however, is (1) to try and discover the method of distribution to be used at the beginning, and (2) to try and find the general tendency of the further development. . . .[259]

Nevertheless, there are in Marx's writings sufficient indications of his views to suggest a number of minimum characteristics, without which a society could not be called communist. There will be no scarcity, and the material abundance of full communism will make it possible to distribute goods according to need and not according to labour performed: 'From each according to his ability, to each according to his needs!' The disappearance of private property in the means of production entails the disappearance of social classes, and 'all social and political inequality arising from them would disappear of itself'.[206] There will be no 'rights of inequality', not even those based on different qualities of labour: 'A *different* form of activity, of labour, does not justify *inequality*, confers no privileges in respect of possession and enjoyment.'[261] Any kind of meritocracy 'tacitly recognises unequal individual endowment and thus productive capacity as natural privileges'.[262] There would therefore be no system of differential reward for social merit. Men would work without incentive.

The theme that a communist society will involve the abolition of the division of labour runs throughout Marx's writings. Basically this is a call for the abolition of any socio-economic system in which the individuals are forced to pursue a single activity. In this wide sense, it refers to the social division of labour as a whole: 'In a communist society there are no painters but at most people who engage in painting among other activities.'[263] In the words of the famous passage in *The German Ideology*,

> In communist society, where no one has one exclusive sphere of activity but each can become accomplished in any branch he wishes, society regulates the general production and thus makes it possible for me to do one thing today and another tomorrow, to hunt in the morning, fish in the afternoon, rear cattle in the evening, criticise just as I have a mind, without ever becoming hunter, fisherman, shepherd, or critic.[264]

Later, however, this Fourier-like picture changes: 'Labour cannot become a game, as Fourier would like it to be. . . .'[265]

There were perhaps two reasons why Marx changed his mind. The viewpoint implied that a range of butterfly-like activities was best for all individuals. But if we think of the painter example, for instance, it is evident that a painter devoted to his art would voluntarily spend the major part of his time painting. If there is any meaning to the notion of 'free activity', it must imply that the individual would have to choose for himself whether or not to engage in one major activity or a whole range of activities. Indeed, 'really free labour, the composing of music, for example, is at the same time damned serious and demands the greatest effort'.[266]

Second, Marx accepted that large-scale industrial organisation requires differentiation of functions and roles: a technical division of labour must remain, though hopefully it will be functions rather than persons that will be specialised. What will disappear is the 'tyrannical subordination' of the individual in the labour process. In *Capital* considerable emphasis is placed on the role of technological development. The new technologies of the automatic machine shop require not 'specialists and craft-idiocy' but generalists with polytechnical education.[267] Implied in this view is the elimination of the distinction between mental and manual labour, for few are so lacking in intelligence that they can do no mental work. Further, free labour will be free if it is social, has a scientific character and is general work: that is, it is not dependent upon purely physical effort but 'appears in the production process . . . as an activity regulating all the forces of nature'.[268] Labour itself no longer sppears to be an essential moment of production. The worker 'steps to the side of the production process instead of being its chief actor'.[269]

Industrial society under communism will create real wealth in the shape of 'socially disposable time'. The realm of freedom begins *beyond* the point at which labour under the compulsion of necessity and external utility is required. 'The shortening of the working day is its basic prerequisite.' [270] This suggests that genuinely creative activity can occur only *outside* industrial production. But Marx goes further: 'Free time . . . has naturally transformed its possessor into a different subject, and he then enters into the direct production process as this different subject.' The apprentice finds discipline, while for the full man the process is 'experimental science, materially creative and objectifying science . . . the accumulated knowledge of society'.[271] The difficulty with this view is transparent. The full man will want more than to be a man in a white coat pressing the odd button. With sufficient experience of creative leisure, tasks of this kind, while more hygienic, may in other respects appear even less attractive than current tasks.

The development of a 'communist consciousness' is correctly seen by Marx as an essential element of a communist society. Social life would be without illusions and hence without ideology. Servility would disappear. Self-determining, reasoning beings, undisturbed by the lust for possession, would act with the power of genuine choice and the knowledge to choose clear-sightedly. In *The German Ideology* it is asserted that 'in revolutionary activity the changing of oneself coincides with the changing of circumstances'. The alteration of men on the mass scale required can only come about in a revolution: only thus can the class 'succeed in ridding itself of all the muck of ages and become fitted to found society anew'.[272] Living before the apocalypse as we do, we are unable to see how such a change could come about. By the same token Marx is not able to tell us. He saw it as some kind of universal event. 'Empirically, communism is only possible as the act of the dominant peoples "all at once" and simultaneously, which presupposes the universal development of productive forces.' [273] It is not surprising that in his later years Marx became very much more cautious in his statements.

In communist society the state will be abolished. It will no longer be necessary to keep order amid scarcity, or to control class antagonisms. There will be no ruling class to employ the state as an instrument. Further, 'in proportion as the antagonism between classes within the nation vanishes, the hostility of one nation to another will come to an end'.[274] The defence and foreign policy functions of the state would therefore become redundant. 'There will be no more political power properly so-called.' [275] If politics is defined as a struggle of social classes for control of the state, then in a classless society there can be no politics, nor a state 'in the present political sense of the word'.[276] But a 'public power' will remain. We need to understand the precise meaning Marx attached to the 'abolition of the state'.

Avineri has suggested that we must understand abolition here in its technical Hegelian meaning of *Aufhebung*. It is Marx's use of this concept that is supposed to distinguish his views on the state from those of reformist social democracy, or of anarchism. Whereas Engels spoke of the *Absterben des Staates* (the 'withering away of the state'), 'Marx always refers to ths abolition and transcendance (*Aufhebung*) of the state'. Thus the state will be *aufgehoben*: abolished, transcended, preserved.[277] There are two major difficulties with this view. First, Engels' normal usage is *Abschaffung* (a straightforward abolition). The 'withering away' phase is infrequently used.[278] Second, Marx's usage is very often *Abschaffung*. In 1877, he was asked to explain the meaning of 'suppression de l'État'. Marx replied that the meaning is the one developed in *The Civil War in France*: 'In short, you can translate; "*Abschaffung (oder Unterdrückung) des Klassenstaats*".' [279] There is no dialectical connotation here. Both Marx and Engels refer to the same phenomenon using a number of different words. There is no systematic usage. Nevertheless, Avineri is right in seeing a problem here: the state is not simply destroyed.

What, then, is abolished? The evidence of *The Civil War in France* suggests, first, that the function of the state as a coercive class instrument *ipso facto* disappears; and second, 'in so far as it forms a special organism separated from society through division of labour', the state disappears as a hierarchical and bureaucratic organisation.[280] Third, although specialised functions of an administrative character would remain, these public functions would be 'real workman's functions, instead of the hidden attributes of a trained caste'.[281] Such legitimate functions presently performed by the state will therefore be controlled by 'the responsible agents of society'.[282] In his critique of the Gotha Programme, Marx raises, but does not answer, the issue concerning the retention of social functions 'that are analogous to present functions of the state'.[283] He assumes, without argument, that they will be 'simple administrative functions'.[284] Marx also believed that the costs of administration not connected with production would diminish 'in proportion as the new society develops', but no reason is given.[285] In any case, the administration of production and distribution would greatly increase. Marx also talks of 'the future state of communist society', 'the future state in the case of future society', and says that 'it is possible to speak of the "present-day state", in contrast with the future. . . .' [286] Presumably if Marx published these remarks he would have reserved 'state' as a term descriptive of the governmental institutions of class societies. But a 'public power' is certainly involved, and this implies some form of 'political' organisation in communist society, though not in Marx's sense of the word.

A clue to what Marx might have meant can be found in his notes on Bakunin's *Statism and Anarchy*. He states that when class rule has disappeared, 'there will no longer be any state in the present political sense of the word'. Marx gives an election as an example of a *political* form in capitalist society. But he emphasises that its character as political

> does not depend upon this name, but on the economic basis, the economic interrelations of the electors, and as soon as the functions have ceased to be political, then there exists (1) no governmental function; (2) the distribution of general functions has become a business matter which does not result in any domination; (3) the election has none of its present political character.[287]

There will be elections, but these will not be political in Marx's sense. Presumably those elected will be tied to their electors in the way outlined in *The Civil War in France*. Politics in the sense of matters pertaining to the *res publica* will remain a feature in communist society. We should note that Marx does not advocate a direct democracy without vertical structures. [288] The methods of election are indirect, while as we have seen, the public functions will be divided in some unspecified way between national and local levels.

The abolition of political authority in Marx's sense does not mean the abolition of all authority relationships. Society will be composed of associations of 'free and equal producers consciously acting upon a common and rational plan'.[289] Such a plan will control, for instance, 'the right proportion of the various work functions to the various needs'.[290] Organisation involves authority. According to Engels, in large-scale production there are technical exigencies which require 'a veritable despotism independent of all social organisation'. Whether decisions are taken by delegates or by a majority vote, 'the will of the individual will always have to subordinate itself'.[291] The free choices of the individual must remain circumscribed by the needs of the community and the technical exigencies of production. Marx envisaged the fully socialised man as one who would see no distinction between private and public interest and whose activity would be attuned to the latter. He drew a significant analogy between the authority relation which would exist in the communist production process and that which he took to exist between a conductor and his orchestra. There must always be 'a directing authority in order to secure the harmonious working of the individual activities'.[292] Marx assumes that the business arrangements of the collective would not lead to new forms of domination, or indeed deep divisions of opinion on what should be done. He is satisfied with having established that authority relationships do not require private property ownership.[293] He seems unable to conceive that there may be other forms of domination with an equal or even greater capacity than capitalism to control the lives of individuals well beyond the needs of the collective. To abolish private property and social classes is not in itself sufficient to abolish all economic inequality, all status hierarchy, or all forms of political authority.

It remains difficult for us to conceive of a society of free opinion in which individual motives do not clash, either with each other or with the public interest; or in which there would not be different conceptions of what constitutes the public interest. Marx's analogy is in any case a strained one. Assuming agreement on what to play, there are often considerable disagreements between the conductor and the members of the orchestra about the interpretation of the music. And in no society of any complexity has it ever been the case that everyone has wanted to play the same tune.

Conclusion

The picture that emerges from this account of Marx's views on history and politics is of a theorist who constantly revised his position in the light of new knowledge, theoretical discoveries and political events. In his relations with others Marx projected an attitude of arrogant certainty; and in his letters there too often appears an unpleasant sense of his own rightness and of the intellectual feebleness of others. But an examination of the record shows that on many issues he was continually reshaping his views to accommodate new data and new theoretical insights. Indeed, this became an obsessive preoccupation. There always seemed to be another book to read or another social development to be observed before Marx felt he could finally commit his views to the public eye. The real difficulty is not that Marx refused to change his views, but that in his later years such changes did not lead to concomitant modifications in his overall perspective.

Marx's authority has been invoked in support of a large and often incompatible range of theoretical positions and practical policies. Yet in the advanced capitalist countries his views have weighed very little with the economic and political leaders of the labour movement. Further, Marx's writings have proved to be only a partial guide to the actual trend of developments within such societies. In his analysis of economic development in France and Britain, Kindleberger concluded that there is no reason to explain 'the course of British economic history since 1850 in terms of . . . the falling rate of profit, the immiseration of the working class, monopoly and capitalistic crises'.[1] The economic systems of western Europe, while changing in some respects anticipated by Marx, still remain, despite some major crises, recognisably capitalist systems despite state economic intervention on a large scale. Marx's mature economic theory stressed the adaptive capacity of capitalism more than his earlier theorising had done, but he still believed that the system would ultimately be undermined by its own tendencies. He assumed that the situation thus created would lead to communism. But despite his claims in his famous letter to Weydemeyer, Marx established no necessary theoretical connection between the collapse of capitalism and the coming of communism.[2] Capitalist crisis gives opportunities to the opponents of political liberalism from the right as well as from the left, and on the whole the political right have proved the more skilful at using conditions of social and economic breakdown to their own advantage. There has been no successful proletarian revolution in any advanced industrial country. Indeed, the German revolution of 1918 is the only case that can lay any kind of claim to being considered such an event.

We have already noted the problem of the social groups which are said to constitute the proletariat. Marx had earlier placed his hopes in the development of a class of factory workers created by the industrial system. Later he realised the considerable differentiation of social groups that was taking place. Marx could continue to think in polarisation terms only if he believed that differentiation and a consequent lack of homogeneity among working-class groups in terms of tasks, outlook and life-style would ultimately be of less importance than the features which bind all wage earners together against their class enemy, the capitalist.[3] In agriculture, for instance, capitalism is said to replace the peasant by the wage-labourer. 'Thus the desire for social changes, and the class antagonisms are brought to the same level in the country as in the towns.'[4] Finally, agricultural, industrial, commercial and domestic workers will all come to an understanding of their common interests. So far this has not happened.

Differentiation has a further consequence. The acceptance of the necessity of a mass organisational basis involves at least a provisional acceptance of current political institutions. Marx saw a favourable sign in the development of a mass electorate. But if a mass party were to remain based on the factory proletariat, it would never win a majority of the votes in an election. In Marx's lifetime this fact was obscured by a continuous rise in the proportion of factory workers to the total population. But the late nineteenth century witnessed the beginnings of a gradual decline in this proportion. Marx's early belief was that the proletariat would be driven to revolt because of the unbearable conditions in which it lived; his mature view, more plausibly, focused on the strategic role of the proletariat in the production process and therefore its power both to organise itself and to paralyse production. This role has passed from the factory proletariat proper to the producers of basic energy resources. But in neither case has the strategic power of the groups concerned been employed in pursuit of other than the traditional objectives concerning wages, hours and conditions of work. There are places where Marx appears to have recognised these facts, but he was too inclined to view them as contingent features which would disappear as the real nature of the capitalist system became more apparent, and he made no adjustments to the kind of political policies he advocated. It was left to others to do so.

With these features in mind, what link remains between socialism and some form of democratic rule? The acceptance of democracy entails the acceptance of electoral politics. To get votes or to retain them requires success in obtaining measures favourable to the voters. No social democratic party can win an election except by appealing to non-proletarian voters or by co-operating with other political groups. From forms of parliamentary collaboration it is only a step to electoral alliances. These themes are writ large in the history of the SPD. The party became organised, not for revolution, but for the winning of elections. Yet success in obtaining reform shows the proletarian that it is possible to better his lot within the existing order.

Even in Marx's lifetime there was little evidence that the new factory workers had revolutionary potential. In many respects the factory proletariat were probably the most conservative and best-off part of the European working class. In 1848 the real radicals in both France and Germany were the uprooted and declining peasant or skilled artisan in a traditional trade subjected to massive technological unemployment. A majority of the members of Cabet's Icarians as well as of the Communist League were of this latter kind. The Paris 'proletariat' in 1848 and 1871 was largely artisan in composition. The perspective of these groups was backward-looking, even though they were prepared to use violence to attain their ends. Marx tended to transfer the revolutionary possibilities he rightly saw among the artisans to the factory workers. Similarly, the main support for the early German labour movement came from the traditional skilled workers fighting a rearguard action against an enforced incorporation in the urban proletariat. We have seen that the main English trade union support for the IWA came from those in relatively backward industries and not from mining, engineering or heavy industry in general. This was true of all countries except Belgium.

Nor is it clear that political failure or economic depression make the worker more revolutionary in Marx's sense. The 1930s give us the classic case of economic depression producing a swing to the political right. But there was evidence in Marx's lifetime. The peak of success for the IWA coincided with a high level of prosperity in which the workers shared. The decline of the IWA began before the Paris Commune, and a certain correlation can be found between a decline in membership and a rise in unemployment. Similarly in the 1880s support for the SPD rose with a rise in the demand for labour and fell in periods of depression with a swing to the right.[5] The labour movement finally engaged in politics. But there is no necessary connection between political participation and socialist political participation, and still less Marxian socialist political participation. The connection remains one of aspiration and hope: 'The masses are sure to come round to us by and by. . . .'[6]

The *Manifesto* implies a model of social development in which economic, political and ideological tendencies are closely dependent on each other. Thus certain economic trends were thought to imply the necessity for certain political changes, ideological stances were thought to arise from, or at least in some way 'reflect' economic trends, and so on. Many of the theoretical problems with which Marx had to grapple in later years arise from the fact that, although he believed that economic, political and ideological changes tended to run in harness, as it were, they rarely did. Such manifestations are problems for him because of his prior assumption of parallel strands. Yet his empirical material is drawn from two major sources. Great Britain is the 'classic ground' for a theory of economic development. France is drawn on for Marx's general conception of politics and revolution. But political development in Great Britain did not follow the French example, while economic development in France was very slow indeed to follow the example of Great Britain. Yet the historical experiences of the two countries are in some way entwined in Marx's mind to produce a model of normal social change.[7]

If we compare the model with actual developments in Great Britain, France and Germany in the nineteenth century, a much more complex picture emerges. Speaking in Marxian terms, the advanced level of economic development in Great Britain was only gradually equalled by what Marx would regard as a concomitant political development, and the high level of bourgeois ideological consciousness was never equalled by a parallel burgeoning of consciousness on the part of the urban proletariat, who had, as Engels put it, 'an indifference to all theory'. In France a high political level was accompanied by a slow rate of economic development wedded to artisanal and petty bourgeois aspirations. Proudhonist, and later anarcho-syndicalist beliefs were of far greater importance than Marxian ones in the French labour movement. In Germany, economic development soon ran far ahead of the political developments assumed to be inevitable in 1848, while the working class was deemed by Engels to be the most theoretically advanced proletariat in Europe. Thus he was able to say enthusiastically in 1874:

For the first time since a workers' movement has existed, the struggle is being conducted pursuant to its three sides – the theoretical, the political, and the practical-economic (resistance to the capitalists) – in harmony and in its interconnections, and in a systematic way.[8]

Such a perspective can easily lend itself to normative conclusions. Engels, for instance, argued that if Bismarck's policies were to be 'in harmony with historical development', then he must follow policies 'directed consciously and resolutely towards the final establishment of bourgeois rule'.[9] If Bismarck failed to conform with the normal course of development, then he would fail in his policies. But, of course, there is no ineluctable necessity which makes the state a handmaiden of the bourgeoisie, and the 'normal' course of development is far from being the norm.

Marx usually attempted to cope with the features to which we have drawn attention by emphasising the need for better organisation and the correct theoretical consciousness among the working class. The creation of an effective organisation, or of a particular theoretical standpoint, can never be a mechanical result of the spontaneous development of the capitalist system. Marx did not completely abandon his view that certain levels of socio-economic development give rise to certain kinds of theorising. In 1871 he was still able to say that Bakunin's views 'found favour . . . in Italy and Spain, where the real conditions for the workers' movement are as yet little developed'.[10] But he argued that a workers' movement in more backward countries can often learn from the experiences of similar movements in more advanced countries. In an important statement in 1869 Marx began by reiterating that where men are placed under widely differing circumstances, 'it seems almost necessary that the theoretical notions, which reflect the real movement, should also diverge'. But he continued:

The community of action, however, called into life by the IWA, the exchange of ideas facilitated by the public organs of the different national sections, and the direct debates at the General Congresses, are sure by and by to engender a common theoretical programme.[11]

Such a view entails a model of normal development, at least for Western Europe, in relation to which a nation is advanced or backward. Yet the *Manifesto* version of what a *normal* development constituted had been effectively discarded both by the changes Marx made to his economic theory and by his recognition of the various changes in political circumstances which followed in the wake of the failure of the 1848 revolutions. No coherent political theory was put forward to cope with the new phenomena. Indeed, both Marx and Engels continued to refer to the *Manifesto* as the classic outline of their political strategy. The disparities between the model and reality are bridged by consciousness. Marx argues that the theoretically backward will learn from their more theoretically advanced neighbours. This view places a far greater reliance on the development of consciousness than is implied by the base-superstructure distinction. The changing of consciousness within the working class remains the major and so far unachieved goal for the Marxist intellectual. It is significant that the most important contributions to Marxist theory since the death of Marx have been by theorists of the superstructure, among whom Gramsci has an outstanding place. It is a matter of controversy whether such contributions conform to the Marxian canon, but in fact the ambiguities of Marx's position mean that there will always be competing orthodoxies of interpretation.

FOOTNOTES TO PART I

1 McLellan (1970), pp. 26–32, points out the importance of Marx's Jewish ancestry.
2 Eleanor Marx, 'Remarks on a Letter by the Young Marx', in *Reminiscences* (n.d.), p. 257.
3 'Thoughts of a Young Man on Choosing a Career', *MEW.EB* 1: 592. See the facsimile on the facing page. The school did nothing for the legibility of Marx's handwriting.
4 D. Riazanov (1927), p. 36; see also Mehring (1936), p. 5.
5 *MEW.EB* 1: 3–12. First published by Eleanor Marx in 1897 and first translated in Rühle (1927). See EG, 40–50.
6 Hegel (1892) I, 40.
7 Hegel, op. cit., p. 57.
8 W. Kaufmann's translation of the preface to the *Phenomenology*, in Kaufmann (1966), p. 390.
9 Hegel (1958), p. 13.
10 Hegel, op. cit., p. 10. The Young Hegelians emphasised the historical aspect of Hegel's thought more than he did himself. *The Science of Logic* is, after all, a timeless dialectic of concepts.
11 See Hammen (1953).
12 *MEW.EB* 1: 262.
13 On these liberals, see Rohr (1963).
14 Marx to Ruge, 30 Nov. 1842; *MEW* 27: 411. The *Freien* group was a successor to the *Doktorklub*.
15 Marx to Oppenheim, 25 Aug. 1842; *MEW* 27: 409.
16 Rohr (1963), p. 145; Camphausen's letter of 25 Jan. 1843, quoted Hammen (1970).
17 *CPE*, preface, p. 19. According to Mehring (1936), p. 41, the wood-theft laws accounted for 150,000 of the 207,000 official legal offences committed in Prussia in 1836.
18 See A. Cornu, 3, p. 11; McLellan (1970), pp. 154ff; Mehring (1936), pp. 73–5.
19 Hexter (1961), p. 14.
20 Note especially Marx to Engels, 27 July 1854, *MEW* 28: 381–2; *SC*, 87–9, discussing Augustin Thierry, *History of the Formation and Progress of the Third Estate* (3rd edn, Paris 1853). Thierry traced the origins of the middle classes to the indigenous early Gauls, whereas the aristocracy was said to derive from later foreign invaders in the shape of the Germanic Franks. For Guizot, see Marx's review of *On the Causes of the Success of the English Revolution of 1640–88* (Paris, 1850), *MEW* 7: 207–12; *On Britain*, pp. 344–50. In December 1847 Marx made some notes on Wade's *History of the Middle and Working Classes* (3rd edn, London, 1835), for some lectures he gave, *MEW* 6: 537–8. The lectures were published as *Wage-Labour and Capital* in 1849. Needless to say, the notion of class in these writers was exceedingly imprecise.
21 Marx to Weydemeyer, 5 Mar. 1852; *MEW* 28: 507–8; *SC*, 69.
22 R. Jones, *An Essay on the Distribution of Wealth and the Sources of Taxation: Part 1, Rent* (London, 1831). Marx took notes on this book in 1851.

Extensive extracts from Jones's writings, with appreciative commentary, can be found in *TSV* III, 399–449. See H. Grossman (1943).

23 H. M. Hyndman (1911), p. 275.

24 *MEW.EB* 1: 554; *EPM*, 155.

25 'Critical Notes on "The King of Prussia and Social Reform"', *MEW* 1: 392–409; EG, 338–58.

26 Marx to Engels, 8 Jan. 1863, and succeeding letters; *MEW* 30: 310–17.

27 Eleanor Marx to Paul Lafargue, 26 Mar. 1883, quoted in Tsuzuki (1967), p. 73.

28 Feuer (1966) claims that Marx was himself much influenced by these communities but his evidence rests solely on quotations from Engels.

29 Engels wrote 21 of the 261 pages in the English edition of *The Holy Family*. *The German Ideology* involved considerable collaboration. Marx amended and extended the manuscript. Part of it is written in Weydemeyer's hand; there is at least one section by Moses Hess.

30 Eleanor Marx wrongly attributed them to her father when republishing them as *Germany: Revolution and Counter-Revolution* (London, 1896). Marx's first article in English was written on 28 Jan. 1853. Marx to Engels, 29 Jan. 1853, *MEW* 28: 209.

31 See Marx to Engels, 2 June 1853; Engels to Marx 6 June 1853, *MEW* 28: 251–4, 259; *SC*, 80–3. This is followed by Marx's 'The British Rule in India' in *NYDT*, 25 June 1853, in which a major portion of Engels' letter is used verbatim. *MEW* 9: 127–33. *On Colonialism* (4th edn, 1968), pp. 34–41, esp. p. 37. On America, see K. Marx and F. Engels, *The Civil War in the United States, passim.*

32 M. Rubel, *Bibliographie*, p. 119, note.

33 See the exchange concerning Pierre Trémaux's book *Origine et transformations de l'homme et des autres êtres* (Paris, 1865), which Marx, despite Engels' opposition, considered a significant advance on Darwin. Marx to Engels, 7 Aug. 1866, Engels to Marx, 2 and 5 Oct. 1866, Marx to Engels, 3 Oct. 1866, Marx to Kugelmann, 9 Oct. 1866, *MEW* 31: 248, 256–61, 530.

34 Marx to Engels, 22 June 1867; *MEW* 31: 305; *SC*, 188.

35 Marx to Engels, 13 Feb. 1866; *MEW* 31: 178.

36 See Engels' prefaces to Capital II and III. Marx must have had a reasonable confidence in Engels' understanding of his economic theories: he allowed Engels to write short accounts in review articles intended to publicise *Capital* I. See *MEW* 16: 207–18; 226–42, 288–309.

37 The leaders of the League of the Just had set up the society (GWES) in 1840. It was a public organisation, and lasted until the First World War.

38 For an examination of the evidence of the personal and intellectual relationship between the two men, see Pickles (1937–8); and Woodcock (1956), pp. 48ff. For Marx's version, which places him in a professor-student relationship with Proudhon, see Marx to J. B. Schweitzer, 24 Jan. 1865, *MEW* 16: 27; *SC*, 153.

39 Woodcock (1956), p. 57.

40 Marx to Proudhon, 5 May 1846; *MEW* 27: 442–4; *SC*, 28–9 (without postscript).

41 Proudhon to Marx, 17 May 1846, in *Lettres de P.-J. Proudhon*, ed. Halévy and Guilloux (Paris, 1929), pp. 71–6; S. Edwards (ed.), *Selected Writings of P.-J. Proudhon* (London, 1971), pp. 150–4.

42 Article 3, *Dokumente* I, 93.

43 Articles 14, 20, 24, 26, 29, *Dokumente* I, 95–7.

44 Article 36, *Dokumente* I, 98.

45 Article 1, *Dokumente* I, 93. According to Ewerbeck, there were also Swiss, Scandinavians and Hungarians in the Just.

46 In this respect, the Icarians were akin to the Just. Of 497 identified Icarians, Johnson (1971) found 379 workers in traditional crafts, of whom 40 per cent were tailors and shoemakers. The appeal to *all* classes establishes Cabet as a Utopian for Marx, but in the late 1840s Cabet began to talk in terms of class conflict and the need for revolution. See Johnson (1966).

47 Letter of 23 Aug. 1843, in A. Lehning (1970), p. 129.

48 Cabet made such attempts in May 1843, May 1844 and mid-1845. His last attempt was in the summer of 1847. Schapper rejected the plan in the only issue of the *Kommunistische Zeitschrift* (Sept. 1847).

49 See *Dokumente* I (1970), no. 64, pp. 214–38, minutes of the GWES.

50 At a meeting on 30 Mar. 1846. There are three extant accounts. The following is based on Annenkov (1968), pp. 168–71. The extract from Annenkov in *Reminiscences*, pp. 269–72, is distorted by omissions.

51 Weitling to Hess, 31 Mar. 1846, in E. Silberner (ed.), *Moses Hess: Briefwechsel*, pp. 150–2. See Engels to Bebel, 25 Oct. 1888, *MEW* 37: 117–19, enclosing Weitling's letter. Engels denied Weitling's claims about Marx's threats, but considered the last two points to be a reasonable summary of the main differences of opinion. Annenkov has nothing to say about threats by Marx.

52 Note in this connection *MEW* 3: 449; *GI*, 508.

53 See the letters of 6 June 1846 and 7 July 1846, *Dokumente* I, 348, 379.

54 *Dokumente* I, 431.

55 Engels to Marx, Dec. 1846; *MEW* 27: 70.

56 For this visit we have the accounts only of Marx, in *Herr Vogt* (1860) and Engels, *History of the Communist League* (1883). According to these, the Just leaders had accepted historical materialism, and the need to rid the organisation 'of its traditional forms and conspiratorial methods' *CM*, 159. In fact, Cabet's influence was more important, and far earlier, in the latter respect, than that of Marx; whilst it took Marx the whole of 1847 to win some form of theoretical acceptance.

57 Feb. 1847 Address, *Dokumente* I, 452.

58 These documents, together with a report of the Congress, were first published by B. Andréas (1969). They were found among the papers of J. F. Martens deposited in the University Library at Hamburg. Also in *Dokumente* I.

59 Andréas (1969), pp. 47–50.

60 *MEW* 4: 596–601. It is unclear as to how the changes in the organisational statutes between June and December reflect the struggle for influence between Marx and the old Just leaders. It *is* clear that there was such a struggle.

61 Engels to Marx, 25–6 Oct. 1847; *MEW* 27: 98. His emphases.

62 Engels to Marx, 23–4 Nov. 1847; *MEW* 27: 104. His emphases.

63 We have no evidence of what happened at the congress.

64 *MEW* 4: 596.

65 Though there is one document extant from the London leading circle to the Cologne *CC*, 18 June 1848, Nicolaievsky (1956), pp. 245–8; *Dokumente* I, 805–7.

66 Mehring (1936), p. 155; Noyes (1966), p. 118.
67 Depositions (Dec. 1853–Feb. 1854), edited in Blumenberg (1964).
68 There was no such power in the statutes.
69 See Nicolaievsky (1961); Kandel (1963).
70 Engels to Marx, 9 May 1848; *MEW* 27: 127.
71 'The Bourgeoisie and the Counter-Revolution.' Note especially the second article, 11 Dec. 1848, *MEW* 6: 106–9; *SW* I, 62–5.
72 Marx to Engels, 1, 17, 23 Aug. 1849; *MEW* 27: 139–42.
73 Marx to Weydemeyer, 19 Dec. 1849; *MEW* 27: 516; *LA*, 18.
74 Published in Nov. 1850 in *NRZ-Revue* (May–Oct. 1850).
75 Lichtheim (1961), pp. 124–6; Wolfe (1967), pp. 153–7.
76 *MEW* 7: 553–4.
77 *MEW* 7: 244–54; *SW* I, 98–108 (1950); Livingstone (1971), pp. 237–45.
78 *MEW* 7: 248; Livingstone (1971), p. 241.
79 Avineri (1968), pp. 196–7, is good on this point.
80 Avineri (1968), pp. 187–96, 218, goes too far in claiming that Marx would never use force. We must discriminate between pointless terror and the disciplined use of force. Note also the passage on 'alchemists of the revolution', published in *NRZ-Revue*, April 1850, *MEW* 7: 273–4, which is usually taken as referring to the Blanquists.
81 *MEW* 8: 412–13; Livingstone (1971), pp. 62–3.
82 *MEW* 7: 414.
83 Marx to Engels, 6 Jan. 1851; *MEW* 27: 156.
84 Marx to Engels, 19 Nov. 1852: *MEW* 28: 195.
85 Marx to Engels, 8 Sept. 1851; *MEW* 28: 128.
86 Marx to Engels, 21 June 1854; *MEW* 28: 371
87 See Tsuzuki (1967), pp. 263ff; Kapp (1972), pp. 289–97.
88 The association lasted from 1851 until 1862.
89 Marx to Weydemeyer, 1 Feb. 1859; *MEW* 29: 570; *LA*, 60. See also Marx to Kugelmann, 9 Oct. 1866; *MEW* 31: 529. Marx once applied for a post as a railway clerk. He was rejected because of his illegible handwriting. Marx to Engels, 10 Sept. 1862; *MEW* 30: 287.
90 Marx to Sorge, 4 Aug. 1874; *MEW* 33: 634; *LA*, 112.
91 Marx to Engels, 30 Apr. 1868; *MEW* 32: 75. A similar comment can be found in Marx to Engels, 20 Aug. 1862; *MEW* 30: 280. In fact, Marx was incapable of handling money matters. He once estimated that he spent between £400 and £500 a year in London, which should have been more than sufficient. Marx to Kugelmann, 17 Mar. 1868; *MEW* 32: 540.
92 Marx to Paul Lafargue, 13 Aug. 1866; *MEW* 31: 518–19. English translation in Kapp (1972), pp. 298–9.
93 This was no idle threat. Marx's displeasure ensured that the engagement between Eleanor and Lissageray, the historian of the Commune, came to nothing.
94 Marx to Weydemeyer, 27 June 1851; *MEW* 27: 560; *LA*, 23.
95 Engels to Marx, 3 Apr. 1851; *MEW* 27: 234–5.
96 Marx to Engels, 8 Dec. 1857; *MEW* 29: 225. The *Grundrisse* editors do, however, mention a manuscript, 'Geldwesen, Kreditwesen, Krisen', dated Nov. 1854–Jan. 1855. See *G*, 1077, 1044 (note).
97 Marx to Lassalle, 22 Feb. 1858; *MEW* 29: 551; *SC*, 103–4.
98 For the equalisation theory, see *G*, 338–9, 549–50; *N*, 434–5, 657–8. For

the tendency of profits to fall, see *G*, 284–9, 632–6; *N*, 380–6, 748–50. In general, see Mandel (1971), chapters 6 and 7.

99   Engels describes the contents of these manuscripts in his *Preface* to *Capital* II (Moscow, 1957), p. 2. Marx gave the manuscripts the title *Zur Kritik der Politschen Oekonomie*. They consist of 23 notebooks, paginated 1–1472, written Aug. 1861–June 1863. Notebooks 1–5 and 19–23 (pp. 1–220, 1159–1472) constitute, according to Engels, 'the first extant draft' of *Capital* I. Notebooks 16–18 (pp. 973–1158) deal with some of the topics of *Capital* III. Notebooks 6–15 (pp. 221–972), written Jan. 1862–Jan. 1863, make up the bulk of the *Theories of Surplus Value*. Engels describes these as constituting a draft of a critical history of economics, in which Marx developed 'in polemics against predecessors, most of the points later investigated separately and in their logical interconnection in the manuscripts for Books II and III'. Engels does not mention the *Grundrisse* in his review of the manuscript material available to him. Either he did not know of the *Grundrisse*, which is unlikely; or he felt that its material was superseded by the later manuscripts. We can only speculate.

100 Marx to Engels, 2 Apr. 1858; *MEW* 29: 311–18; *SC*, 104–8.

101 Marx called the three theoretical parts of *Capital* first chapters, then sections, and then books. These changes in nomenclature themselves reflect the growth in scale. We now refer to the three volumes of *Capital*. *Theories of Surplus Value* was first published by Karl Kautsky 1904–10.

102 Marx to Engels, 31 July 1865; *MEW* 31: 132. Marx is referring to Grimm's German dictionary.

103 *MEW* 3: 537; *GI*, 655; *EG*, 399.

105 *MEW.EB* 1: 467; *EPM*, 63.

104 See Marx to Weydemeyer, 1 Feb. 1859; *MEW* 29: 570; *LA*, 61.

106 See Marx to Kugelmann, 23 Feb. 1865; *MEW* 31: 451–5; *SC*, 167–71, for a summary of his views on Lassalle and German politics.

107 Marx to Weydemeyer, 29 Nov. 1864; *MEW* 31: 428; *LA*, 65; Engels to Marx, 7 Nov. 1864; *MEW* 31: 17: 'It is good that we should once more be coming into contact with people who at least represent their class.'

108 Marx to Engels, Nov. 1864; *MEW* 31: 10–16; *SC*, 146–9. The word 'profit-mongers' was cut out of the *Address*. For the minutes of the meetings leading up to the adoption of Marx's material, see *Documents* I, 35–44, and notes, 375–7. Ironically, in the same letter to Engels, Marx spoke enthusiastically of a visit by Bakunin: 'He is one of the very few people who after sixteen years has not receded but has gone on developing.' Bakunin was to become a major catalyst in the collapse of Marx's hopes for the IWA.

109 For the *Address*, see *Documents* I, 277–87.

110 Collins and Abramsky (1965), p. 46.

111 This is pointed out by Harrison (1964), p. 304. His account of the *Address* is invaluable; however, he is mistaken in speaking of the 'conspiratorial and vanguardist conception of revolution' in the *Manifesto*. This is to misread Marx's activities in the Communist League culminating in the break of September 1850.

112 In March 1850 Engels had written on the Act in Harney's *Democratic Review* I, 371–7, *MEW* 7: 226–32, claiming that it had no chance of success in face of the necessities of the capitalist economic system.

113 'In mining, engineering and in heavy industry generally, its strength was

to remain small or non-existent.' Collins and Abramsky (1965), p. 70.

114 Marx to Engels, 4 Nov. 1864; *MEW* 31: 16; *SC*, 149.

115 Marx to Kugelmann, 9 Oct. 1866; *MEW* 31: 529–30; *SC*, 183–4. For passages in official documents disclaiming any theoretical stance see *Documents* I, 346 (Aug. 1866); II, 329 (Sept. 1868); and III, 310–11 (Mar. 1869). In the last case, however, Marx had tactical considerations in mind when he wrote as he did. See Marx to Engels, 5 Mar. 1869; *MEW* 32: 273–4; *SC*, 219–21; and Engels' reply, 7 Mar. 1869; *MEW* 32: 276.

116 The major references are in *Freymond* I, 56, 297, 360, 429–30.

117 The first example after the *Address* is the *Address to Abraham Lincoln*. See *Documents* I, 50–3 (Nov. 1864); and cf. Marx to Engels, 2 Dec. 1864; *MEW* 31: 33; *CWUS*, 273.

118 Rubel (1965), p. 10.

119 *Freymond* I, 231–3.

120 *Freymond* I, 151. See also I, 323, note 16.

121 *Freymond* I, 361–71.

122 *Freymond* II, 63–74, discussion; 74–5, votes; 75–92, reports.

123 *Freymond* II, 63–5 (Tolain, Richard and Langlois), 67, 70.

124 *Documents* III, 322–4. *Report of the General Council on the Right of Inheritance* (Aug. 1869).

125 *Freymond* II, 94. Three years later Bakunin said, 'I remember the exclamation made on this occasion in my presence . . . 'Marx will be very annoyed!' And so he was. . . .' *Freymond* II, 302. Eccarius, Marx's friend, is credited with the remark.

126 *Documents* I, 286. It is significant that in the French translation '*the* great duty' becomes '*un* grand devoir'.

127 *Freymond* I, 10, 79.

128 *Documents* I, 345, 346; *Freymond* I, 32, 33, 46.

129 *Freymond* I, 234. Note also the declaration of the General Council on the eve of the French referendum, *Documents* III, 231–2, 4 May 1869.

130 *Documents* III, 268–9, GC Minutes 12 July 1870; see facsimile opposite p. 368.

131 *Documents* IV, 340–1. *Second Address . . . on the Franco-Prussian War*, 9 Sept. 1870.

132 Stafford (1971), p. 20. Lichtheim (1961), p. 105, holds a similar view. Probably about 38 of the 81 members of the Communal Assembly were also members of the IWA; most of the 38 were Proudhonists, though there were 10 Jacobins and 2 Blanquists. See the list in J.-P. Azema and M. Winock (1971), pp. 182–3. At no point could it be said that the 38, or a proportion of them, were following any official IWA policy. Neither the General Council nor Marx had any influence on the course of events.

133 *Freymond* II, 157.

134 *Freymond* II, 162. In this respect, Marx and the General Council were equally open to criticism. Thus their publication of the Geneva and Brussels resolutions (Documents III, 284–98) omitted many of the resolutions actually passed at those congresses.

135 *Documents* IV, 445.

136 *Documents* III, 268–9.

137 Marx and Engels envisaged national workers' parties on the German model. Engels to the Spanish Federal Council, 13 Feb. 1871, *MEW* 17: 288; *SC*, 259. Vaillant went much further, advocating a centralised,

disciplined 'international revolutionary workers' party' with the General Council as its 'vanguard'. Collins and Abramsky (1965), p. 230, note 1. See also Steklov (1928), p. 181.

138 *Documents* I, 290–1.

139 *Freymond* I, 54–7. These were numbers 4, concerning subscriptions, and 11: 'Each member of the International has the right to vote and is eligible.' Tolain argued that working-class representatives should themselves be manual workers. A resolution to this effect was defeated 20–25.

140 *Freymond* I, 134.

141 Administrative Resolution IV–VII of the Basle congress, in *Freymond* II, 129.

142 General Rules, Administrative Regulations II, 4–7, in *Documents* IV, 455–456. See Carr (1937), p. 366.

143 Carr (1937), p. 130; see also pp. 146, 163, 246–7, 251.

144 The full passage is given in *Freymond* I, 451.

145 A position argued at length in *Statism and Anarchy*, which Marx annotated.

146 Quoted Carr (1937), p. 343.

147 Engels was later to see this support as tactical, in that Bakunin hoped at this point to take over the General Council. *Documents* V, 512.

148 James Guillaume, quoted Carr (1937), p. 421.

149 *Documents* III, 299–301. See Marx to Engels, 15 Dec. 1868, *MEW* 32: 234. 'Mr Bakunin . . . is kind enough to want to take the workers' movement under *Russian* control.' Marx enclosed the Programme and Rules of the Alliance, with his own marginal comments. *Documents* III, 379–83.

150 *Documents* III, 310–11. Marx drafted the reply with the following tactical considerations in mind: 'Bakunin thinks: if we approve his "radical programme" he can make a big noise about this and compromise us, even if only just a little. If we declare ourselves against it we shall be designated as counter-revolutionaries. Moreover: if we admit them he will see to it that he is supported by some of the riff-raff at the Congress in Basle. . . .' Marx to Engels, 5 Mar. 1869, *MEW* 32: 273; *SC*, 219–21.

151 Bakunin to Herzen, 28 Oct. 1869, quoted Carr (1937), pp. 370–1.

152 *MEW* 16: 409–20. Dated *c.* 28 Mar. 1870. At this point Marx had no real evidence for his interpretation, and was beginning to betray a tendency to regard the IWA as his personal organisation.

153 The reasoning being that the 21 delegates represented 600 members; while the 18 delegates represented 2,000. See Jung in GC Minutes 19 Apr. 1870, in *Documents* III, 226. The report of the pro-General Council Fédération Romande committee to the London conference (dated 11 Sept. 1871) gives the figures as: Majority, 22 delegates, 13 sections, 628 members; Minority, 18 delegates, 22 sections, 1,394 members. See Molnar (1963), Annexe I, pp. 199–204.

154 *Documents* III, 368, 412. Resolution dated 29 June 1870.

155 Sonvilliers Circular, 12 Nov. 1871, in *Freymond* II, 260–5, espec. 263.

156 *Freymond* II, 265.

157 Mar. 1872. *Documents* V, 356–409; *Freymond* II, 266–96.

158 Collins (1964), pp. 32–3.

159 See Engels' *Report on the Alliance* . . . in *Documents* V, 463–76, 505–18, espec. 468, 510–11 (Sept. 1872). He had hard evidence for only certain of the Spanish sections, which he illegitimately generalised as evidence for the IWA as a whole.

160   For the report, see Gerth (1958), pp. 225–7; *Freymond* II, 365. A compila-
tion of contradictory parts, the report, which had found 'insufficient
evidence' for the continued existence of the Alliance, nevertheless recom-
mended the expulsion of Bakunin, Guillaume and Schwitzguebel because
they still belonged to it. Five Spanish delegates were spared, though the
evidence against them was no less (and no more) than against those con-
victed. The report adds weight to the picture of the authoritarian Marx.
The reason for its recommendations lay in an 'in the wings' manœuvre by
Marx. Bakunin had been advanced 300 roubles for a translation of *Capital*.
He soon tired of the job. Unknown to him, Nechaev (soon to become
notorious for the Ivanov murder) wrote to the publisher threatening
reprisals if he should ask for his money back. Marx heard of it, procured
the letter from Danielson, and read it confidentially to the committee. See
Marx to Danielson, 15 Aug. 1872, 12 Dec. 1872, *MEW* 33: 516. 548. For
Nechaev's letter, see Nicolaievsky and Maenchen-Helfen (1973), pp.
373–4.

161   Engels to Bebel, 20 June 1872; *MEW* 33: 591; *SC*, 283–5.

162   See Engels' speech, in Gerth (1958), pp. 212–14.

163   Marx to César de Paepe, 28 May 1872; *MEW* 33: 479–80; to Danielson,
p. 477.

164   Marx had suggested Brussels as a new seat in July 1870. *Documents* III,
256–7, 261, 266–8.

165   Steklov (1928), p. 261.

166   Marx to Kwasniewski, 29 Sept. 1871; *MEW* 33: 287. Also Engels to
Cuno, 7–8 May 1872; *MEW* 33: 461. On this issue, see Morgan (1965),
passim.

167   'The working class would have to conquer the right to emancipate themselves on the battlefield. The task of the International was to organise and
combine the forces of labour for the coming struggle.' New York *World*,
15 Oct. 1871, reporting Marx's speech of 26 Sept. 1871. In full in Molnar
(1963), p. 238.

168   Rubel (1965), p. 21.

169   Marx to Engels, 9 Apr. 1863; *MEW* 30: 343; *SC*, 140–1.

170   Marx to Lassalle, 22 Feb. 1858; *MEW* 29: 551; *SC*, 103.

171   Marx to Danielson, 10 Apr. 1879; *MEW* 34: 370–2; *SC*, 315–17.

172   Marx to Kugelmann, 29 Nov. 1869; *MEW* 32, 637; *SC*, 229; Marx to
Engels, 10 Feb. 1870; *MEW* 32: 437; Marx to S. Meyer, 21 Jan. 1871;
MEW 33: 173; *SC*, 256.

173   Reported by Paul Lafargue in *Reminiscences*, p. 93.

174   Engels to Marx, 27 Apr. 1867; *MEW* 31: 292.

175   Engels to Bebel, 30 Aug. 1883; *MEW* 36: 56.

176   Engels to Danielson, 13 Nov. 1885; *MEW* 36: 385; *SC*, 388–9.

177   But we should note the marginal notes written by Marx on Adolph
Wagner's *Textbook of Political Economy* in 1879, which are important for
a re-statement of his methodological principles in *Capital*.

178   *MEW* 19: 230–7. The original English version may be found in T. B.
Bottomore and M. Rubel (eds.), *Karl Marx: Selected Writings in Sociology
and Social Philosophy* (London, 1956), pp. 204–12.

179   Engels to Bernstein, 2–3 Nov. 1882; *MEW* 35: 388; also to Schmidt, Aug.
1890; *MEW* 37: 436; *SC*, 415.

180   'Do not let any political considerations stop you, as one London news-

paper is as bad as another and the idea is to get the widest publicity,' wrote Marx to Engels 20 June 1866; *MEW* 31; 288; *SC*, 178. This attitude helps to account for the otherwise bizarre relationships with the Russophobe David Urquhart, and the Tory agent Maltman Barry, who spent many years seeking a Tory alliance with the working class.

181   Marx to Engels, 4 Aug. 1874; *MEW* 33: 108. See Marx to Engels, 20 Mar. 1869; *MEW* 32: 283.

182   Quoted in Kapp (1972), pp. 173–4.

183   On this episode, see F. Harrison, *Autobiographic Memoirs* (2 vols, London, 1911), II, 33–4; Carr (1937), pp. 284–5. There are relevant letters in *MEW* 33: Marx to Engels 30 Aug. 1873, Engels to Marx 3 Sept. 1873, 5 Dec. 1873, pp. 89, 90–1, 97; and Marx to George Moore 26 Mar. 1874, 28 Mar. 1874, pp. 620–1.

184   Marx to Engels, 11 Nov. 1882; *MEW* 35: 110.

185   Sir M. E. Grant-Duff, *Notes from a Diary 1873–81* (London, 1898), II, 103–6.

186   A full, though not complete, list of periodicals and contributions can be found in the *Marx-Engels Verzeichnis: Werke, Schriften, Artikel* (Berlin, Dietz Verlag, 1966), pp. 283–319.

187   See M. Rubel, *Bibliographie des œuvres de Karl Marx* (Paris, 1956), no. 879, pp. 225–7, for a general account of the notebooks. Summaries of notes and extracts 1839–48 are given in *MEGA* I, 1, 2, pp. 107–36 (Berlin, Bonn, Kreuznach); *MEGA*, I, 3, pp. 411–583 (Paris); *MEGA* I, 6, pp. 597–618 (Brussels and Manchester). Two pieces by M. Rubel (1957 and 1960) give an account of the notebooks 1840–56.

188   *TSV* and *GI* are examples. There are two quite different arrangements of *TSV*, the first by Kautsky, the second by the Institute of Marxism-Leninism in Moscow. Owing to the state of the manuscript, different arrangements of Part I of *GI* have been proposed.

189   Other candidates have included the *Critique* (Avineri) and Marx's marginal notes on Adolph Wagner's *Lehrbuch* (Althusser). No doubt *Herr Vogt* will soon be proposed.

190   Marx to A. Cluss, 15 Sept. 1853; *MEW* 28: 592. However, the articles embody a substantial amount of work. There has been little systematic examination of Marx's journalistic output after 1852.

191   The claim that 'we abandoned the manuscript to the growing criticism of the mice all the more willingly since we had achieved our main purpose – self-clarification' is a later gloss by Marx which does not stand up to scrutiny so far as *GI* is concerned. *CPE: Preface*, p. 22.

192   Engels to Gurvitsch, 27 May 1893; *MEW* 39: 75. See also Engels to Schmidt, 5 Aug. 1890; *MEW* 31: 436; *SC* 416.

FOOTNOTES TO PART II

1   Marx himself said of scientific socialism that it was 'used only in opposition to utopian socialism which tries to saddle the people with new phantasmagorias, instead of confining its science to the recognition of the social movement made by the people itself'. *MEW* 18: 636. Marginal notes on Bakunin's *Statism and Anarchy*.

2   Baron (1963), p. 287.

3   *MEW* 3: 6; *EG*, 402 (early 1845).

4   *MEW* 1: 378; *EG*, 250. Note the much later statement: 'My *analytic* method does not proceed from Man, but from the economically given social period.' *MEW* 19: 371; *Notes on Adolph Wagner's Lehrbuch (c.* 1880), p. 52.

5   For Feuerbach, see Kamenka (1970); for his relation to Marx, McLellan (1969), pp. 85–116. Despite Marx's use of Feuerbachian concepts, such as species or generic being (*Gattungswesen*) in the *EPM*, it is clear that he has already a historical conception of human nature.

6   *MEW* 23: 184; *Cap.* I, 150. The following suggests plasticity even in physical human nature: 'Even differences that have arisen naturally within the species, such as racial differences, etc. . . . can and must be abolished in the course of human development.' *MEW* 3: 410; *GI*, 467.

7   Engels to Lavrov, 12 Nov. 1875; *MEW* 34: 169; *SC*, 303. See also *MEW* 3: 21 *GI*, 31.

8   *MEW.EB* 1: 517; *EPM*, 76; *MEW* 23: 194, 346; *Cap.* I, 159, 316; *MEW. EB* 1: 543; *EPM*, 111; *MEW* 3: 30; *GI*, 42.

9   *MEW* 23: 193; *Cap.* I, 157.

10   *MEW* 23: 346; *Cap.* I, 316. This passage should be considered by those who see 'Man the toolmaker' as *the* definition of man by Marx.

11   *MEW.EB* 1: 579; *EPM*, 158, cf. *MEW* 3: 18, *GI*, 28.

12   *MEW* 23: 393; *Cap.* I, 367 (note).

13   *MEW.EB* 1: 543, 546; see also 570, 574, 583–4; *EPM*, 111, 113, 146, 151–2, 164–5.

14   *MEW* 23: 535; *Cap.* I, 521.

15   *MEW* 13: 640; *CPE*, 215 (Introduction).

16   *MEW* 23: 181; *Cap.* I, 145.

17   *G*, 206; *N*, 298; also *G*, 208; *N*, 301.

18   *MEW* 23: 198; *Cap.* I, 163–4. See also *MEW* 25: 798, 828; *Cap.* III, 771, 799.

19   *G*, 266, 270; *N*, 361, 364.

20   *G*, 265; *N*, 360.

21   'It is not the tropics with their luxurious vegetation but the temperate zone, that is the mother country of capital. . . .' *MEW* 23: 536–7; *Cap.* I, 522–3, see also 535, 521; and *TSV* II, 407.

22   *G*, 157; *N*, 245. Marx tends to use *need* and *want* interchangeably.

23   *G*, 426; *N*, 528.

24   *MEW* 3: 28; *GI*, 39.

25   *MEW* 13: 624; *CPE*, 197 (Introduction).

26   *MEW* 23: 185; *Cap.* I, 150.

27   *MEW* 23: 249; *Cap.* I, 218.

28 For the distinction between individual and productive consumption, see also *MEW* 23: 198; *Cap.* I, 163. Bober (1962), pp. 177–8, notes that surplus value is not unique to capitalism. But for Marx 'the production of surplus value . . . is the specific end and aim, the sum and substance, of capitalist production'. *MEW* 23: 315; *Cap.* I, 284.
29 *MEW* 4: 467; *CM*, 94.
30 *G*, 231: *N*, 325.
31 *G*, 425–6; *N*, 527.
32 *MEW* 3: 44; *GI*, 58.
33 Schmidt (1971), p. 80. He attributes the use to Moleschott's influence.
34 *MEW* 23: 528; *Cap.* I, 513. Marx had great admiration for the work of J. von Leibig (1803–73), who had been the first to show that soil exhaustion occurred because the crops had extracted substances from the soil which were not returned into it.
35 *MEW* 13: 616; *CPE*, 189 (Introduction).
36 *MEW* 13: 617; *CPE*, 190 (Introduction).
37 *MEW* 13: 619; *CPE*, 192 (Introduction).
38 *MEW* 2: 98; *HF*, 125 (written by Engels). See *MEW* 3: 45, 71–2; *GI*, 59, 87–8.
39 *G*, 176; *N*, 265.
40 *G*, 111; *N*, 196–7.
41 *MEW* 3: 30; *GI*, 42. 'All relations can be expressed in language only in the form of concepts.' *MEW* 3: 347; *GI*, 396. 'Ideas do not exist separately from language.' *G*, 80; *N*, 163.
42 *G*, 61; *N*, 143.
43 *G*, 82; *N*, 164–5.
44 *G*, 366–7; *N*, 463.
45 Schmidt (1971), p. 63.
46 Marx to Schweitzer, 24 Jan. 1865; *MEW* 16: 28; *SC*, 154. We shall take up this theme when considering Marx's critique of political economy.
47 Korsch (1938), p. 55 (his emphasis).
48 This is stated explicitly in *MEW* 23: 96; *Cap.* I, 54 (note).
49 *G*, 376; *N*, 472.
50 'Apparently' because in fact Marx emphasises 'the illusion of the "purely personal relations" of feudal times'. *G*, 82; *N*, 165.
51 *G*, 389; *N*, 489.
52 *MEW* 13: 638; *CPE*, 213.
53 *G*, 375–414; *N*, 471–514.
54 *G*, 389; *N*, 489.
55 Note also *MEW* 3: 65–6; *GI*, 80-1.
56 *MEW* 13: 638; *CPE*, 213.
57 *G*, 365; *N*, 460–1. See also *MEW* 13: 636; *CPE*, 211: 'The anatomy of man is a key to the anatomy of the ape.'
58 *MEW* 13: 8–9; *CPE*, 20–2. Earlier versions of the passage may be found in *MEW* 3: 38, 69–70; *GI*, 50, 85–6; and *MEW* 6: 408; *WLC*, 28.
59 Jordan (1971), p. 37, argues that the purely methodological position of the *German Ideology* has been replaced in the *Preface* by 'a rigid metaphysical theory of historical causation'. I prefer to assume that Marx meant what he said when he spoke of 'the guiding thread of my studies'.
60 Prinz (1969).
61 Marx also talks of 'feudal economic structure' and 'feudal society', etc.

This is the same distinction, used of a group of similar societies. See *MEW* 3: 72; *GI*, 88–9.

62 *MEW* 23: 96 (note 33); *Cap.* I, 54 (note).
63 *MEW* 3: 27; *GI*, 38.
64 *MEW* 23: 194; *Cap.* I, 158.
65 *MEW* 23: 195; *Cap.* I, 160.
66 *MEW* 23: 196; *Cap.* I, 160–1.
67 *MEW* 23: 197; *Cap.* I, 162.
68 *MEW* 4: 181; *PP*, 174.
69 *MEW* 23: 506; *Cap.* I, 487.
70 *MEW* 23: 390; *Cap.* I, 363.
71 *MEW* 23: 512; *Cap.* I, 494.
72 A terminology used by Cohen (1971), pp. 126–7. He lists 10 ownership and 5 work relations. 'It is . . . required to show sufficient continuity between them to justify their common appellation "production relations".' This is indeed the crucial question.
73 *MEW* 13: 615; *CPE*, 188.
74 Fleischer (1973), p. 109, points out that the strongest relationship is posited of the most indefinite statement of the three, which is a near-tautology.
75 But Marx also talks of A 'naturally corresponding' with B.
76 In the *Introduction* to the *CPE*, the following terms are also used: *knüpfen* (bound up with), *erzeugen* (create) and *produzieren* (produce).
77 The main *GI* passages are as follows: *MEW* 3: 21, 22, 25, 30, 37–8, 43, 72; *GI*, 32, 36, 41, 49–50, 57, 88, 93. There are sentences of the form 'A conditions (32), determines (32), conditions and determines (93), corresponds with (88), is connected with (36), is combined with (41) B.' Two sentences emphasise a reciprocal action of A and B (49–50, 57). The multiple usages are obscured in the English translation by the use of *determine* to translate *bedingen* (condition), e.g., *GI*, 32, 41, 57.
78 *MEW* 13: 619–20; *CPE*, 192–3.
79 *MEW* 13: 626; *CPE*, 199.
80 *MEW* 13: 626–9; *CPE*, 199–203.
81 *MEW* 13: 630–1; *CPE*, 204–5.
82 *MEW* 13: 640; *CPE*, 215.
83 *G*, 157; *N*, 245–6. Probably written two months after the *Introduction* passage.
84 *MEW* 13: 640–2; *CPE*, 215–17. Kamenka (1972), p. 135, makes some useful comments.
85 ibid.
86 Nearly, because it is logically possible for the conqueror to decide on a totally new mode of production. We can agree with Marx that this is not very likely.
87 *MEW* 13: 629; *CPE*, 203.
88 Note the brilliant critique in Habermas (1972), pp. 326–9.
89 A point made neatly by Plamenatz (1963), II, 278, who also uses the formulas above to point the dilemma, pp. 281–2.
90 *MEW* 23: 96; *Cap.* I, 54 (note).
91 *MEW* 23: 231; *Cap.* I, 200.
92 For a version of this approach see Hook (1955), pp. 21–2.
93 *MEW* 25: 799–800; *Cap.* III, 772.

94 Acton (1955), p. 137. His unsympathetic account is modified in Acton (1967), pp. 45–57.
95 Acton quotes *MEW* 23: 194; *Cap.* I, 159, without noticing *MEW* 23: 346; *Cap.* I, 316, quoted above.
96 *MEW* 3: 21; *GI*, 32.
97 *MEW* 23: 194–5, 393; *Cap.* I, 159, 367. Also *MEW* 4: 130; *PP*, 109. Acton (1967), p. 64.
98 *MEW* 23: 315, 391, 404–5; *Cap.* I, 284–5, 366, 379–80. Note that in all three examples, which are typical, the term *mode of production* is employed to designate the stage of Manufacture and the stage of Modern Industry (both *within* the capitalist epoch) as distinguishable modes of production.
99 *MEW* 23: 419; *Cap.* I, 394.
100 *MEW* 23: 444; *Cap.* I, 422.
101 *MEW* 23: 320; *Cap.* I, 288.
102 *MEW* 23: 779; *Cap.* I, 776. Also G, 407, N, 507. Factory legislation, Marx noted, reacted back on production: it accelerated 'the concentration of capital and the exclusive predominance of the factory system'. *MEW* 23: 526; *Cap.* I, 511.
103 *MEW* 25: 800; *Cap.* III, 772.
104. Jordan (1971), p. 33, quotes Marx as saying that any alteration in the mode of production 'except in trivial matters, is solely owing to a revolution in the instruments of labour' (*MEW* 23: 385; *Cap.* I, 358). But it is quite clear that this statement refers to 'the division of labour peculiar to Manufacture', and *not* to a mode of production, in whatever sense.
105 *MEW* 23: 779; Cap. I, 776. See also Engels, in letters to Schmidt, 27 Oct. 1890, *MEW* 37: 493; *SC*, 424, and to Borgius, 25 Jan. 1894, *MEW* 39: 206; *SC*, 467. Starkenburg was formerly thought to be the recipient of the letter to Borgius, *MEW* 39: 580, note 245.
106 *MEW* 3: 23–4; *GI*, 33–4.
107 G, 375–413, N, 471–514. Hobsbawm (1964), pp. 27–59, gives a good account of the development of Marx's thinking in these matters.
108 Marx to Engels, 14 Mar. 1868; *MEW* 32: 42; Hobsbawm (1964), p. 139.
109 *MEW* 23: 15–16; *Cap.* I, xvii, xviii–xix.
110 *MEW* 23: 26; *Cap.* I, xxvi–xxviii.
111 Fleischer (1973), pp. 109–21, has a useful discussion.
112 *MEW* 23: 15; *Cap.* I, xvii.
113 In 1843–4 Marx used the concept of dialectical necessity to explain historical developments, e.g. *MEW* 1: 367–70; *EG*, 238–41 (*JQ*); *MEW.EB* 1: 529; *EPM*, 126–7. There is a useful analysis of the *JQ* example by Maguire (1972), pp. 25–6. Howard (1972) argues that this usage is central to Marx throughout his work. Thus, of the development from feudalism into capitalism, he says: 'The "necessity" in this process is the logical necessity revealed by the dialectical process' (p. 148). But it is clear that Marx has abandoned this peculiar view by 1846. See *MEW* 3: 229, 287, 445; *GI*, 267, 331, 504–5.
114 G, 716; *N*, 831.
115 Marx to Annenkov, 28 Dec. 1846; *MEW* 27: 452; *SC*, 35. Also *MEW* 8: 115; *EB*, 15.
116 Quoted Walicki (1969), p. 46. On Mikhailovsky, see Billington (1958).
117 This is quoted by Marx from the French edition of *Capital* I (Paris, 1875), p. 315. The text differs from that in the German edition, on which the

English translation is based: 'The history of this expropriation, in different countries, assumes different aspects, and runs through its various phases in different orders of succession, and at different periods. In England alone . . . has it the classical form.' *MEW* 23: 744; *Cap.* I, 739. This statement could be read as applying to all countries: the French edition limits it to Western Europe. But clearly no set pattern is indicated in either version.

118 Marx in reply to *Notes of the Fatherland*, Nov. 1877, *MEW* 19: 108–12; *SC*, 312–13.
119 Zasulich to Marx, 16 Feb. 1881, in Blackstock and Hoselitz (1952), pp. 276–7.
120 Marx to Zasulich, 8 Mar. 1881; *MEW* 19: 242–3; *SC*, 339–40. In a letter of 1884, Engels enclosed Marx's letter of 1877. Engels to Zasulich 6 Mar. 1884, *MEW* 36: 121, *SC*, 370. Neither the 1877 nor the 1881 letter was published by the Russian Marxists in Geneva. The 1877 letter first appeared in a Populist journal in Geneva in 1886; the 1881 letter was first published in 1924 by Nicolaievsky. See Walicki (1969), pp. 186–8.
121 *MEW* 19: 384–406 contains 3 of the 4 drafts. First published by Riazanov in 1927. A conflated version in Blackstock and Hoselitz (1952), pp. 218–26.
122 *MEW* 19: 404–5; Blackstock and Hoselitz (1952), p. 221.
123 *MEW* 19: 400; Blackstock and Hoselitz (1952), p. 224.
124 *MEW* 19: 296; *CM*, 132.
125 *MEW* 3: 338; *GI*, 386; see also 66, 81.
126 *G*, 386, *N*, 486. Indeed, our analysis brings us close to Hobsbawm (1964), p. 34, who suggests that we should see the stages of the *Preface* as a set of 'analytical, though not chronological, stages'.
127 *MEW* 23: 512; *Cap.* I, 494.
128 *MEW* 23: 16; *Cap.* I, xx.
129 *MEW* 23: 791; *Cap.* I, 789.
130 *MEW* 23: 743; *Cap.* I, 738.
131 *G*, 168; *N*, 256–7, suggests that Marx was aware of this.
132 See the discussions in Sweezy (ed.) (1954); and Dobb (1967). Sweezy used Pirenne's views in elaborating his own explanation, but his views were contested on methodological grounds.
133 *MEW* 25: 809; *Cap.* III, 781. Indeed, Hobsbawm (1964), p. 46, feels that Sweezy's view is the nearest approximation to Marx's own view.
134 *G*, 379, 393; *N*, 476, 494.
135 *G*, 375–85; *N*, 472–85.
136 Marx to Sorge, 27 Sept. 1877; *MEW* 34: 296; *SC*, 308.
137 For two useful discussions of this explanation, see Runkle (1963–4); Genovese (1958).
138 Marx to Engels, 2 and 14 June 1853; Engels to Marx, 6 June 1853; *MEW* 28: 251–4, 259–61, 267–9; *SC*, 80–6.
139 'Revolution in China and Europe', *NYDT* 14 June 1853; and 'The British Rule in India', *NYDT* 25 June 1853; *On Colonialism*, pp. 21, 40.
140 *MEW* 23: 379; *Cap.* I, 352.
141 'Chinese Affairs', *Die Presse* 7 July 1862; Avineri (ed.) (1968), pp. 418–20; *MEW* 15: 514–16.
142 'The Future Results of the British Rule in India', *NYDT* 8 Aug. 1853; *On Colonialism*, p. 82.
143 *MEW* 25: 346, 799; *Cap.* III, 328, 771–2.

144 *MEW* 13: 21; *CPE*, 33.
145 *G*, 377; *N*, 473. For discussion of the Asiatic mode, see Mandel (1971); Lichtheim (1967); and Avineri (ed.) (1968).
146 *MEW* 18: 556–7; Blackstock and Hoselitz (1952), pp. 205–13, 'Soziales aus Russland', in *Volksstaat*, 16, 18 and 21 Apr. 1875. In 1894 Engels reiterated his views: 'The initiative for . . . a higher form of communal property . . . can only originate, not in the [village] community itself, but solely among the industrial proletariat of the West. . . .' *MEW* 22: 426–7; Blackstock and Hoselitz (1952), pp. 232–3; see also Engels to Danielson, 17 Oct. 1893; *MEW* 39: 148–50; *SC*, 463.
147 Engels to Ernst, 5 June 1890; to Schmidt, 5 Aug. 1890; *MEW* 37: 411, 436; *SC*, 413, 415; to Sombart 11 Mar. 1895; *MEW* 39: 427–9; *SC*, 479–81.
148 Engels to Bloch, 21–2 Sept. 1890; to Schmidt, 27 Oct. 1890; *MEW* 37: 463–5, 488–95; *SC*, 417–24; to Mehring, 14 July 1893; to Borgius, 25 Jan. 1894; *MEW* 39: 96–100, 205; *SC*, 459–60, 466.
149 *MEW* 4: 462; *CM*, 89. Marx later became convinced that there had been many forms of non-class primitive communalism, out of which, for reasons which remain obscure, 'society begins to be differentiated into separate and finally antagonistic classes' (Engels' note to the 1888 edn). See Krader (1973).
150 *MEW* 4: 91–2; *PP*, 61.
151 Aron (1965), p. 162; Jordan (1971), p. 29.
152 *MEW* 25: 892–3; *Cap.* III, 862–3. For one attempt to complete it see Ollman (1967–8). Aron (1965), p. 161, is wrong to take Marx's preliminary comments as an answer.
153 The development of share-holding, unit trusts, mutual insurance and pension funds greatly complicates the task of making the distinction.
154 *MEW* 8: 198; *EB*, 124.
155 *MEW* 4: 472; *CM*, 100; *MEW* 7: 26; *CSF*, 50; *MEW* 8: 160–1; *EB*, 75.
156 *MEW* 7: 19–20; *CSF*, 42–3.
157 *MEW* 4: 141; *PP*, 123; *MEW* 8: 172, 185; *EB*, 90, 107; *MEW* 3: 316; *GI*, 363.
158 *MEW* 7: 79; *CSF*, 113; *TSV* III, 123. See also *MEW* 6: 195–6.
159 *MEW* 8: 182–4; *EB*, 103–6.
160 *MEW* 4: 471–2; *CM*, 99.
161 *MEW* 25: 614; *Cap.* III, 587; *G*, 81; *N*, 164.
162 *MEW* 8: 122–3; *EB*, 25.
163 *MEW* 4: 480; *CM*, 109.
164 See the discussion in Plamenatz (1970), pp. 50ff.
165 Engels to Schmidt, 27 Oct. 1890; *MEW* 37: 490; *SC*, 421.
166 *MEW* 3: 26; *GI*, 37.
167 *MEW* 3: 27; *GI*, 38. This is a favourite metaphor.
168 *MEW* 23: 765; *Cap.* I, 761.
169 *MEW* 3: 46; *GI*, 60–1.
170 *MEW* 25: 218–19; *Cap.* III, 205.
171 *MEW* 3: 212–13; *GI*, 249, also 257–9, 347, 432; 297–9, 396, 491–2.
172 *TSV* III, 485.
173 *MEW* 25: 825; *Cap.* III, 797.
174 *MEW* 23: 95; *Cap.* I, 53 (note). Smith and Ricardo are the two major classical economists.

175 *TSV* I, 291–2.
176 *TSV* II, 117–18.
177 *TSV* II, 119.
178 *TSV* II, 165.
179 *TSV* II, 166.
180 For examples, see *TSV* II, 497–8, 525.
181 For examples, see *TSV* II, 236–40 (rent); III, 527–34 (interest).
182 *TSV* II, 18; III, 500–1.
183 *TSV* III, 501.
184 *TSV* II, 238–40; 157.
185 *TSV* III, 399–449.
186 *TSV* III, 258–60.
187 *MEW* 23: 21; *Cap.* I, xxiii. Vulgar economists included James Mill, MacCulloch, Torrens and Senior. Marx excluded Jones and J. S. Mill from the list, though both wrote well after 1830. See *TSV* III, 429. Despite his criticisms of J. S. Mill, Marx thought it unjust to place him with 'the herd of vulgar economic apologists'. *MEW* 23: 638; *Cap.* I, 623 (note).
188 *TSV* III, 84–5.
189 *TSV* III, 501–2,453.
190 *MEW* 23: 471; *Cap.* I, 449.
191 *MEW.EB* 1: 561; *EPM*, 163, also 557, 159.
192 *G*, 76; *N*, 158.
193 *MEW.EB* 1: 551; *EPM*, 152.
194 *MEW.EB* 1: 446; *EG*, 266.
195 See A. Ferguson, *An Essay on the History of Civil Society* (1767), Book IV, ss. I and 2 (ed. Forbes 1966), pp. 182–6. Marx quotes these passages in *MEW* 4: 130–1; *PP*, 129–30; and *MEW* 23: 137, 375, 382, 383–4; *Cap.* I, 99, 347, 355–6. Marx considered Ferguson 'the master' of Adam Smith, but in fact the reverse was the case. Smith had arrived at his conclusions well before 1767: see *Early Draft* in Scott (1937), pp. 325–8; and *Lectures* (ed. Cannon 1896), pp. 161–72 (corresponding with *Wealth of Nations*, Book I, Chapters 1–3), and 255–9 (corresponding with *Wealth of Nations*, Book V, Chap. 1). Ferguson's *Essay* was published in German in 1772, whereas the *Wealth of Nations* (1776) was not really known until the second German translation in 1794. See Hasek (1925), pp. 64–8. Both Herder and Schiller read and admired Ferguson's work.
196 *MEW* 4: 146; *PP*, 129. See Scott (1937), pp. 341–4; *Lectures* (ed. Cannon 1896), p. 170; *Wealth of Nations*, Book 1, Chap. 1.
197 *MEW* 4: 151; *PP*, 135.
198 *MEW* 3: 22, 32, 33, 422; *GI*, 32–3, 44, 45, 480.
199 He gives no reasons. Engels later explained that some took advantage of their social (and especially political) functions and seized economic power.
200 *MEW* 3: 50; *GI*, 64–5.
201 *MEW* 23: 349; *Cap.* I, 319.
202 *MEW* 23: 358; *Cap.* I, 329.
203 *MEW* 23: 372; *Cap.* I, 344.
204 *MEW* 23: 375; *Cap.* I, 347.
205 *MEW* 23: 377; *Cap.* I, 349.
206 *MEW* 23: 384; *Cap.* I, 357.
207 *MEW* 23: 386; *Cap.* I, 359.

208 *MEW* 23: 390; *Cap.* I, 363.
209 *MEW* 23; 391; *Cap.* I, 366.
210 *MEW* 23: 442; *Cap.* I, 419.
211 *MEW* 23: 455; *Cap.* I, 432.
212 *MEW* 23: 469; *Cap.* I, 447.
213 *MEW* 25: 310–11; *Cap.* I, 294–5.
214 *MEW* 23: 475; *Cap.* I, 454. Cf. note 1: 'In their present form (1866) the states must still be considered a European colony.'
215 *G*, 80, *N*, 163. The same basic points about exchange are made in both the *Grundrisse* and *Capital* I, but the analysis is more extensive in the former.
216 *G*, 114, *N*, 200.
217 *G*. 75, *N*, 157.
218 *G*. 155, *N*, 243.
219 *MEW* 1: 366; *EG*, 236–7.
220 *G*, 156, *N*, 245.
221 *G*. 159–60, *N*, 247–8.
222 *MEW* 23: 189–90; *Cap.* I, 155.
223 *G*, 200; *N*, 289.
224 *G*, 214; *N*, 307.
225 *MEW.EB* 1: 451; *EG*, 272 (*Notes on James Mill*).
226 Marx had little to say about alienation in other forms of society. But it is clear that in all societies involving division of labour, private property and classes, there will be *some* form of alienation.
227 *MEW.EB* 1: 521; *EPM*, 118.
228 *MEW.EB* 1: 537; *EPM*, 136.
229 There are two full English translations, by Bottomore (1963) and Milligan (1959), in the version edited by D. J. Struik. The latter is a more precise translation. For accounts of the *EPM*, see McLellan (1970), and Maguire (1972), who also suggests some emendations and additions to Bottomore's translation (pp. 148–52). Of the four manuscripts, only three are translated. The fourth may be found in Karl Marx: *Frühe Schriften* I (*ed.* Lieber and Furth), pp. 958–64.
230 See Milligan's useful remarks, *EPM*, 58; also Schacht (1972), Chap. 1.
231 *MEW* 1: 376; *EG*, 248.
232 *MEW.EB* 1: 579–80; *EPM*, 183.
233 Because of these and related complexities, there is no fixity of usage among the English translations, as the following table shows:

	Entäusserung	*Entfremdung*
Bottomore	alienation	alienation
Milligan	alienation; or externalisation	estrangement
Easton and Guddart, McLellan	externalisation	alienation

In the *Grundrisse*, Marx occasionally uses the term *Fremdartigkeit*.
234 *MEW.EB* 1: 510; *EPM*, 106.
235 *MEW.EB* 1: 474; *EPM*, 68.
236 *MEW.EB* 1: 511; *EPM*, 107. Tucker (1961) mistranslates: 'The only wheels that set political economy in motion . . .', and goes on to claim that for Marx it is the passion of greed that is the 'inhuman force' that dominates human existence (pp. 138–9). This view reflects a complete mis-

understanding of what Marx is saying. For a general criticism of Tucker, see Ryan (1965). In the *Grundrisse* Marx says that 'greed itself is the product of a definite social development, not *natural*, as opposed to historical'. *G*, 134; *N*, 222–3.

237   *MEW.EB* 1: 512; *EPM*, 108.
238   *MEW.EB* 1: 512; *EPM*, 108.
239   *MEW.EB* 1: 515; *EPM*, 111.
240   *MEW.EB* 1: 514; *EPM*, 111.
241   *MEW.EB* 1: 557; *EPM*, 159.
242   *MEW.EB* 1: 520; *EPM*, 117.
243   *MEW.EB* 1: 537; *EPM*, 136.
244   *MEW.EB* 1: 522; *EPM*, 119.
245   *MEW* 2: 37; *HF*, 51.
246   *MEW.EB* 1: 554; *EPM*, 156.
247   *G*, 715–16; *N*, 831.
248   For passages where alienation is employed in these three senses, see *MEW* 3: 32, 34, 37, 212, 227–8, 245–6, 276, 287, 392 (*GI*); *Grundrisse*, 65, 78, 80, 111, 214, 374, 387, 413–15, 514–15, 439–40, 449, 565–6, 584, 586, 715–17; *MEW* 26: 1; 53, 64, 321 (*TSV* I); *TSV* II, 347, 416, 504; *TSV* III, 245, 251, 255, 256, 264, 271, 272, 293, 296, 314, 495, 530; *MEW* 23: 445, 596, 635, 674 (*Cap*. I); *MEW* 24: 37 (*Cap*. II); *MEW* 25: 95, 274, 802, 453 (*Cap*. III).
        Only the main passages are listed. Marx dropped neither the term, nor its uses as noted above, in his mature work, though the term itself appears to be used less frequently in *Capital* than in the *Grundrisse*.
249   *MEW* 3: 69, 206, 217–18, 475–6; *GI*, 84–5, 242, 254, 536–7.
250   *MEW* 3: 217–18; *GI*, 254. Marx had criticised Feuerbach's lack of concern with politics as early as March 1843. But he remained known as a Feuerbachian. It was the challenge of Max Stirner which decided Marx and Engels 'to settle accounts with our former philosophical conscience'. See McLellan (1969), pp. 101–16, 219–32; Lobkowicz in Adelmann (ed.) 1969.
251   *MEW* 3: 475–6; *GI*, 536–7.
252   *MEW.EB* 1: 574; *EPM*, 151. Cf. *MEW* 23: 192; *Cap*. I, 157. See O'Malley (1966).
253   Note *MEW* 3: 38; *GI*, 50. As we have seen, Marx always distinguished between 'human nature in general' and 'human nature as modified in each historical epoch'. The distinction is made in the context of a critique of Bentham who, according to Marx, thought the English shopkeeper to be the normal man. 'Whatever is useful to this queer normal man, and to his world, is absolutely useful. This yardstick he applies to past, present and future.' But what is considered 'useful' varies widely over space and time. *MEW* 23: 636–7; *Cap*. I, 622.
254   *MEW* 23: 742; *Cap*. I, 737.
255   *MEW* 23: 789–91; *Cap*. I, 786–90.
256   *MEW* 23: 779; *Cap*. I, 776.
257   *MEW* 23: 621; *Cap*. I, 606.
258   *MEW* 23: 54; *Cap*. I, 6–7.
259   *MEW* 23: 59; *Cap*. I, 12.
260   *MEW* 23: 55; *Cap*. I, 8.
261   Marx's early vision of the creativity of human labour is reduced here to a definition of productive labour as that which creates surplus value. See

Arendt (1959), p. 81. But the definition is historically specific to capitalism. Marx's own view comes out in this passage: 'Milton, who wrote *Paradise Lost* for five pounds, was an *unproductive labourer*. . . . Milton turned out *Paradise Lost* for the same reason as a silkworm produces silk. It was an activity of *his* nature. But the literary proletarian . . . who fabricates books. . . . under the direction of his publisher, is a productive labourer; for his product . . . comes into being only for the purpose of increasing . . . capital.' *MEW* 26: 1, 377; *TSV* I, 389. On the distinction, see Gough (1972).

262 *MEW* 23: 181; *Cap*. I, 145.
263 *MEW* 23: 185; *Cap*. I, 150.
264 *MEW* 23: 223–4; *Cap*. I, 191–2.
265 *MEW* 23: 230–1; *Cap*. I, 199–201. Necessary labour is the amount required for the reproduction of the labourer. This does not entail that a non-exploitative situation is one in which the worker gets the equivalent of his reproduction *plus* surplus value. Marx never posits a right to the full product of labour for the direct producer. There will always be necessary but unproductive labour, as well as numerous social functions to be financed by the surplus.
266 *MEW* 25: 253–4; *Cap*. III, 238–9.
267 *MEW* 23: 322, 324–5; *Cap*. I, 290–1, 292–3.
268 Bober (1962), p. 191.
269 *MEW* 23: 325; *Cap*. I, 293. See also *MEW* 25: 162; *Cap*. III, 151.
270 Marx to Engels, 2 Aug. 1862; *MEW* 30: 265; *SC*, 130.
271 *MEW* 25: 169, 171; *Cap*. III, 157, 159.
272 *MEW* 25: 186; *Cap*. III, 174. Marx's solution failed to win acceptance from economists. Recently, however, with the publication of P. Sraffa, *The Production of Commodities by Means of Commodities* (Cambridge, 1960), there has been renewed interest. See Hunt and Schwartz (eds.) (1972). The classic critique is that by Böhm-Bawerk (1896). It should be noted that the law of value will not apply to socialist production: 'The measure of wealth is then not . . . labour time, but rather disposable time.' *G*. 596; *N*, 708.
273 *MEW* 23: 621; *Cap*. I, 606.
274 *MEW* 23: 645–6; *Cap*. I, 630–1. See also *MEW* 6: 411–12.
275 *MEW* 23: 650; *Cap*. I, 635.
276 *MEW* 23: 655; *Cap*. I, 641.
277 *MEW* 23: 658; *Cap*. I, 643–4.
278 *MEW* 23: 664; *Cap*. I, 649.
279 *MEW* 23: 673–4; *Cap*. I, 659–60.
280 *MEW* 25: 274; *Cap*. III, 259.
281 *MEW* 25: 260; *Cap*. III, 245. See also *G*, 318–19; *N*, 415–16.
282 *MEW* 25: 242; *Cap*. III, 227.
283 *MEW* 25; *Cap*. III, Chap. 14.
284 *G*, 632–7; *N*, 746–51.
285 Bober (1962), pp. 224–5; Robinson (1966), pp. 35–42.
286 Meek (1967), pp. 129–32.
287 *MEW* 25: 501; *Cap*. III, 472–3. See also *MEW* 25: 254–5, 277; *Cap*. III, 239–40, 261; *MEW* 24: 318; *Cap*. II, 316.
288 *MEW* 23: 512; *Cap*. I, 494.
289 *MEW* 25: 456; *Cap*. III, 431.

290 *MEW* 25: 454; *Cap.* III, 429.

291 *MEW* 23: 658; *Cap.* I, 643.

292 *MEW* 23: 675; *Cap.* I, 661.

293 *MEW* 23: 683; *Cap.* I, 669. One suspects that polemical reasons were equally compelling.

294 *MEW* 4: 469; *CM*, 96; *MEW* 6: 407.

295 *MEW* 23: 476; *Cap.* I, 456.

296 *TSV* III, 259. Cf. *MEW* 23: 681; *Cap.* I, 668; *TSV* III, 126, 306, 335.

297 *MEW* 26: 1, 189–90; *TSV* I, 212. Marx refers to 'government officials, priests, lawyers, soldiers, etc.' as the ideological estates (*Stände*). *MEW* 23: 470; *Cap.* I, 448.

298 *MEW* 23: 469–70; *Cap.* I, 447–8. See also *TSV* II, 571; *G*, 304–5; *N*, 401–402.

299 *MEW* 25: 310–11; *Cap.* III, 294–5.

300 *TSV* III, 573.

301 *TSV* III, 63. See also *TSV* III, 352, 360.

302 Nicolaus (1967), p. 45.

303 *TSV* II, 96, 153.

304 *MEW* 23: 108; *Cap.* I, 65.

305 *MEW* 25: 839; *Cap.* III, 810.

306 *MEW* 23: 12, 89; *Cap.* I, xviii, 46.

307 *MEW* 23: 12; *Cap.* I, xvi–xvii.

308 Gregor (1971), pp. 164–6.

309 *MEW* 25: 242; *Cap.* III, 227. See also *G*, 543; *N*, 650.

310 *MEW* 23: 12; *Cap.* I, xvii.

311 *MEW* 25: 171; 182, 836; *Cap.* III, 159, 170, 807.

312 Marx to Kugelmann, 3 Mar. 1869; *MEW* 32: 596.

313 *MEW* 8: 508–9, *Articles on Britain*, pp. 152–3. 'Capital Punishment' in *NYDT* 18 Feb. 1853.

314 *MEW* 25: 868; *Cap.* III, 839. Marx first read Quetelet's *Treatise on Man* (Edinburgh 1842), in 1851.

315 *MEW* 23: 286; *Cap.* I, 255; Marx to Kugelmann, 17 Mar. 1868; *MEW* 32: 541.

316 *MEW* 25: 184; *Cap.* III, 172.

317 *G*, 454–5; *N.* 559–60.

318 *MEW* 3: 229, 362; *GI*, 267, 413.

319 *MEW* 19: 21.

320 *MEW* 23: 249; *Cap.* I, 218.

321 *TSV* II, 185.

322 *MEW* 23: 16; *Cap.* I, xix.

323 *MEW* 23: 286; *Cap.* I, 255.

324 Marx to Kugelmann, 17 Mar. 1868; *MEW* 32: 541.

325 *MEW* 3: 45; *GI*, 59.

326 *MEW.EB* 1: 577, 578, 516; *EPM*, 180, 181, 116.

327 *G*, 270; *N*, 364. Note *G*, 585, *N*, 693: 'The science which compels . . . the machinery to act purposefully, as an automaton, does not exist in the worker's consciousness. . . . The productive process has ceased to be a labour process . . . dominated by labour as its governing unity.'

328 *MEW* 23: 199–200; *Cap.* I, 165.

329 *MEW* 25: 838; *Cap.* III, 800.

330 Colletti (1972), pp. 229–36.

FOOTNOTES TO PART III

1   *MEW* 4: 482; *CM*, 112.
2   Marx to Bolte, 23 Nov. 1871; *MEW* 33: 332–3; *SC*, 271.
3   *MEW* 18: 634.
4   *MEW* 4: 482; *CM*, 112.
5   *MEW* 1: 407, 409; *EG*, 355, 357.
6   *MEW* 21: 165, 166–7; *Origin of the Family*, pp. 280, 283.
7   *MEW* 20: 166–7; *Anti-Dühring*, pp. 247–9.
8   Hegel (1958), ss. 182, 183, 185, 188, 236 and Remark (p. 276). A good dis-
    cussion of the difficulties of Hegel's account can be found in Foster (1968),
    Chap. 5.
9   *MEW* 1: 277; *Critique*, p. 73.
10 *MEW* 1: 364; *EG*, 235 (*JQ*).
11 For an example, see *MEW* 1: 318–19; *Critique*, pp. 113–14. Marx men-
    tions the need to criticise Hegel's treatment of civil society (*Critique*,
    pp. 81, 82, 121), but no extant manuscript exists.
12 *MEW* 1: 252; *Critique*, p. 50.
13 *MEW* 1: 281, 283; *Critique*, pp. 77, 79. On the phrases in the latter passage,
    see Lobowicz (1967), p. 268, note 73.
14 Hegel (1958), ss. 296, 294 Remark, 297.
15 *MEW* 1: 248; *Critique*, p. 46.
16 *MEW* 1: 249; *Critique*, p. 47.
17 *MEW* 1: 253; *Critique*, p. 51.
18 *MEW* 1: 250; *Critique*, p. 48.
19 *MEW* 1: 327; *Critique*, p. 121.
20 *MEW* 1: 324; *Critique*, p. 119.
21 *MEW* 1: 320; *Critique*, p. 115.
22 *MEW* 1: 233; *Critique*, p. 32.
23 *MEW* 1: 283; *Critique*, p. 80.
24 *MEW* 1: 285; *Critique*, p. 81. The word *Klasse* is not used in the *Critique*.
    In the English translation, *Stand* is translated by class, which is mis-
    leading. In *The German Ideology* we find: 'By the mere fact that it is a *class*
    (*Klasse*) and not an *estate* (*Stand*), the bourgeoisie is forced to organise
    itself no longer locally, but nationally.' *MEW* 3: 62; *GI*, 78. This and
    other statements suggest that in 1846 Marx saw class as a modern pheno-
    menon, e.g. *MEW* 6: 187–8, 253. As we have seen, a different view
    appears in the *Manifesto*.
25 Avineri (1968), p. 38.
26 *MEW* 1: 344; *EG*, 212.
27 Avineri (1968), pp. 33, 34. Lichtheim (1961), pp. 39, 55.
28 Especially in *The Eighteenth Brumaire* and *The Civil War in France*.
29 *MEW* 3: 62; *GI*, 78. Marx's view is made clear in the 1859 *Preface*:
    'Legal relations [and] political forms . . . originate in the material con-
    ditions of life, the totality of which Hegel . . . [calls] . . . "civil society";
    . . . the anatomy of this civil society . . . has to be sought in political
    economy.' *MEW* 13: 8; *CPE*, 20.
30 *MEW* 19: 28; *CGP*, 31.
31 *The Ethnological Notebooks*, p. 329.

32 *MEW* 19: 29; *CGP*, 32–3.
33 *MEW* 25: 297; *Cap.* III, 376–7.
34 *G*, 377; *N*, 473.
35 Hobsbawm (1964), p. 34.
36 Lichtheim (1967), pp. 72, 90.
37 *MEW* 25: 799; *Cap.* III, 771–2.
38 Mandel (1970), p. 131.
39 *MEW* 3: 178; *GI*, 208. See also *MEW* 3: 62; *GI*, 78.
40 Engels to Marx, 3 Dec. 1851; *MEW* 27: 381; *SC*, 62–3.
41 Marx to Engels, 9 Dec. 1851; *MEW* 27: 383; *SC* (1956), p. 77.
42 *MEW* 8: 460, 188–9; *EB*, 8, 111–12. A good comparison of *EB* and *CSF* may be found in Krieger (1953).
43 *MEW* 8: 138; *EB*, 47. This was also Tocqueville's interpretation. Recent historical work throws doubt on this claim.
44 *MEW* 8: 122–3; *EB*, 24–5. The June Days involved an insurrection of artisans from traditional trades, with a small minority from mechanical industry. The Paris 'proletariat' were in no sense a modern industrial proletariat. De Luna (1969), p. 129.
45 De Luna (1969), p. 173, refuses to see June as 'the triumph of the counter-revolution', arguing that the Cavaignac cabinet pressed on with moderate republican reforms, and were equally critical of utopian socialism *and* *laissez-faire* dogma.
46 *MEW* 8: 131; *EB*, 36. In fact Louis Napoleon also won, though by much smaller majorities, in most of the urban areas, including Paris. His largest majorities in urban areas came in working-class districts. De Luna (1969), p. 390.
47 *MEW* 8: 138–9; *EB*, 46–7.
48 *MEW* 8: 140, 153; *EB*, 48, 66.
49 *MEW* 8: 153; *EB*, 65.
50 *MEW* 8: 161; *EB*, 75.
51 *MEW* 8: 177; *EB*, 96–7.
52 *MEW* 8: 193; *EB*, 117.
53 *MEW* 8: 198; *EB*, 123–4.
54 *MEW* 8: 203; *EB*, 130.
55 *MEW* 8: 201; *EB*, 127–8.
56 *MEW* 8: 205–6; *EB*, 132–3.
57 Price (1972), pp. 19–29.
58 *NRZ* 29 June 1848; *MEW* 5: 136; *Articles from the NRZ*, p. 49.
59 *G*, 844; *N*, 884.
60 *G*, 655; *N*, 769.
61 Rubel (1962), p. 83. The object of Rubel's paper is to argue that 'Marx was a revolutionary communist only in theory, while he was a bourgeois democrat in practice' (p. 79). The evidence seems to be against this view.
62 Hamilton (1843), p. 175. About 50 excerpts appear in the Kreuznach notebooks in the IISH.
63 *MEW* 4: 372–3; *CM*, 180.
64 *MEW* 4: 481; *CM*, 111.
65 Marx to Engels, 13 July 1851; *MEW* 27; 278.
66 *MEW* 7: 43; *CSF*, 69–70 (Feb. 1850).
67 *MEW* 7: 100; *CSF*, 138 (Oct. 1850).

68 'The Chartists', *NYDT* 25 Aug. 1852; *MEW* 8: 344; *Articles on Britain*, p. 119.
69 'Louis Napoleon and Italy', *NYDT* 29 Aug. 1859; *MEW* 13: 485.
70 Marx to Schweitzer, 13 Oct. 1868; *MEW* 32: 569; *SC*, 214.
71 Preamble to the Programme of the French Workers' Party (May 1880), *MEW* 19: 328.
72 *MEW* 19: 29; *CGP*, 31–2.
73 Marx to Kugelmann, 28 Dec. 1862; *MEW* 30: 639.
74 For examples, see *G*, 406–7; *N*, 507; *MEW* 23: 779; *Cap.* I, 776; *MEW* 19: 400; Blackstock and Hoselitz (1952), p. 224.
75 *MEW* 25: 799–800; *Cap.* III, 772.
76 *MEW* 4: 466, 479; *CM*, 93, 109. Engels in the *Principles* was more explicit, predicting communist revolution in England, America, France and Germany 'at one and the same time'. *MEW* 4: 375; *CM*, 182.
77 *MEW* 5: 282; *Articles from the NRZ*, p. 76; *NRZ* 30 July 1848.
78 *MEW* 4: 466, 479; *CM*, 93, 109.
79 *MEW* 6: 275; *NRZ* 15 Feb. 1849, 'Democratic Pan-Slavism'.
80 'The Danish-Prussian Armistice', *NRZ* 10 Sept. 1848; *MEW* 5: 395; *Articles from the NRZ*, p. 115.
81 'The Magyar Struggle', *NRZ* 13 Jan. 1849; *MEW* 6: 173; *The Revolutions of 1848*, p. 222.
82 Talmon (1960), p. 485.
83 *MEW* 6: 174. Note the comments of Pech (1969), pp. 304 ff.
84 'The Poland Debates at Frankfurt', *NRZ* 20 Aug. 1848; *MEW* 5: 332; *Articles from the NRZ*, p. 98.
85 In 1866 Marx still held the view that 'both aristocrats and bourgeois, see the dark Asiatic power in the background as a last resource against the advancing tide of working-class ascendancy. That power can only be put down by the restoration of Poland upon a democratic basis.' *Documents* I, 350. Marx's obsessive concern with the Russian threat tended to warp his judgement. Reading from right to left, the Whigs, Palmerston, Gladstone, *The Times*, Proudhon, Lassalle and Bakunin were all accused of pro-Russian attitudes or policies.
86 *NRZ* 12 July 1848; *MEW* 5: 202.
87 Marx to the Brunswick Committee, 22–30 Aug. 1870; *MEW* 17: 270; *SC*, 247. Note Engels to Marx, 15 Aug. 1870; *MEW* 33: 40; *SC*, 242: 'Bismarck . . . is doing a bit of our work, in *his own* way and without meaning to. . . . He is clearing the deck for us better than before.'
88 The argument portrayed in this paragraph first appeared in the article 'The Bourgeoisie and the Counter-Revolution', *NRZ*, 10, 15, 16, 31 Dec. 1848; *MEW* 6: 102–24; *Articles from the NRZ*, pp. 177–202.
89 Engels to Marx, 23 Sept. 1852; *MEW* 28: 139. (English in original.)
90 *NRZ* 21 Jan. 1849; *MEW* 6: 191–5; *Articles from the NRZ*, pp. 221–5. Marx is alluding to the various measures being taken to propitiate the artisanate.
91 'The Chartists', *NYDT* 25 Aug. 1852; *Articles on Britain*, p. 118 (see also pp. 112, 226).
92 *NYDT* 8 Aug. 1856; *MEW* 12: 42; *Revolution in Spain*, p. 147.
93 'The Chartists', *NYDT* 25 Aug. 1852; *Articles on Britain*, p. 117.
94 *G*, 431; *N*, 533.
95 Hamerow (1969), pp. 152–63.

96 Engels to Marx, 13 Apr. 1866; *MEW* 31: 208; *SC*, 177.
97 *CWF*, 65–6; see also 165 (first draft), and 251 (second draft).
98 *MEW* 19: 29; *CGP*, 32–3.
99 Nicolaus (1967), (1968); Mandel (1971).
100 *MEW* 4: 481; *CM*, 111.
101 *MEW.EB* 1: 509–10; *EPM*, 105.
102 *MEW* 3: 200, *GI*, 235.
103 *MEW* 2: 38; HF, 52–3.
104 *MEW* 6: 387; *WLC*, 17–18.
105 *MEW* 7: 33; *CSF*, 58.
106 Nicolaus (1968), p. 61, argues that apart from the critique of the Gotha Programme, 'there exists no programmatic political statement which is based squarely on the theory of surplus value . . . the most important Marxian political manifesto remains to be written'. The *Address* is the nearest thing we have, but was, of course, written to satisfy a number of disparate elements in the IWA.
107 *MEW* 16: 103, 148, 149; *WPP*, 2, 72, 74. Marx read his paper to the Council on 20 and 27 June 1865. See Marx to Engels, 20 May 1865; *MEW* 31: 122–3; *SC*, 174–5.
108 *MEW* 16: 151; *WPP*, 77. Marx was well aware of the extreme over-simplification of his presentation, and sought Engels' view on 'whether it is advisable, to anticipate things', and publish his lecture in advance of *Capital* itself. Marx to Engels, 24 June 1865; *MEW* 31: 125. No reply from Engels is extant, but *WPP* was left unpublished until 1898.
109 *MEW* 23: 670; *Cap.* I, 655.
110 *MEW* 25: 892; *Cap.* III, 862.
111 *TSV* II, 579–80.
112 *MEW* 16: 152; *WPP*, 78–9. Another version of this passage was found among Marx's papers. See *Documents* I, 272.
113 *Documents* III, 292. Resolutions at Brussels (1868).
114 Marx to Engels, 16 Sept. 1868; *MEW* 32: 151.
115 *Documents* I, 347–9 (Aug. 1866); III, 290–2.
116 Whereas there was a decisive rupture with liberalism in both France and Germany. Lichtheim (1961), pp. 102–3.
117 In *The Eastern Post*, 8 Feb. 1873, quoted Collins (1960), p. 258.
118 Gerth (1958), p. 186. Ironically, Barry was a Tory party agent. Barry's account (p. 262) reads: 'for almost every recognised leader of English working men was sold to Gladstone, Morley, Dilke and others'.
119 *Documents* I, 285.
120 *Documents* I, 346–7.
121 *MEW* 19: 27; *CGP*, 29–30.
122 *Documents* I, 345; also III, 288. See also *MEW* 23: 320; *Cap.* I, 288.
123 *Documents* I, 345.
124 Marx firmly believed that 'a *general prohibition* of child labour is incompatible with the existence of large-scale industry and hence an empty, pious wish'. *MEW* 19: 32; *CGP*, 35.
125 *Documents* I, 343–6; also III, 287–9 (Aug. 1866).
126 *MEW* 19: 32; *CGP*, 36.
127 *Documents* III, 140, 147. The General Council reviewed the Geneva resolutions on education in 1869. GC Minutes 10, 17 Aug. 1869.
128 *MEW* 19: 30; *CGP*, 34.

129   Marx to Bolte, 23 Nov. 1871; *MEW* 33; 328; *SC*, 269.
130   Marx to Freiligrath, 29 Feb. 1860; *MEW* 30: 490; *SC* (1956), 147.
131   *Documents* II, 329.
132   He added that Lassalle's error was 'to prescribe the course to be followed by this movement according to a certain doctrinaire recipe'. Marx to Schweitzer, 13 Oct. 1868; *MEW* 32: 569; *SC*, 214.
133   *MEW* 4: 474; *CM*, 103.
134   Marx to Schweitzer, 13 Oct. 1868; *MEW* 32; 570; *SC*, 215.
135   Marx to Blos, 10 Oct. 1877; *MEW* 34: 308; *SC*, 310.
136   Marx and Engels to the leaders of the SPD (circular letter), 17–18 Sept. 1879; *MEW* 34: 407–8; *SC*, 326–7.
137   *MEW* 6: 115; *Articles from the NRZ*, p. 192.
138   *MEW* 16: 76.
139   *MEW* 4: 492–3; *CM*, 124–5.
140   *MEW* 19: 22–3; *CGP*, 24. See Lidtke (1966) pp. 333–4, for the agreed programme.
141   *MEW* 38: 179–80; *SC*, 432.
142   Marx to Siebel, 22 Dec. 1864; *MEW* 31: 437.
143   Stafford (1971), pp. 158–69.
144   Engels to Bebel, 20 June 1873; *MEW* 33: 591; *SC*, 285.
145   *MEW* 4: 182; *PP*, 175.
146   *MEW* 7: 273–4 (Apr. 1850).
147   *MEW* 18: 530. See Schulkind (1972), pp. 235–40.
148   Avineri (1968), p. 218.
149   Note the strictures in Thompson (1965).
150   *MEW* 4: 493; *CM*, 125.
151   *MEW* 3: 70, 195; *GI*, 86, 230.
152   *MEW* 5: 457; see also 506.
153   Lichtheim (1961), p. 125. We have argued that the *Address* does not yield such an interpretation. See above, pp. 30–1.
154   *MEW* 23: 779; *Cap.* I, 776.
155   *La liberté* (Brussels) 15 Feb. 1872; Algemeen Handelsblad (Amsterdam), 10 Sept. 1872. The Brussels version was the basis of the account in the German social democratic *Der Volksstaat* (Leipzig). The Brussels version in translated in *On Britain*; the Amsterdam version may be found in de Jong (1951). The German version was altered to avoid the censor.
156   *MEW* 18: 160; *On Britain*, pp. 494–5. In *Der Volksstaat*, the last sentence reads: 'But this is not the state of affairs in all countries.'
157   de Jong (1951), p. 12.
158   The need to *smash* the state machine, and not merely transfer it to new hands, emphasised by the later Marx, means also a strong probability of the use of force. Marx added that 'this is the preliminary condition for every real people's revolution on the Continent'. Marx to Kugelmann, 12 Apr. 1871; *MEW* 33: 205. See below for a discussion of the problems which arise from this.
159   Marx to Hyndman, 8 Dec. 1880; *MEW* 34: 482; *SC*, 334.
160   Interview in New York *World*, 18 July 1871; cf. *Cap.* I, xiv. The views of Marx and Engels were essentially the same. For the latter, see *MEW* 22: 78, 234, 280; Engels to Fischer, 8 Mar. 1895; *MEW* 39: 424–6; and his (unexpurgated) introduction to the 1895 edition of *CSF*, which was cut by Liebknecht 'in such a fashion that I am made to appear a peaceful wor-

shipper of legality at any price'. See also his letters to Kautsky and Lafargue, 1 and 3 Apr. 1895; *MEW* 39: 452, 458; *SC*, 486, 487. Engels would not have agreed with Lichtheim (1961), p. 230, who argues that the omissions make no difference.

161 Hill (1948), p. 135.
162 Guizot (1850), pp. 12–13. The argument that the political balance was upset by a change in the property balance was first advanced by James Harrington in the 1650s.
163 *MEW* 7: 210; *On Britain*, p. 348.
164 Guizot (1850), pp. 135, 129.
165 *MEW* 7: 210–11; *On Britain*, pp. 348–9.
166 The assertions of this paragraph rely on the work of Ashton, Habakkuk, Stone, Thirsk, Zagorin, cited in the bibliography.
167 Christopher Hill, in a discussion with Lawrence Stone in *The Listener*, 4 Oct. 1973, p. 449. Stone rightly objected that it was methodologically incorrect to argue from the *results* of an event back to its *nature* at the time it occurred. It is also misleading from the point of view of consistent usage. Historians, for instance, refer to the *révolte nobiliaire* of 1787, by which is meant a revolt of an identifiable group, the nobles.
168 For references see *MEW* 7: 432–3; 27: 598; 28: 520, 116; 8: 367; 28: 592; 10: 602; 29: 41–2, 76, 204.
169 Mandel (1971), pp. 74–8.
170 Marx to Engels, 26 Sept. 1856; *MEW* 29: 76.
171 Marx to Engels, 31 May 1873; *MEW* 33: 82.
172 *G*, 231; *N*, 325; see *G*, 198; *N*, 287.
173 *G*, 635; *N*, 749; see *G*, 440, 442; *N*, 541–2, 543.
174 *MEW* 25: 456; *Cap*. III, 431; Marx to Engels, 2 Apr. 1858; *MEW* 29: 312; *SC*, 104 ('*zum Kommunismus überschlagend*').
175 *G*, 77; *N*, 159.
176 *Documents* III, 357; 402. See also Marx's letter to the Labour Parliament (9 Mar. 1854); *MEW* 10: 125; *On Britain*, p. 416. Chang (1965), p. 19, claims that it is 'revisionism' to insist on 'certain specific preliminary conditions such as a highly developed and numerous proletariat, a democratic state, a majority with developed managerial ability'. Thus revisionism began with Marx.
177 At the London conference, Sept. 1871, Marx himself proposed the establishment of a Federal Council. He had formerly opposed this move 'because he wanted to ensure that the English are imbued with the spirit of the *Socialist* International. In fact, on the General Council their education is complete. . . .' The many branches founded since the Commune required a united organisation (*Freymond* II, 217–18). The reason given fits the argument of the circular and also perhaps Marx's post-Commune optimism about the more revolutionary character of the movement. Abramsky suggested that Marx may have hoped for more support from the English members of the General Council as a result of his move, but Collins thinks there is no evidence of this. *SSLH Bulletin* 9 (1964).
178 *Documents* III, 357–8; 402–3. The spirit of tutelage in this circular, together with Marx's views on the Irish question, could not have endeared him to the English trade union leaders.
179 Marx to Meyer and Vogt, 9 Apr. 1870; *MEW* 32: 667–9; *SC*, 235–8.
180 Marx to Engels, 10 Dec. 1869; *MEW* 32: 414–15; *SC*, 232.

181   Marx to Kugelmann, 29 Nov. 1869; *MEW* 32; 638; *SC*, 230. More succinctly, 'Ireland gone, the British "Empire" is gone, and the class war in England, till now somnolent and chronic, will assume acute forms.' Marx to Paul and Laura Lafargue, 5 Mar. 1870; *MEW* 32: 656; *On Ireland*, p. 290.

182   *MEW* 3: 35; *GI*, 46–7.

183   *MEW* 7: 79; *CSF*, 113.

184   For opposed views about the 'labour aristocracy', see Hobsbawm (1964), and Pelling (1968).

185   Plamenatz (1963), II, 399, accepts that this is Marx's view, but argues that there is no necessity for a country to have a strong industrial base and a literate working class before it can establish socialism. The Russian example merely warns us that there are methods to avoid (p. 401). For an orthodox Marxist like Plekhanov, however, the development in Russia was to be expected, for in the absence of the necessary preconditions, the revolution was bound to become yet another oriental despotism.

186   *MEW* 18: 633 (1874–5).

187   The late 1843 essay, 'An Introduction to a Critique of Hegel's *Philosophy of Right*'. has been seen as such an analysis. Marx asked whether Germany could have a revolution which would 'raise it to the human level which will be the immediate future' of more advanced countries. His answer was that theoretical development in Germany was equal to that in advanced countries, and theory itself 'becomes a material force once it has seized the masses'. The material basis of revolution will be provided by the emerging industrial proletariat, and *not* by the bourgeoisie (*MEW* 1: 385, 390; *EG*, 257, 263). Alexander Ulyanov, Lenin's brother, concluded that Germany, and therefore Russia, could launch a proletarian revolution without completing a bourgeois revolution. But the 1843 essay was written well before Marx's first draft of his theory in *The German Ideology*, and should not be used as evidence of his mature views. See Walicki (1969), pp. 152–3.

188   *MEW* 4: 493; *CM*, 125.

189   *MEW* 7: 246–8; Livingstone (1971), pp. 239–40.

190   Marx to Engels, 23 May 1856; *MEW* 29: 47; *SC*, 92.

191   *MEW* 4: 475; *CM*, 104.

192   See Mayer (1960), for a useful tabulation.

193   *MEW* 8: 198; *EB*, 123.

194   *MEW* 25: 815; *Cap.* III, 787.

195   *MEW* 25: 821; *Cap.* III, 793.

196   *MEW* 8: 202; *EB*, 128.

197   *MEW* 8: 204; *EB*, 148. This passage was cut out of the 2nd edition in 1869. Marx spoke in the preface of 'striking out allusions no longer intelligible', presumably because small-holding property had not yet collapsed.

198   Price (1972), pp. 22–9.

199   *Documents* III, 123. (GC Minutes 13 July 1869.)

200   Note the paper 'Nationalisation of Land' (Dec. 1869), in which Marx wrote out the main points for the trade union leader Robert Applegarth. See Marx to Engels, 4 Dec. 1869; *MEW* 32: 409.

201   *CWF*, 173–7.

202   *CWF*, 176–7. A similar statement appeared in his paper for Applegarth:

'The French peasant has been thrown into a most fatal antagonism to the industrial working class.'

203 *CWF*, 76.

204 Marx to Sorge, 27 Sept. 1877; *MEW* 34: 296; *SC*, 308.

205 Marx to Zasulich, 8 Mar. 1881; *MEW* 19: 242–3; *SC*, 339–40. As we have noted, a few months later Marx added the rider that two revolutions must complement each other (*MEW* 19: 296; *CM*, 132). Engels, who in his polemic against Tkachev insisted on the need for the socio-economic pre-requisites of revolution, even allowed for the possibility of a Blanquist-type *coup d'état*. Following the assassination of Alexander II he wrote: 'The Russians are approaching their 1789. . . . This is one of the exceptional cases where it is possible for a handful of people to *make* a revolution, i.e. with one little push, to cause a whole system . . . to come crashing down. . . . If ever Blanquism . . . had a certain *raison d'être*, that is certainly now in Petersburg.' Engels to Zasulich, 23 Apr. 1885; *MEW* 26: 304; *SC*, 384.

206 *MEW* 5: 402; *NRZ* 12 Sept. 1848.

207 Marx to Weydemeyer, 5 Mar. 1852; *MEW* 28: 508; *SC*, 69. An exhaustive account may be found in Draper (1962).

208 *MEW* 7: 89–90; *CSF*, 126. References to the dictatorship of the prole-tariat are infrequent, and occur in two date-clusters, 1850–2 and 1871–5. See *MEW* 7: 323; 17: 433; 18: 300; 19: 28. Avineri (1968), p. 204, claims that Marx does not use the term in the context of proletarian rule, that it is used only 'two or three times in his life, and then always in what is basically a private communication'. In fact, four references are to *public* statements. In any case, private use does not disqualify such use as evi-dence, unless, of course, Avineri wishes to argue that (e.g.) the *Critique of the Gotha Programme* should be disregarded as evidence for Marx's views.

209 *MEW* 18: 529.

210 *MEW* 4: 472, 481; *CM*, 101, 111.

211 *MEW* 7: 323; *Neue Deutsche Zeitung*, 4 July 1850. The references are in *MEW* 4: 181–2, 481; 7: 89–90.

212 *MEW* 18: 634. Here Marx uses the term '*Klassenherrschaft der Arbeiter*'.

213 *MEW* 17: 433. New York *World* 15 Oct. 1871, reporting speech of 26 Sept. 1871, in full in Molnar (1963), pp. 238 ff.

214 See McLellan (1970), p. 182 for identifications.

215 *MEW.EB* 1: 534–6; *EPM*, 133–5.

216 Tucker (1961), pp. 154–6.

217 Avineri (1968), pp. 221–30, espec. p. 225.

218 Engels to Cuno, 24 Jan. 1872; *MEW* 33: 388; *SC*, 274. See also Engels to Bebel, 18–28 Mar. 1875: *MEW* 34: 128–9; *SC*, 293–4.

219 *MEW* 18: 634; *Marginal Notes*, also p. 635: 'If Mr Bakunin were familiar with only the position of a manager in a workers' co-operative . . . all his nightmares about authority would go to the devil. He should have asked himself: What forms can administrative functions take . . .?'

220 *MEW* 8: 196; *EB*, 121.

221 Marx to Kugelmann, 12 Apr. 1871; *MEW* 33: 205. Marx adds: 'This is the preliminary condition for every real people's revolution on the Con-tinent.' By this does he mean to exclude Great Britain and the United States?

222 *CWF*, 228 (second draft).
223 Marx to Kugelmann, 17 Apr. 1871; *MEW* 33: 209.
224 *CWF*, 170 (first draft). In fact the Commune proliferated executive organs throughout its short existence.
225 *CWF*, 189 (first draft); 71 (published version); 189 (first draft). Marx based himself upon the Communal Declaration of 19 Apr. At this time, the National Assembly at Versailles was split between republican centralisers and monarchist decentralisers. A Municipal Election Law had been passed on 15 Apr. which allowed Paris the right to elect its own municipal council, but which otherwise confined the right of electing the mayor to towns of a population of under 20,000.
226 *CWF*, 70. Fränkel had urged Marx to make this point. *MEW* 33: 749, note 259.
227 *CWF*, 233 (second draft); 69 (published version).
228 *CWF*, 69, 71, 74 (published version). Marx is disingenuous here. As we have seen, he was aware of the antagonism between proletarian and peasant (*CWF*, 176). The scheme outlined in the Declaration of 19 Apr. would have placed effective control in peasant hands. The political motivation behind the Declaration was to counteract Versaillaise propaganda, which portrayed the Commune as a threat to individual liberty and property ownership.
229 *CWF*, 162 (first draft).
230 For the Declaration, see Schulkind (1972), pp. 149–51. Mason (1930), p. 58, gives evidence of the parallels with Proudhon's views.
231 *MEW* 7: 252; Livingstone (1971), 243–4; see also *MEW* 5: 42, 321, 409.
232 *MEW* 8: 204 (note); *EB*, 148 (omitted from the 2nd edition in 1869).
233 Marx to Engels, 20 July 1879; *MEW* 33: 5.
234 *MEW* 7: 252–3 (note); *Select Works* I, 106–7 (note to the 1885 edition). The sentences quoted above from the *Eighteenth Brumaire* were cut out of the 2nd edition (1869) by Marx and replaced by a more ambiguous phrasing. In his criticism of the draft SPD programme of 1891, Engels suggested the following inclusion under political demands: 'Complete self-government in province, district, town and village through civil servants elected by universal suffrage. Abolition of all local and provincial bodies appointed by the State.' *MEW* 22: 237; *CGP*, 61.
235 Rougerie (1971), p. 157. Johnstone (1971), makes some apposite comments. For a view which emphasises the propagandist aim of the Declaration, see Greenberg (1971), pp. 126–31.
236 *MEW* 4: 481–2; *CM*, 111–12. There are two earlier drafts of the *CM* extant, both by Engels: the June 1847 draft, and the *Principles of Communism* (Oct. 1847). The June draft mentions 4 points (equivalent to points 2, 3, 7, 10 in the *CM* (*CM*, 168). The *Principles* contain 12 points (*CM*, 181–2), of which points 10 (slum clearance) and 11 (equal right of inheritance for illegitimate as for legitimate children) are dropped from *CM* list. Point 2 of the *Principles* is much modified in point 1 of the *CM*: '2. Gradual expropriation of landed proprietors, factory owners, railway owners and owners of shipping concerns, partly through competition by State industries and in part directly through payment of compensation in currency notes.' *MEW* 4: 373.
237 *MEW* 4: 481; *CM*, 111.
238 Wagner and Strauss (1969).

239 Note Marx's comments on this conflict of interest, *MEW* 25: 530, 575, 577; *Cap.* III, 502, 547, 549.

240 *MEW* 25: 621; *Cap.* III, 593–4.

241 It is possible that the 10 measures were the result of a compromise agreement at the Congress of Dec. 1847.

242 *MEW* 5: 3–5 (with facsimile); *CM*, 190–2. Written between 21 and 29 Mar. 1848.

243 *MEW* 4: 475; *CM*, 104.

244 In the original text, in place of '*an die Revolution zu knüpfen*' one read '*an die Regierungen zu fesseln*'— 'to chain . . . to the governments'.

245 *MEW* 4: 573–4; *CM*, 129–30. Preface dated 24 June 1872. Marx's letters reveal a curious reluctance to publish. Liebknecht had asked for a reprint in early 1871. Marx pointed to the need for a new preface, but showed no urgency in producing it. *MEW* 33: 207, 323, 362. The reader is told, misleadingly, that 'that this reprint was too unexpected to leave us time' to insert a section on 1847–72.

246 *Documents* III, 324.

247 *MEW* 18: 633.

248 *MEW* 17: 625; *CWF*, 18 (Engels' introduction to the 1891 edition).

249 *CWF*, 171 (first draft).

250 *CWF*, 78 (published version); 182 (first draft). Avineri (1968), p. 247, claims that for Marx the Commune was 'a petty bourgeois democratic-radical *émeute*' but this has no basis in the drafts.

251 Marx to Domela-Nieuwenhuis, 22 Feb. 1881; *MEW* 35: 160; *SC*, 338.

252 *CWF*, 179. Defined as 'a Republic which disowns the capital and landowner class . . . that frankly avows 'social emancipation' as the great goal of the Republic'. Note Engels in *Documents* IV, 165.

253 With these qualifications, we can accept the Commune as 'the initial stage of a proletarian dictatorship, neither fully developed nor nationally based'. Johnstone (1971), p. 458.

254 Marx to Liebknecht, 6 Apr. 1871, to Kugelmann, 12 Apr. 1871; *MEW* 33: 200, 205. See also Engels, *Documents* IV, 171.

255 *CWF*, 162 (first draft).

256 Marx to Domela-Nieuwenhuis, 22 Feb. 1881; *MEW* 35; 161; *SC*, 338.

257 Marx to Sorge, 19 Oct. 1877; *MEW* 34: 303; *LA*, 117.

258 *MEW* 17: 343; *CWF*, 73.

259 Engels to Schmidt, 5 Aug. 1890; *MEW* 37: 436; *SC*, 415–16.

260 *MEW* 19: 21; *CGP*, 21.

261 *MEW* 3: 528; *GI*, 593. This was probably drafted by Moses Hess.

262 *MEW* 19: 21; *CGP*, 21.

263 *MEW* 3: 379; *GI*, 432.

264 *MEW* 3: 33; *GI*, 44–5. 'This . . . is a rather limited version of a summer's day on the Phalanx . . . betraying a Germanic penchant for higher intellectual activities. . . .' Beecher and Bienvenu (1972), pp. 70–1. Marx and Engels saw in Fourier's work 'a vein of true poetry'. *MEW* 3: 448; *GI*, 508.

265 *G*, 599; *N*, 712.

266 *G*, 505; *N*, 611.

267 *MEW* 4: 157; *PP*, 144.

268 *G*, 505; *N*, 612.

269 *G*, 593; *N*, 705.

270   *MEW* 25: 828; *Cap.* III, 800. Yet Marx sees child labour as a necessity of large-scale industry, as late as 1875. *MEW* 19: 32; *CGP*, 35.
271   *G*, 599–600; *N*, 712.
272   *MEW* 3: 195, 70; *GI*, 230, 86. See also *MEW* 4: 376; *CM*, 184.
273   *MEW* 3: 35; *GI*, 46–7.
274   *MEW* 4: 479; *CM*, 109. On Marx and nationalism, see Bloom (1941), McDonald (1941), Martin (1968), Petrus 1971).
275   *MEW* 4: 182; *PP*, 174.
276   *MEW* 18: 634.
277   Avineri (1968), pp. 210, 239, 203–4.
278   The phrase was first inserted into the second edition of *Anti-Dühring*, three years after Marx's death. 'The State is not "abolished". *It withers away.*' *MEW* 20: 262; *A–D*, 386.
279   Marx to Blos, 10 Nov. 1877; *MEW* 34: 308.
280   *MEW* 19: 29; *CGP*, 33.
281   *CWF*, 170 (first draft).
282   *CWF*, 69.
283   *MEW* 19: 28; *CGP*, 31.
284   *Documents* V, 407. See also Engels, *MEW* 18: 308; *Select Works* I, 577.
285   *MEW* 19: 19; *CGP*, 19.
286   *MEW* 19: 28; *CGP*, 30, 31.
287   *MEW* 18: 635.
288   As claimed by Sartori (1962), p. 424. A more apposite criticism is that Marx nowhere considers the need for conflict resolution of some institutionalised kind. See Dahl (1948).
289   'Nationalisation of the Land' (1869), p. 417. See Marx to Engels, 4 Dec. 1869; *MEW* 32: 409.
290   *MEW* 23: 93; *Cap.* I, 50.
291   'On Authority' (1873); *MEW* 18: 306, 308; *Select Works* I, 576, 577.
292   *MEW* 23: 350; *Cap.* I, 321. See *MEW* 25: 397; *Cap.* III, 376. Discipline and control because of class conflict will not be necessary. *MEW* 23: 352; *Cap.* I, 323. Similarly, Marx believes that efficient use of resources will not require control once 'the labourers work for their own account'. *MEW* 25: 93; *Cap.* III, 83.
293   *MEW* 25: 400; *Cap.* III, 379.

FOOTNOTES TO CONCLUSION

1 Kindleberger (1964), p. 323.
2 Marx to Weydemeyer, 5 Mar. 1852; *MEW* 28: 508; *SC*, 69.
3 Gough (1972), pp. 69–72, makes some useful comments in the light of the distinction between productive and unproductive labour.
4 *MEW* 23: 528; *Cap.* I, 513.
5 Lidtke (1968).
6 Engels to Laura Lafargue, 19 Oct. 1890. *MEW* 37: 484.
7 Plamenatz (1963), II, 388, is right to stress that Marx and Engels assumed there to be 'a normal course of social change'.
8 *MEW* 18: 516–17.
9 *MEW* 21: 454.
10 Marx to Bolte, 23 Nov. 1871; *MEW* 33: 329; *SC*, 270.
11 *Documents* III, 310.

BIBLIOGRAPHY

1. THE WRITINGS OF MARX AND ENGELS

A. *Bibliographies*

Andréas, B. (ed.), *Le manifeste communiste de Marx and Engels. Histoire et bibliographie 1848–1918* (Milan 1963)

Kliem, M., Merbach, H. and Sperl, R. (eds.), *Marx-Engels Verzeichnis: Werke-Schriften-Artikel* (Berlin 1966)

Lachs, J. (ed.), *Marxist Philosophy: A Bibliographical Guide* (Chapel Hill 1967)

Rubel, M. (ed.), *Bibliographie des œuvres de Karl Marx* (Paris 1956). Includes a list of Engels' writings

Rubel, M. (ed.), *Supplément à la bibliographie des œuvres de Karl Marx* (Paris 1960)

Uroyeva, A., *For all Time and all Men* (Moscow 1969). An account of the publications, translations and spread of *Capital* I, 1867–95

B. *Major Editions*

Marx, K. and Engels, F., *Historisch-Kritische-Gesamtausgabe. Werke-Briefe-Schriften*, ed. D. Riazanov (Frankfurt and Moscow, Marx-Engels Institute, 1927–36). Of 40 projected volumes, only 12 were published. This is so far the only attempt at a critical edition with texts in the original language of composition

Marx and Engels, *Marx-Engels Werke* (Berlin, Dietz Verlag 1956–68). 39 volumes plus 2 supplementary volumes. There is a subject index to the letters (27–39). All texts are in German. This is the fullest edition available, but there are a number of omissions

Marx, *Œuvres: Économie* I and II, ed. M. Rubel (Bibliothèque de la Pléiade, Gallimard, Paris 1963, 1968). The notes to this edition are indispensable

Marx, *Frühe Schriften* I and II (1837–47), ed. P. Lieber and H.-J. Furth (Darmstadt 1971). This edition includes alternate readings of Marx's manuscripts

Marx, *Grundrisse der Kritik der Politischen Oekonomie. Rohentwurf.* (1857–8) (Berlin 1953). First published in Moscow 1939–40.

C. *Individual Writings in English*

(A collected edition is projected based on the *MEW* edition.)

Marx, *Critique of Hegel's Philosophy of Right* (1843), ed. with an introduction and notes by J. O'Malley (Cambridge 1970)

    Economic and Philosophical Manuscripts of 1844, ed. D. J. Struik, translated by M. Milligan (New York 1971)

Marx and Engels, *The Holy Family: or Critique of Critical Critique* (1845) (Moscow 1956)

Marx and Engels, *The German Ideology* (1846) (London 1965)

Marx and Engels, *Feuerbach: Opposition of the Materialist and Idealist Outlooks* (London 1973). Part I of *The German Ideology* published in accordance with the text and arrangement of the original manuscripts. See *Deutsche Zeitschrift für Philosophie* (Berlin), 14 (1966), 1192–1354

Marx, *The Poverty of Philosophy* (1847) (Moscow 1956)

Marx and Engels, *The Birth of the Communist Manifesto*, ed. D. J. Struik (New York 1971). In addition to the *Manifesto* itself, this edition includes the draft of June 1847, *The Principles of Communism* (Oct. 1847), and the *Demands of the Communist Party in Germany* (Mar. 1848)

Marx and Engels, *The Communist Manifesto of Karl Marx and Friedrich Engels*, ed. D. Riazanov (New York 1963). A large number of supplementary documents, including the *Principles*, the *Demands*, and the *Kommunistische Zeitung* (Sept. 1847)

Marx, *The Class Struggles in France* (1850) (London, n.d.)

Marx, *The Eighteenth Brumaire of Louis Napoleon* (1852) (Moscow 1967)

Marx, *Secret Diplomatic History of the Eighteenth Century*, ed. L. Hutchinson (London 1969). Also includes *The Story of the Life of Lord Palmerston*

Marx, *Grundrisse: Foundations of the Critique of Political Economy (Rough Draft)* (*1857–8*), translated with a foreword by M. Nicolaus (Harmondsworth 1973)

Marx, *Contribution to the Critique of Political Economy* (1859), ed. M. Dobb (London 1971)

Marx, *Theories of Surplus Value* (3 vols., London 1969–72)

Marx, *Un Chapitre inédit de Kapital*, ed. R. Dangeville (Paris 1971). French translation of Marx's 1865 manuscript, *The Results of the Immediate Process of Production*, first published in *Archiv Marksa i Engelsa* II (VIII) (1939)

Marx, *Wages, Price and Profit* (1865) (Peking 1969)

Marx, *Capital: A Critical Analysis of Capitalist Production*, I, translated by S. Moore and E. Aveling, ed. Dona Torr (London 1938)

Marx, *Capital* II and III (Moscow 1957, 1962)

Marx, 'Nationalisation of Land', *The Labour Monthly* 34 (1952), 415–17

Marx, *The Civil War in France* (1871) (Peking 1966). Includes the 2 drafts of *CWF*, first published in *Archiv Marksa i Engelsa* III (VIII) (1934). The latter includes newspaper excerpts made by Marx in 1870–1871

Marx, 'An Interview with Karl Marx' (by R. Landor in the New York *World* 18 July 1871), *The Labour Monthly* 54 (1972), 261–70

Marx, 'Deux interviews de Karl Marx sur la commune', ed. M. Rubel, *Le Mouvement Social* 38 (Jan.–Mar. 1962), 3–27

Marx, 'Political Indifferentism' (1873), *Society for the Study of Labour History: Bulletin 20* (Spring 1970), 19–23

Marx, 'Marx on Bakunin: a Neglected Text'. The Marginal Notes on

Bakunin's *Statism and Anarchy* (1874), translated with an introduction by H. Mayer. *Études de Marxologie* 2 (1959), 91–117. (Cahiers de l'ISEA, 91, series S, no. 2)

Marx, *Critique of the Gotha Programme* (1875) (Moscow, n.d.)

Marx, 'Interview with the Founder of Modern Socialism' (*Chicago Tribune*, 5 Jan. 1879), in *L'Homme et la société* (Jan.–Mar. 1968)

Marx, 'Marginal Notes on Adolph Wagner's *Lehrbuch der politischen Oekonomie*' (1879–80).
   Theoretical Practice 5 (Spring 1972), 40–65

Marx, *The Ethnological Notebooks* (1880–2). Studies of Morgan, Maine, Phear and Lubbock. Transcribed and edited, with an introduction by L. Krader (Assen 1972)

Engels, *The Condition of the Working Class in England in 1844*, ed. Chaloner and Henderson (2nd edn, Oxford 1971)
   Anti-Dühring: Herr Eugene Dühring's Revolution in Science (2nd edn, Moscow 1959)
   The Origin of the Family, Private Property and the State (Mar.–June 1884) (Moscow, n.d.)
   Frederick Engels and Paul and Laura Lafargue: *Correspondence* (3 vols., 1868–95) (London and Moscow 1959–60)

D. *Collections*

Marx, *Writings of the Young Marx on Philosophy and Society* (New York 1967), ed. L. D. Easton and K. H. Guddat. Includes 'On the Jewish Question'

Marx and Engels, *Select Works* (2 vols., Moscow, n.d.)
   Articles from the Neue Rheinische Zeitung 1848–9 (Moscow 1972)
   The Revolutions of 1848, ed. D. Fernbach (Moscow 1973)

Marx, *The Cologne Communist Trial*, ed. R. Livingstone (London 1971). Includes *Great Men of the Exile, History of the Communist League*, and other important documents

Marx and Engels, *Revolution in Spain 1854–6*) (New York 1939)

Marx, *The Eastern Question 1853–6*, ed. E. M. Aveling (London 1969)

Marx and Engels, *On the Paris Commune* (Moscow 1971)

Marx and Engels, *On Britain* (2nd edn, Moscow 1962)

Marx and Engels, *Articles on Britain* (Moscow 1971)

Marx and Engels, *On Ireland* (Moscow 1971)

Marx and Engels, *On Colonialism* (4th edn, Moscow 1968)

Marx, *Karl Marx on Colonialism and Modernisation*, ed. S. Avineri (New York 1968)

Marx and Engels, *The Civil War in the United States* (New York 1969). Articles and letters

Marx and Engels, *Marx and Engels: The Russian Menace to Europe*, ed. P. W. Blackstock and B. F. Hoselitz (Glencoe, Illinois 1952)

Marx and Engels, *Selected Correspondence* (Moscow 1956)

Marx and Engels, *Selected Correspondence* (2nd edn, Moscow 1965).

Described as 'revised and supplemented'. Thirteen letters of the 1956 edition are left out; 36 new letters are included
Marx and Engels, *Letters to Americans 1848–95* (New York 1969)

2. WORKS CITED IN THE TEXT

Acton, H. B., *The Illusion of the Epoch* (London 1959); *What Marx Really Said* (London 1967)

Adelmann, F. J. (ed.), *Demythologising Marxism: A Series of Studies On Marxism*. Boston Studies in Philosophy II (The Hague 1969)

Andréas, B. (ed.), *Gründungsdokuments des Bundes der Kommunisten (Juni bis September 1847)* (Hamburg 1969); *La Ligue des Communistes (1847)* (Paris 1972)

Annenkov, P., *An Extraordinary Decade: Literary Memoirs*, ed. A. P. Mendel (Ann Arbor 1968)

Arendt, H., *The Human Condition* (New York 1959)

Aron, R., *Main Currents in Sociological Thought* I (London 1965)

Ashton, R., 'The Civil War and the Class Struggle', in R. H. Parry (ed.), *The English Civil War and After 1642–58* (London 1970)

Avineri, S., *The Social and Political Thought of Karl Marx* (Cambridge 1968); (ed.), *Karl Marx on Colonisation and Modernisation* (New York 1968)

Azéma, J.-P. and Winock, M., *Les Communards* (Paris 1971)

Baron, S. H., *Plekhanov: The Father of Russian Marxism* (London 1963)

Beecher, J. and Bienvenu, R. (eds.), *The Utopian Vision of Charles Fourier* (London 1972)

Billington, J. H., *Mikhailovsky and Russian Populism* (Oxford 1958)

Blackstock, P. W., and Hoselitz, B. F. (eds.), *Karl Marx and Friedrich Engels: The Russian Menace to Europe* (Glencoe, Illinois 1952)

Bloom, S. F., *The World of Nations: A Study of the National Implications in the World of Karl Marx* (New York 1941, 2nd edn 1961)

Blumenberg, W., 'Zur Geschichte des Bundes der Kommunisten. Die Aussagen der Peter Gerhard Röser', *International Review of Social History* 9 (1964), 81–122

Bober, M. M., *Karl Marx's Interpretation of History* (2nd edn revised, Cambridge, Mass. 1962)

Böhm-Bawerk, E., *Karl Marx and the Close of his System* (1896), ed. P. Sweezy (New York 1949)

Carr, E. H., *Karl Marx: A Study in Fanaticism* (London 1934); *Michael Bakunin* (London 1937)

Chang, S. H. M., *The Marxian Theory of the State* (New York 1965)

Cohen, G., and Acton, H. B., 'Symposium: On some Criticisms of Historical Materialism', *Aristotelian Society Supplementary Volume* 44 (1970), 121–56

Colletti, L., *From Rousseau to Lenin: Studies in Ideology and Society* (London 1972)

Collins, H., 'The English Branches of the First International', in A. Briggs and J. Saville (eds.), *Essays in Labour History* (London 1960), 242–75; 'The International and the British Labour Movement', *Society for the Study of Labour History: Bulletin* 9 (Autumn 1964), 26–39

Collins, H., and Abramsky, C., *Karl Marx and the British Labour Movement* (London 1965)

Cornu, A., *Karl Marx et Friedrich Engels: Leur vie et leur œuvre*, vols. 1–4 (1818–46) (Paris 1955–)

Dahl, R., 'Marxism and Free Parties', *Journal of Politics* 10 (1948), 787–813

De Jong, F., 'Amsterdam Meetings of the First International in 1872', *Bulletin of the International Institute of Social History* 6 (1951), 1–15

De Luna, F. A., *The French Republic Under Cavaignac* (Princeton 1969)

Dobb, M., *Papers on Capitalism, Development and Planning* (London 1967)

Dokumente I, *Der Bund der Kommunisten. Dokumente und Materialen*, vol. I, 1836–49 (Berlin 1970)

Documents, Documents of the First International (5 vols., 1864–72) (London, n.d.)

Draper, H., 'Marx and the Dictatorship of the Proletariat', *Études de Marxologie* 6 (1962), 5–73 (Cahiers de l'ISEA, series S, no. 6)

Feuer, L. S., 'The Influence of the American Communist Colonies on Marx and Engels', *Western Political Quarterly* 19 (1966), 456–74

Fleischer, H., *Marxism and History* (London 1973)

Foster, M. B., *The Political Philosophies of Plato and Hegel* (Oxford 1968)

Freymond, J. (ed.), *La Première Internationale: Recueil de Documents* (4 vols, 1864–77) (Geneva 1962, 1971)

Genovese, E., 'Marxian Interpretations of the Slave South' in B. Bernstein (ed.), *Towards a New Past* (New York 1968), 90–125

Gerth, H. (ed.), *The First International: Minutes of the Hague Congress of 1872* (Madison 1958)

Gough, I., 'Marx's Theory of Productive and Unproductive Labour', *New Left Review* 76 (Nov.–Dec. 1972), 47–72

Greenberg, L. M., 'The Commune of 1871 as a Decentralist Reaction', *Journal of Modern History* 41 (1969), 304–18; *Sisters of Liberty: Marseilles, Lyons, Paris and the Reaction to a Centralised State 1869–71* (Cambridge, Mass. 1971)

Gregor, A. J., *An Introduction to Metapolitics. A Brief Inquiry into the Conceptual Language of Political Science* (New York 1971)

Grossmann, H., 'The Evolutionist Revolt against Classical Economics', *Journal of Political Economy* 51 (1943), 381–96; 506–22

Guizot, F. P. G., *On the Causes of the Success of the English Revolution 1640–88* (London 1850)

Habakkuk, H. J., 'Landowners and the Civil War', *Economic History Review* 18 (1965), 130–51

Habermas, J., *Knowledge and Human Interests* (London 1972)

Hamerow, T. S., *The Social Foundations of German Unification 1858–71.*
I: *Ideas and Institutions* (Princeton, N.J. 1969)

Hamilton, T., *Men and Manners in America* (2nd edn, London 1843)

Hammen, O. J., 'The Spectre of Communism in the 1840s', *Journal of the History of Ideas* 14 (1953), 404–20; 'The Young Marx, Reconsidered', *Journal of the History of Ideas* 31 (1970), 109–20

Harrison, R., 'The British Labour Movement and the International in 1864', *The Socialist Register* (1964), 293–308

Hasek, C. W., *The Introduction of Adam Smith's Doctrines into Germany* (New York 1925)

Hegel, G. W. F., *The History of Philosophy*, translated by E. S. Haldane (3 vols., London 1892); *The Philosophy of Right*, translated with notes by T. M. Knox (Oxford 1958)

Hexter, J. H., *Reappraisals in History* (London 1961)

Hill, C., 'The English Civil War Interpreted by Marx and Engels', *Science and Society* 12 (1948), 130–46

Hobsbawm, E. *Labouring Men: Studies in the History of Labour* (London 1964); (ed.) *Karl Marx: Pre-Capitalist Economic Formations* (London 1964)

Hook, S. (ed.), *Marx and the Marxists: An Ambiguous Legacy* (Princeton, N.J. 1955)

Howard, D., *The Development of the Marxian Dialectic* (Carbondale and Edswardsville 1972)

Hunt, E. K., and Schwartz, J. G. (eds.), *A Critique of Economic Theory* (Harmondsworth 1972)

Hyndman, H. M., *The Record of an Adventurous Life* (London 1911)

Johnson, C. H., 'Communism and the Working Class Before Marx: The Icarian Experiment', *American Historical Review* 76 (1971), 642–89; 'Étienne Cabet and the Problem of Class Antagonism', *International Review of Social History* 11 (1966), 403–43

Johnstone, M., 'The Paris Commune and Marx's Conception of the Dictatorship of the Proletariat', *Massachusetts Review* 12 (1971), 447–62

Jordan, Z. A., *Karl Marx: Economics, Class and Social Revolution* (London 1971)

Kamenka, E., *The Philosophy of Ludwig Feuerbach* (London 1970); *The Ethical Foundations of Marxism* (2nd edn, London 1972)

Kandel, E., 'Eine schlechte Verteidigung einer schlechten Sache', *Beiträge zur Geschichte der Arbeiterbewegung* 5 (1963), 290–303

Kapp, Y., *Eleanor Marx. I: Family Life (1855–83)* (London 1972)

Kaufmann, W., *Hegel: Reinterpretation, Texts, and Commentary* (London 1966)

Kindleberger, C. P., *Economic Growth in France and Britain 1851–1950* (Cambridge, Mass. 1964)

Korsch, J., *Karl Marx* (London 1938)

Krader, L., 'The Works of Marx and Engels in Ethnology Compared', *International Review of Social History* 18 (1973), 223–75

Krieger, L., 'Marx and Engels as Historians', *Journal of the History of Ideas* 14 (1953), 381–403

Lehning, A., *From Buonarroti to Bakunin: Studies in International Socialism* (Leiden 1970)

Lichtheim, G., *Marxism: An Historical and Critical Survey* (London 1961); *The Concept of Ideology and Other Essays* (New York 1967); *From Marx to Hegel* (London 1971)

Lidtke, V. L., *The Outlawed Party: Social Democracy in Germany 1878–1890* (Princeton 1966)

Lobkowicz, N., *Theory and Practice: History of a Concept from Aristotle to Marx* (Notre Dame, Indiana 1967)

Macdonald, H. M., 'Marx, Engels and the Polish National Movement', *Journal of Modern History* 13 (1941), 321–34

Maguire, J., *Marx's Paris Writings: An Analysis* (London 1972)

Mandel, E., *The Formation of the Economic Thought of Karl Marx: From 1843 to Capital* (London 1971)

Martin, N. A., 'Marxism, Nationalism and Russia', *Journal of the History of Ideas* 29 (1968), 231–52

Mason, E. S., *The Paris Commune* (New York 1930)

Mayer, H., 'Marx, Engels and the Politics of the Peasantry', *Études de Marxologie* 3 (1960), 91–152 (Cahiers de l'ISEA, series S, no. 6)

McGovern, R. F., 'Karl Marx's First Political Writings: The *Rheinische Zeitung*, 1842–3' in Adelmann (ed.), *Demythologising Marxism* (1969), 19–63

McLellan, D., *The Young Hegelians and Karl Marx* (London 1969); *Marx Before Marxism* (London 1970); *The Thought of Karl Marx* (London 1971)

Meek, R. L., *Economics and Ideology and Other Essays: Studies in the Development of Economic Thought* (London 1967)

Mehring, F., *Karl Marx: The Story of his Life* (London 1936)

Molnar, M., *Le Déclin de la Première Internationale: La Conférence de Londres de 1871* (Geneva 1963)

Morgan, R. P., *The German Social Democrats and the First International 1864–72* (Cambridge 1965)

Nicolaievsky, B., 'Towards a History of the "Communist League" 1847–52', *International Review of Social History* 1 (1956), 234–52; 'Who is Distorting History? (*Voprosy Istorii* and Karl Marx in 1848–1849)', *Proceedings of the American Philosophical Society* 105 (1961), 209–36

Nicolaievsky, B., and Maenchen-Helfen, O., *Karl Marx: Man and Fighter* (London 1973)

Nicolaus, M., 'Proletariat and Middle Class. Hegelian Choreography and the Capitalist Dialectic', *Studies on the Left* 7 (1967), 22–49; 'The Unknown Marx', *New Left Review* 48 (Mar.–Apr. 1968), 41–61

Noyes, P. R., *Organisation and Revolution. Working-Class Associations in the German Revolutions of 1848–9* (Princeton, N.J. 1966)

Ollman, B., 'Marx's Use of "Class"', *American Journal of Sociology* 73 (1967–8), 573–80; *Alienation: Marx's Concept of Man in Capitalist Society* (Cambridge 1971)

O'Malley, J., 'History and "Man's Nature" in Marx', *Review of Politics* 28 (1966), 508–27

Ossowski, S., *Class Structure in the Social Consciousness* (London 1963)

Pech, S. Z., *The Czech Revolution of 1848* (Chapel Hill 1969)

Pelling, H., *Popular Politics and Society in Late Victorian Britain* (London 1968)

Petrus, J. A., 'Marx and Engels on the National Question', *Journal of Politics* 33 (1971), 797–824

Pickles, W., 'Marx and Proudhon', *Politica* III (1937–8), 236–60

Plamenatz, J., *Man and Society. A Critical Examination of Some Important Social and Political Theories from Machiavelli to Marx* (2 vols., London 1963); *Ideology* (London 1970)

Price, R., *The French Second Republic: A Social History* (London 1972)

Prinz, A. M., 'Background and Ulterior Motive of Marx's *Preface* of 1859', *Journal of the History of Ideas* 30 (1969), 437–50;

Reminiscences of Marx and Engels (Moscow, n.d.)

Riazanov, D., *Karl Marx and Friedrich Engels* (London 1927)

Robinson, J., *An Essay on Marxian Economics* (London 1966)

Rohr, D. G., *The Origins of Social Liberalism in Germany* (Chicago 1963)

Rougerie, J., *Paris libre 1871* (Paris 1971)

Rubel, M., *Karl Marx: Essai de Biographie Intellectuelle* (Paris 1957); 'Les cahiers de lecture de Karl Marx. I: 1840–53', *International Review of Social History* 2 (1957), 392–420; 'Les cahiers d'étude de Karl Marx. II: 1853–6', *International Review of Social History* 5 (1960), 39–76; 'Notes on Marx's Conception of Democracy', *New Politics* 1 (1962), 78–90; 'La Charte de l'Internationale. Essai sur le "marxisme" dans l'A.I.T.', *Le Mouvement Social* 51 (Apr.–June 1965), 3–22

Rühle, O., *Karl Marx: His Life and Work* (London 1929)

Runkle, G., 'Karl Marx and the American Civil War', *Comparative Studies in Society and History* VI (1964), 117–41

Ryan, A., 'A New Look at Professor Tucker's Marx', *Political Studies* 15 (1967), 202–10

Sartori, G., *Democratic Theory* (New York 1962)

Schacht, R., *Alienation* (London 1972)

Schmidt, A., *The Concept of Nature in Marx* (London 1971)

Scott, W. R., *Adam Smith as Student and Professor* (Glasgow 1937)

Schulkind, E. (ed.), *The Paris Commune of 1871: The View from the Left* (London 1972)

Sraffa, P., *The Production of Commodities by Means of Commodities* (Cambridge 1960)

Stafford, D., *From Anarchism to Reformism: A Study of the Political Activities of Paul Brousse 1870–90* (London 1971)

Steklov, G. M., *History of the First International* (London 1928)

Stone, L., *The Causes of the English Revolution 1529–1642* (London 1972)

Sweezy, P. (ed.), *The Transition from Feudalism to Capitalism: A Symposium* (New York 1954)

Talmon, J. L., *Political Messianism: the Romantic Phase* (London 1960)

Thirsk, J., 'The Restoration Land Settlement', *Journal of Modern History* 26 (1954), 315–28

Thompson, E. P., 'The Peculiarities of the English', *The Socialist Register* (1965), 311–62

Tsuzuki, C., *The Life of Eleanor Marx 1855–98: A Socialist Tragedy* (Oxford 1967)

Tucker, R. C., *Philosophy and Myth in Marl Karx* (Cambridge 1961)

Wagner, Y., and Strauss, M., 'The Programme of the Communist Manifesto and its Theoretical Foundations', *Political Studies* 17 (1969), 470–84

Walicki, A., *The Controversy over Capitalism: Studies in the Social Philosophy of the Russian Populists* (Oxford 1969)

Wolfe, B., *Marxism: One Hundred Years in the Life of a Doctrine* (London 1967)

Woodcock, G., *Pierre-Joseph Proudhon* (London 1956)

Zagorin, P., *The Court and the Country: The Beginnings of the English Revolution* (London 1969)

INDEX